Style

Ten Lessons in Clarity and Grace

Fifth Edition

Joseph M. Williams
The University of Chicago

LONGMAN

An imprint of Addison Wesley Longman, Inc.

New York • Reading, Massachusetts • Menlo Park, California • Harlow, England
Don Mills, Ontario • Sydney • Mexico City • Madrid • Amsterdam

Executive Editor: Anne Elizabeth Smith
Developmental Editor: Matthew A. Rohrer
Project Coordination, Text and Cover Design: York Production Services
Art Coordination: York Production Services
Electronic Production Manager: Valerie Zaborski
Manufacturing Manager: Helene G. Landers
Electronic Page Makeup: York Production Services
Printer and Binder: R. R. Donnelley & Sons Company
Cover Printer: The Lehigh Press, Inc.

For permission to use copyrighted material, grateful acknowledgment is made to the copyright holder on p. 268, which is hereby made part of this copyright page.

Library of Congress Cataloging-in-Publication Data

Williams, Joseph M.
Style: ten lessons in clarity and grace/Joseph M. Williams.—5th ed.
p. cm.
Includes index.
ISBN 0-673-98243-2 (pbk.)
1. English language—Rhetoric. 2. English language—Technical English. 3. English language—Business English. 4. English language—Style. I. Title.
PE1421.W545 1996
808′.042—dc20 96–4541
CIP

ISBN 0-673-98243-2

5678910—DOC—9998

To my mother and father

. . . English style, familiar but not coarse, elegant, but not ostentatious. . . .

SAMUEL JOHNSON

Contents

Preface

Most people won't realize that writing is a craft.
You have to take your apprenticeship in it like anything else.

KATHERINE ANNE PORTER

WHAT'S THE SAME IN THIS EDITION

Most of you require no convincing that the ability to write clearly is important, especially those of you who have to struggle daily with the prose of those who never learned how. Unfortunately, people who haven't learned to write clearly don't get much help from the standard advice about writing better, because it consists mostly of truisms like "Make a plan" or trivia like "Don't begin a sentence with *and* or end it with *up*." Getting beyond the trivia and behind the self-evident has been the object of every edition of this book, so this fifth edition still aims at answering these same three questions:

- What features *in* a sentence determine how readers judge its clarity?
- How can you diagnose your own prose to anticipate their judgments?
- How can you revise your prose so that your readers will think well of it?

WHAT'S NEW

This fifth edition, however, differs from earlier ones in ways that I think are important. (As I always say, you can't write a book too often; eventually you might get it right.)

First, I have reshuffled the lessons into three larger and more coherent parts.

- The first two original lessons are now in an introductory part called "Style as Choice."

- Five lessons on agent/action, cohesion, and emphasis are now in a single unified part called "Clarity."
- Three lessons on the finer points of style—concision, managing long sentences, and elegance—are now grouped into a final part called "Grace."

This organization gives the book a structure far more coherent than any of the prior editions.

Second, a new page design has improved a format so cramped that it made earlier editions a pain in the eyes to read. Moreover, important principles are now boxed and shaded to make them easier to identify and review. And I have indicated which of two paired sentences or passages to take as the model.

Third, to make room for a new lesson carved out of material on cohesion and coherence, I have moved the section on punctuation into an Appendix. (Actually, I wanted to avoid the subtitle, *Eleven Lessons in Clarity and Grace.*)

Fourth, I have added new material to almost every lesson. In Lesson Two on correctness, I have added some advice that some might think too conservative (a sign of aging?) but that I intend as purely objective predictions about the way some especially careful readers read. In Lessons Three and Four, I have added new material on nominalizations and characters. In Lesson Six, I offer a long analysis of another of our "sacred secular texts," Abraham Lincoln's Second Inaugural Address. This goes along with the analyses of the Declaration of Independence and the Gettysburg Address in earlier editions. In Lesson Eight, I have added new material on metadiscourse, hedging, and emphasizing. In Lesson Nine, I suggest what I think is a generally reliable new principle about constructing long but shapely sentences. And in Lesson 10, I discuss an element of self-conscious grace observed by especially elegant writers: chiasmus. There is more added throughout.

Fifth, I have slowed the pace of the explanations a bit further, unpacking the density that made some of the analysis of nominalizations and topics perhaps more demanding than necessary.

And sixth, I have recast the (now) Appendix on punctuation from the point of view of the reader, something I now realize I should have done in the first edition. Live and learn.

The Importance of Revision

Despite those changes, this book is still not about writing; it is about *re*writing. If I knew reliable principles that would help you *write* better, that is, help you put words down on paper or up on the screen that were right the first time—I would offer them cheerfully. But most advice specifically about drafting consists of more banalities: "Don't stop to edit," "Think of your audience," and so on. It is also advice that most of us ignore as we wrestle our ideas out onto the page for the first time. As I first drafted this paragraph, I wasn't thinking about you; I was struggling to get my own ideas straight; I had no plan for it, much less the next one; and the first time I wrote this sentence, I stopped to edit it several times before I finished it.

What I did know was that I would go back to that paragraph again and again, and that I could rely on a few principles that would help me know whether I was revising it in the right direction. It was only then—as I was revising—that I could think about you, the reader; that I could find a plan that fit my draft. I also knew that as I did so, there were a few good principles that I could rely on. This book is about those principles.

Predictions, Not Prescriptions

Those principles may seem to some readers prescriptive. That is not how I intend them. What I offer here are not rules for writing, but principles that will help you read your prose so that you can predict how your readers will, and then *choose* whether to revise it, depending on how you want your readers to respond. If you choose to write in ways that your readers will think obscure, so be it. It's a free country.

In fact, to get the most out of this book, you should be ready to write against the principles just to see what happens. Try writing in the bureaucratic style, just to get the feel of it (something that you will, in fact, be asked to do). Try creating a passage in a style elegant beyond your needs, just to see whether you can pull it off. Or try writing the longest sentence you can, just so that you can stretch it to its breaking point. Do not let habits of style box you in, even good habits.

You may find that at first you are writing more slowly. That's inevitable. Anytime you reflect on what you are doing *as you do it,* you become self-conscious, sometimes to the point of paralysis. It will pass. But in fact, you can avoid the paralysis, even the slowdown, if you remember that the principles offered here have little to do with how you *write,* but with how you *re*write. In fact, the first principle of drafting is to forget the principles for diagnosing and revising.

Some Demands on Your Time

To revise efficiently, though, you have to know a few things and learn a few more:

- You have to know a few grammatical terms: *SUBJECT, VERB, NOUN, ACTIVE, PASSIVE, CLAUSE, PREPOSITION,* and *COORDINATION.* They are defined the first time they appear or are defined in the Glossary (it defines all capitalized words).
- You will have to learn new meanings for two familiar words: *TOPIC* and *STRESS.*
- You will have to learn five terms that you may never have heard. Two are important: *NOMINALIZATION* and *METADISCOURSE;* three are useful: *RESUMPTIVE MODIFIER, SUMMATIVE MODIFIER,* and *FREE MODIFIER.*

Some students complain at having to learn new words, an understandable complaint from those who want to learn nothing new. But anyone who expects to learn new ideas has to learn new words. Style is new for many of you: it has a vocabulary of its own. But just knowing how to define a noun or verb won't help you write more clearly. To do that, you must develop a sense of how nouns and verbs differ and what they do in a sentence and *to* a sentence, and most important what they do to readers. Only then will you understand why some writing seems clear and other writing does not. And *that* will help you rewrite more quickly.

Some students also wonder that since they see so much unclear writing in print, a clear style must be less important than good ideas. But the truth is that even good ideas need all the help they can get, especially when you have to communicate them to readers who have neither the time nor the patience to dig them out of muddy prose. Indeed, whenever professionals are asked what they wish they had studied more diligently, first or second on the list is always communication, especially writing. In any field, the person who can deliver a clear and readable document quickly has an invaluable skill.

If you are reading this book on your own, go slowly. It is not an amiable essay that you can read in a sitting or two. Take the lessons a section at a time, up to the exercises. Do the exercises, edit someone else's writing, then edit some of your own that you wrote a while ago. You will be surprised at how much its quality has declined. Then look hard at what you've written today, first for elements addressed by the current lesson, then for another point, and if you have the time, for others.

Acknowledgments

So many of you have provided support that I cannot thank you all. But I again begin with my English 194 students, who too many years ago put up with faintly dittoed pages (that tells you how many years) and with a teacher who at times was as puzzled as they. I remain grateful to you all.

In more recent years, I have learned much from those undergraduates, graduate and professional students, and post-docs who have gone through the Little Red Schoolhouse writing program here at the University of Chicago (a.k.a. Advanced Academic and Professional Writing). I am equally grateful to the graduate students who have taught these principles and offered important feedback. They all have encouraged us that this way of thinking about writing and of teaching it continues to pay off long after they leave the university, and perhaps most of all to those who have taught it.

I have debts to those who broke ground in psycholinguistics, text linguistics, and functional sentence perspective. Those who keep up with such matters will recognize the influence of Charles Filmore, Jan Firbas, Nils Enkvist, Michael Halliday, Noam Chomsky, Thomas Bever, Vic Yngve, and others. More recently, the work of Eleanore Rosch has provided a rich explanation for why verbs *should* be actions and characters *should* be subjects. Her work in prototype semantics is a powerful theoretical account for the kind of style urged here.

I am indebted to colleagues who have taken time to read the work of another. For reading earlier versions of this book, I must thank in particular Randy Berlin, Ken Bruffee, Douglas Butturff, Donald Byker, Bruce Campbell, Elaine Chaika, Avon Crismore, Constance Gefvert, Maxine Hairston, George Hoffman, Ted Lowe, Susan Miller, Neil Nakadate, Mike Pownall, Peter Priest, Margaret Shaklee, Nancy Sommers, Mary Taylor, and Stephen Witte.

I am grateful for the feedback from the class taught by Stan Henning at the University of Wisconsin–Madison, and for the error in usage caught by Linda Ziff at Johns Hopkins University.

For this edition, I must thank the following reviewers for their thoughtful and useful feedback: John Ruszkiewicz, Bill Vande Kopple, and Margaret Batschelet. I am indebted to Christina Devlin for the Wesley quotation in Lesson Eight and to James Vanden Bosch for the Montaigne quotation in the Glossary. I acknowledge the assistance of Frederick C. Mish, editorial director, G. & C. Merriam Company, in locating the best examples of three citations in Lesson Two, and Charles Bazerman, whose work on Crick and Watson led me to the first paragraph of their DNA paper. I have used (and changed) Bill Vande Kopple's Hart Queen paragraph in Lesson Five.

The editors of Addison Wesley Longman have saved me from more than a few gaffes. I remain in the debt of the editor who first urged me to write this book, Harriett Prentiss, and my current editor, Anne Smith, who has more than restored my faith in the competence of editors, and to her assistant Matt Rohrer (who is also quite a good poet). And to Stephanie Magean, copyeditor, and Susan Free, coordinator for York Production Services, who, with great skill and tact, have guided the manuscript to what you now hold in your hands. And finally, my thanks to my always reliable and careful assistant, James Donato, who helped proof the galleys and assemble the index.

For several years, I have had the good fortune to work with two people who have been both good colleagues and good friends and whose careful thinking has helped me think better about many matters, both professional and personal: Greg Colomb and Don Freeman. Don's careful readings have saved me from more than a few howlers, and I am indebted to him for the quote from William Blake in Lesson Nine. It has been a pleasure and a privilege to work and hang out with them for almost 20 years now. Until three years ago, Frank Kinahan made us four. We are diminished by his death; I have almost forgiven him for that.

And again, the five who have contributed more to the quality of my life than I have probably let them know: Chris, Megan, Oliver, Dave, and Joe. And at the beginning and end still, Joan, whose depths of patience and good judgment I have not yet plumbed.

J. M. W.   December 1995

Part One

Style as Choice

Essentially style resembles good manners. It comes of endeavouring to understand others, of thinking for them rather than yourself—or thinking, that is, with the heart as well as the head.

Sir Arthur Quiller-Couch

Lesson One

Understanding Style

Style is the physiognomy of the mind.
ARTHUR SCHOPENHAUER

Have something to say, and say it as clearly as you can.
That is the only secret of style.
MATTHEW ARNOLD

To me, style is just the outside of content, and content the inside of style, like the outside and inside of the human body—both go together, they can't be separated.
JEAN-LUC GODARD

The great enemy of clear language is insincerity.
GEORGE ORWELL

In matters of grave importance, style, not sincerity, is the vital thing.
OSCAR WILDE

Principles and Aims

This book rests on two principles: It's good to write clearly, and anyone can. That first principle is self-evident, especially to those who regularly have to deal with prose like this:

> Better evaluation of responses to treatment modalities depends on the standardization of an index allowing accurate descriptions of learning disorder behaviors.

But that second principle may seem optimistic to those writers who hide their ideas not only from their readers, but sometimes even from themselves. Hard as they struggle, they can't get close to this:

> We could better evaluate how those with learning disorders respond to treatment if we could standardize an index that accurately describes how they behave.

We might say that such writers have a problem with their style, but they don't, because they have no style, if by style we mean how we choose to arrange our words to the best effect: They do not *choose* how to write, any more than they choose to put *the* before *dog* rather than after. But choice is at the heart of clear writing, because to meet the needs of different readers, we always have to choose between this word and that, between this order of words and some other order that helps a reader get from the beginning of a sentence to its end without feeling she is slogging through a field of wet mud.

Our writing can fail for reasons more serious than its style, of course. We bewilder our readers when we cannot organize new and complex ideas in a way that seems coherent to them. We lose any chance of gaining their assent when we ignore their predictable questions and objections. As important as those issues are, this book addresses a different matter: Once we've assembled our materials, formulated our claims, supported them with good reasons, and organized our text coherently, we still have to express ourselves in a way that our readers think is readable. Before our readers can accept our claims, they have to understand them.

That's the aim of this book: to explain how to overcome a problem that has afflicted generations of writers—a style that, instead of revealing ideas, hides them. When we read that kind of writing in government regulations, we call it *bureaucratese;* when we find it in contracts and judicial pronouncements, *legalese;* in scholarly articles and books that inflate modest ideas into gassy abstractions, *academese.* Intended or not, it is the style of pretension and intimidation, a kind of exclusionary language that a democratic society cannot tolerate as its standard of civic discourse. Unfortunately, it is also a style so common that it seems to bespeak institutional success, and so inexperienced writers adopt it not because they have anything to hide, but because by reading so much of it, they cannot resist imitating it. They feel they have no choice. It is a problem with a long history.

A SHORT HISTORY OF UNCLEAR WRITING

The Past

It was not until the late sixteenth century that English writers finally decided that their language was sufficiently eloquent to replace Latin and French in intellectual discourse, but their first choice toward elegance was a style complex beyond the needs of their readers:

> If use and custom, having the help of so long time and continuance wherein to [re]fine our tongue, of so great learning and experience which furnish matter for the [re]fining, of so good wits and judgments which can tell how to refine, have griped at nothing in all that time, with all that cunning, by all those wits which they will not let go but hold for most certain in the right of our writing, that then our tongue has no certainty to trust to, but write all at random.
>
> —Richard Mulcaster, *The First Part of the Elementary,* 1582

Within a century, this inflated style had spread to scientific prose. As one critic of that style complained,

> Of all the studies of men, nothing may sooner be obtained than this vicious abundance of phrase, this trick of metaphors, this volubility of tongue which makes so great a noise in the world.
>
> —Thomas Sprat, *History of the Royal Society,* 1667

When the New World was settled, American writers had an opportunity to choose a new prose style, one not viciously voluble, but lean and direct. In 1776, Thomas Paine wrote *Common*

Sense, a pamphlet whose plain language helped rouse American colonists to a revolution. It was a good start—a style that was deliberately clear, direct, unselfconsciously straightforward:

> In the following pages I offer nothing more than simple facts, plain arguments, and common sense; and have no other preliminaries to settle with the reader, than that he will divest himself of prejudice.

His plain arguments helped spark a revolution in our form of government but not, sad to say, in the style of our prose.

By the early nineteenth century, James Fenimore Cooper was complaining that "the common faults of American language were an ambition of effect, a want of simplicity, and a turgid abuse of terms":

> The love of turgid expressions is gaining ground, and ought to be corrected. One of the most certain evidences of a man of high breeding, is his simplicity of speech: a simplicity that is equally removed from vulgarity and exaggeration. . . . He does not say, in speaking of a dance, that "the attire of the ladies was exceedingly elegant and peculiarly becoming at the late assembly," but that "the women were well dressed at the last ball"; nor is he apt to remark, "that the Rev. Mr. G—gave us an elegant and searching discourse the past sabbath," but that "the parson preached a good sermon last sunday."
>
> The utterance of a gentleman ought to be deliberate and clear, without being measured. . . . Simplicity should be the firm aim, after one is removed from vulgarity, and let the finer shades of accomplishment be acquired as they can be attained. In no case, however, can one who aims at turgid language, exaggerated sentiments, or pedantic utterances, lay claim to be either a man or a woman of the world.
>
> —James Fenimore Cooper, *The American Democrat,* 1838

Unfortunately, Cooper could not resist abusing his own terms, for he adopted that turgid style in the act of condemning it. He criticizes the *attire of the ladies was elegant,* but in his next sentence echoes it: *The utterance of a gentleman ought to be deliberate.* Had he followed his own advice, he might chosen to write this:

> We should discourage writers who love turgid language. A well-bred person speaks simply, in a way that is neither vulgar nor ex-

> aggerated. We should not measure our words, but speak them clearly and deliberately. After we rid our language of vulgarity, we should aim at simplicity, and then as we can, acquire the finer shades of accomplishment. No one can claim to be a man or woman of the world who exaggerates sentiments or deliberately speaks in language that is turgid or pedantic.

About 50 years later, Mark Twain wrote what we now like to think is classic American prose—clear, concise, direct, emphatic:

> There have been daring people in the world who claimed that Cooper could write English, but they are all dead now—all dead but Lounsbury [an academic who praised Cooper's writing]. I don't remember that Lounsbury makes the claim in so many words, still he makes it, for he says that *Deerslayer* is a "pure work of art." Pure, in that connection, means faultless—faultless in all details—and language is a detail. If Mr. Lounsbury had only compared Cooper's English with the English which he writes himself—but it is plain that he didn't; and so it is likely that he imagines until this day that Cooper's [style] is as clean and compact as his own. Now I feel sure, deep down in my heart, that Cooper wrote about the poorest English that exists in our language, and that the English of *Deerslayer* is the very worst tha[t] even Cooper ever wrote.

Everyone admires Twain's easy directness; few choose to emulate it.

The Present

In the best-known essay on English style, "Politics and the English Language," George Orwell anatomized the inflated language of twentieth-century politicians, bureaucrats, and other chronic dodgers of responsibility:

> The keynote [of a pretentious style] is the elimination of simple verbs. Instead of being a single word, such as *break, stop, spoil, mend, kill,* a verb becomes a *phrase,* made up of a noun or adjective tacked on to some general-purposes verb such as *prove, serve, form, play, render.* In addition, the passive voice is wherever possible used in preference to the active, and noun constructions are used instead of gerunds (*by examination of* instead of *by examining*). The range of verbs is further cut down by means of the *-ize* and *de*-formations, and the banal statements are given an appearance of profundity by means of the *not un*-formation.

But just as Cooper did, in the act of abusing that style, Orwell modeled it. Had *he* avoided making a VERB a phrase or using PASSIVES and NOUN constructions (capitalized words are defined in the Glossary), he could have written more directly, something closer to this perhaps:

> Those who write pretentiously eliminate simple verbs. Instead of using one word, such as *break, stop, spoil, mend, kill,* they turn a verb into a noun or adjective and then tack it on to a general-purpose verb such as *prove, serve, form, play, render.* Wherever possible, they use the passive voice instead of the active and noun constructions instead of gerunds (*by examination* instead of *by examining*). They cut down the range of verbs with *-ize* and *de-*, and try to make banal statements profound by the *not -un* formation.

If in the act of attacking this style Orwell could not avoid imitating it (I don't think he was being ironic), we should not be surprised that today's academic and professional writers fare worse. On the language of the social sciences:

> A turgid and polysyllabic prose does seem to prevail in the social sciences. . . . Such a lack of ready intelligibility, I believe, usually has little or nothing to do with the complexity of thought. It has to do almost entirely with certain confusions of the academic writer about his own status.
>
> —C. Wright Mills, *The Sociological Imagination*

On the language of medicine:

> It now appears that obligatory obfuscation is a firm tradition within the medical profession. . . . [Medical writing] is a highly skilled, calculated attempt to confuse the reader. . . . A doctor feels he might get passed over for an assistant professorship because he wrote his papers too clearly—because he made his ideas seem too simple.
>
> —Michael Crichton, *New England Journal of Medicine*

On the language of law:

> In law journals, in speeches, in classrooms and in courtrooms, lawyers and judges are beginning to worry about how often they have been misunderstood, and they are discovering that sometimes they cannot even understand each other.
>
> —Tom Goldstein, *New York Times*

On the language of scholarship (from a review of a book about teaching apes to communicate):

> There are times when the more the authors explain, the less we understand. Apes certainly seem capable of using language to communicate. Whether scientists are remains doubtful.
>
> —Douglas Chadwick, *New York Times*

Students first confront that kind of writing in textbook sentences like this next one, a sentence clearer than many, but less readable than it might have been:

> Recognition of the fact that systems [of grammar] differ from one language to another can serve as the basis for serious consideration of the problems confronting translators of the great works of world literature originally written in a language other than English.

More concisely:

> When we recognize that languages have different grammars, we can consider the problems of those who translate great works of literature into English.

Generations of students have struggled through prose that they could not understand, blaming themselves because they thought that they could not read well enough or were not smart enough to comprehend ideas so seemingly complex. Some have been right about that, but most could have blamed the tangled writing they were trying to understand.

Some students, sad to say, give up, but sadder still, many who learn to read that style also choose to imitate it and then go on to write their own books in the same way, causing more grief to more students, some of whom master that same tangled style and go on to write yet more books. . . . And thus the style of each generation insinuates itself into that of the next, sustaining a 400-year-old tradition of wretched prose.

Some Private Causes of Unclear Writing

Hiding Behind Language

But if the historical sources of unclear English go back more than 400 years, other causes spring from motives more immediate, and more private. Michael Crichton mentioned the most common one: Some writers choose complicated language not only to plump up their ideas, but to mask their absence, hoping that turgidity will impress those who confuse difficulty with substance. When we don't know what we're talking about, our first recourse is usually to put up a smoke screen of big words in long sentences.

Others choose intimidating language to protect what they have from those who want a piece of it—the power and privilege that go with the ruling class. We control information by locking it up, but we can also conceal it behind a style of such Latinate complexity that it can be understood only by those trained in the academy or in government to endure and interpret it. It is ironic that in these postmodern days, it is also, oddly, the style of many academic critics who want to free us from our attachments to what they consider outmoded academic values.

Bad Memories

Others write graceless prose because they are gripped by the memory of someone who taught them that writing was good only when it was free of errors that only a teacher of grammar could explain. Too many of us now approach a blank page not as a space for fresh thinking, but as a minefield to be traversed timidly. We inch our way from word to word, concerned less with our readers' understanding than with our own sheer survival.

Temporary Aphasia

Finally, many of us write unclearly not because we choose to, but because we are seized by a kind of literary aphasia, a dismaying experience during which we can no longer write as well as we thought we once could, or in some cases even write at all. This typically happens when we start to write about matters that we do not entirely understand, for readers who do. We are most afflicted when we are learning to think and write in a new academic or professional area, for a new "community of discourse." The afflicted include not just undergraduates taking their first course in economics or psychology, but graduate students, business people, doctors, lawyers, professors—anyone who has ever written about knowledge that seems difficult for an audience that is new and intimidating.

As we struggle to master complex ideas, many of us, perhaps most of us, have to pass through this period of stylistic confusion. Our floundering should dismay us less when we realize that we are sharing an experience with generations of writers before us. We usually find that we are able to write more clearly once we more clearly understand what we are writing about.

There is in all this, of course, a great irony: When we have to write about a subject that confuses us, we will almost invariably write in ways that confuse others. But when we struggle through a piece of prose not just because of its intrinsically difficult subject, but also because of its gratuitously difficult style, we too easily assume that such complexity of language must indicate complexity of thought, and so we try to imitate that language in our own prose, confounding our confused writing even more. Thus it is that our inability to avoid one kind of writing conspires with our desire to choose something that turns out to be similar, a conspiracy that can so thoroughly confuse our readers that they may choose to stop reading.

The point of this book is to cut through that confusion by giving you more choices.

A Disclaimer

Now a disclaimer: As I emphasized in the Preface, this book is not, in fact, about writing. It is about *re*writing. Principles are useful before we write and after we have written, but they help no one caught up in the *act* of writing. In fact, if we had to think about principles *as* we wrote, we'd probably never write anything. Experienced writers get something down on paper as fast as they can, just so they can revise it into something clearer, and if they are lucky, in the process discover something new.

It's when we revise our early confusion into something clearer that we understand our ideas better. And when we understand our ideas better, we express them more clearly, and when we express them more clearly, we understand them even better . . . and so it goes, writing to help us think better, thinking to help us write better, until we run out of energy, interest, or time. For a fortunate few, that moment comes weeks, months, even years after they begin. (Over the last 15 years, this book has been through dozens of drafts, and there are parts I still can't get right.) For the rest of us, it's closer to tomorrow morning. And so we have to settle for an essay or report that is less than perfect, but does the job—a document as readable as the complexity of its subject and the time available allows. Perfection is an admirable goal, but it can also be the enemy of done.

As important as clarity is, though, some occasions call for more:

> Now the trumpet summons us again—not as a call to bear arms, though arms we need; not as a call to battle, though embattled we are; but a call to bear the burden of a long twilight struggle, year in and year out, "rejoicing in hope, patient in tribulation," a struggle against the common enemies of man: tyranny, poverty, disease and war itself.
>
> —John F. Kennedy, Inaugural Address, January 20, 1961

Few of us are asked to write a presidential address. But in even our most modest prose, we may want to be more than just readable, especially when we have something to say that demands special dignity. Or when we just want to take a moment of pleasure in our craft, regardless whether anyone will notice, like a cabinetmaker who wants even the invisible joints to be right. That is the object of the last section.

About 60 years ago, H. L. Mencken wrote

> With precious few exceptions, all the books on style in English are by writers quite unable to write. The subject, indeed, seems to exercise a special and dreadful fascination over school ma'ams, bucolic college professors, and other such pseudoliterates. . . . Their central aim, of course, is to reduce the whole thing to a series of simple rules—the overmastering passion of their melancholy order, at all times and everywhere.

That melancholy judgment has hovered over every sentence I've written. Mencken was right: No one can teach good writing by rule, especially to those who cannot feel or think or see. But I know that many do see clearly, feel deeply, and think carefully, but cannot write clearly enough to share their feelings and thoughts and visions. I also know that when we write clearly, we see and feel and think more clearly, and that we can find some help not in inviolate rules, but in a few reliable principles.

Here they are.

Lesson Two

Correctness

No grammatical rules have sufficient authority to control the firm and established usage of language. Established custom, in speaking and writing, is the standard to which we must at last resort for determining every controverted point in language and style.

HUGH BLAIR

It is not the business of grammar, as some critics seem preposterously to imagine, to give law to the fashions which regulate our speech. On the contrary, from its conformity to these, and from that alone, it derives all its authority and value.

GEORGE CAMPBELL

English usage is sometimes more than mere taste, judgment, and education—sometimes it's sheer luck, like getting across the street.

E. B. WHITE

God does not much mind bad grammar, but He does not take any particular pleasure in it.

ERASMUS

Any fool can make a rule and every fool will mind it.

HENRY DAVID THOREAU

Choice versus Obedience

To a competent writer, no ability is more important than being able to choose not just what to write but how to write it. In some matters of language, of course, we have no choice—whether to put *up* before or after a NOUN, as in *up the street* versus *the street up.* But for other matters, choice is always at the front of the writer's mind. For example, which of these sentences would you *choose* to write if you wanted your readers to think you wrote clearly and directly?

1. There was a lack of evidence in support for their claim.
2. Their claim suffered from a lack of evidence in its support.
3. They could not support their claim because they lacked evidence.

All three are grammatically "correct," but most of us would choose (3).

In some other matters, though, what is choice and what is not is contested: whether to split an infinitive, or begin a sentence with *and,* or end it with *up.* And it is choices like these that cause some writers anxiety: Which choice is "correct"?

We must write English correctly. But we must also understand that some points of "Correctness" are less important than many think (in fact, are not important at all), and that if you concern yourself with these points of usage too much, they can interfere with writing quickly and easily. I want to address this matter now, before we turn to matters of clarity, where choice governs everything, not because I think clarity is secondary to "good" grammar. Quite the contrary: I want to put this matter of correctness where it belongs—behind us.

Unlike matters of style, correctness seems not to offer choices, but to require obedience. When the *American Heritage Dictionary* says that *irregardless* is "nonstandard . . . never acceptable" (except, they say, for humor), the choice between it and *regardless* seems at best academic. In this matter, we are choosing not between better and worse, but between right and utterly, irredeemably, unequivocally, existentially Wrong.

That seems to simplify things: "correctness" requires neither good taste nor sound judgment, much less choice, but only a good memory. If you can remember that *irregardless* is always Wrong, it ought no more rise to even the lowest level of your conscious choice than does *dog the.* Some teachers and editors think that we should do the same with dozens of other "rules" like these:

- Don't begin a sentence with *and* or *but.*
- Don't use double negatives.
- Don't split INFINITIVES.
- Don't end a sentence with a PREPOSITION.

Unfortunately, it's not that simple:

- Many such rules are not linguistic fact, but classroom folklore, invented by eighteenth-century grammarians out of whole cloth and still taught by those who repeat what textbooks tell them, even though such "rules" are widely ignored by respected writers and by their careful readers.
- Other rules are real rules, imperatives whose violation marks us as at least careless, if not illiterate. These rules are observed by even the less-than-best writers.
- And then there are points of usage that are in fact choices that we may choose to make or not, depending on how we want our readers to respond.

Before we look at these points in detail, though, we might take a moment to think about where rules come from in the first place.

REASONS FOR RULES

Two Extreme Views

Opinion is split about the social role of Standard English. To some, it is just another device invented by one class to repress the others: a standard grammar helps keep the underclasses under. To others, Standard English is the refined product of a sifting and winnowing conducted by generations of grammarians, the best of all possible Englishes, now captured in rules observed by the best writers, or at least, according to some grammarians, they should be.

Both views are correct, partly. For centuries, most of those who govern our affairs have always believed that "errors" in grammar identify those who are unwilling or unable to acquire the habits of diligence, self-discipline, and obedience—values that the gatekeepers of our institutions look for in those whom they screen for admission. But the conservatives are also right;

many features of Standard English did originate in efficiencies of expression: We no longer use the complex set of verb endings required a thousand years ago, so that today we can omit present tense endings in all but one context:

Singular:	*I leave* + _.	*You leave* + _.	<u>*She leave* + **S.**</u>
Plural:	*We leave* + _.	*You leave* + _.	*They leave* + _.

So by any measure of logical consistency, an -s in *You know***S** *him* seems not just ungrammatical, but logically redundant and so, in the very nature of things, Wrong.

A More Informed View

In fact, the history and logic of Standard English are more complicated.

Historical Accidents

The radical critics are wrong when they claim that Standard English has been *devised* to achieve socially vicious ends. Linguistic standards arise from historical accidents of geography and economic power. When a country has different regional dialects, that of the wealthiest region is likely to become most prestigious and the basis for that nation's standard form of writing. Thus if a thousand years ago, Scotland had been closer to the Continent than was London, if it had a great port and had become the center of Britain's economic, political, and literary life, Standard English today might look and sound less like the English of London and more like that of Edinburgh, something like this (from Robert Burns):

A ye wha are sae guid yourself,	All you who are so good yourselves,
Sae pious and sae holy,	So pious and so holy,
Ye've nought to do but mark and tell	You've nothing to do but talk about
Your neebours' fauts and folly!	Your neighbors' faults and folly!

But the conservative critics are also wrong to claim that Standard English is intrinsically superior to other forms just because it has been refined by the logic of countless educated speakers. True, many features of Standard English seem to reflect an evolution toward efficiency. But most of those features are shared by native speakers of all dialects, whether they speak Standard English or not. Every speaker of Modern English, for example, enjoys (or should) the demise of the distinction that made nouns grammatically masculine, feminine, or neuter.

Logic and the System of Grammar

But if Standard English is not defined by features that are historically inevitable, neither is it defined by features that are intrinsically logical, if by logical we mean systematic and therefore predictable. In fact, many features of nonstandard English are more "logical" than their corresponding features in Standard English.

- The person who says *I knowed* makes the same "mistake" as the first person who said *I* ***climbed*** *the tree* instead of the earlier "correct" *clum.* Both speakers regularized an inconsistent pattern, an act that in any other context is taken as a sign of intelligence.
- The person who says *hisself* and *theirselves* similarly regularizes an inconsistency among the reflexive pronouns that mostly use the possessive: If we have ***my****self,* ***our****selves,* ***your****self,* ***your****selves,* ***her****self,* and ***its***[*s*]*elf,* why not ***his****self* and ***their****selves?*
- The person who says, *I'm here, ain't I?* uses a wholly logical (and once widely acceptable) contraction of *am + not:*

  I am here, [am + not → amn't →] ain't I?

  What is illogical is the "correct" form—*I'm here,* ***aren't I?***—because that *aren't* derives from the "ungrammatical" *I are not.*

We could cite a dozen other examples where, strictly applied, principles of logic and historical precedent should approve a form that we condemn as nonstandard, because that nonstandard form in fact reflects a logical mind deducing principles of regularity.

Those determined to discriminate will choose to do so, of course, by any social difference available. But since our language seems to reflect the quality of our minds more directly than do our ZIP codes, it is easier to imagine that certain linguistic "errors" reliably signal mental or moral deficiency. Anyone who takes language seriously, however, must reject the idea that the historical *accidents* of conventional usage reflect any intrinsic goodness.

Here's the point: We must reject the notion that Standard English has any special natural logic or goodness that makes its speakers intellectually or morally superior. That belief is not just wrong: In a democracy, it is destructive. Yet even if logic does predict *hisself* and *knowed* and history attests to a once-respectable *ain't,* so much greater is the power of social convention that we must nevertheless exclude those usages when we write for serious purposes.

THREE KINDS OF RULES

These confused attitudes have been encouraged by grammarians who, in their zeal to accumulate principles of "good" English, have since the eighteenth century confounded three kinds of rules:

1. Rules that govern the fundamental structure of English;
2. Rules that define its standard written form;
3. Rules invented by grammarians about trivial points of usage.

1. Some rules define the fundamental structure of English—ARTICLES precede nouns: *the book,* not *book the;* SUBJECTS usually precede verbs: *I see you,* not *See I you.* These rules are observed without conscious choice by every native speaker of English.
2. A handful of rules distinguish standard speech from nonstandard: *you were* versus *you was, I don't know anything* versus *I don't know nothing.* The only writers who choose whether to obey these rules are those striving to join the ed-

ucated class. Schooled writers think about such rules only when they see them violated.

3. Finally, some grammarians have *invented* rules that they think all educated writers *should* observe. Most such rules date from the last half of the eighteenth century:

   - Don't split infinitives, as in *to quietly leave.*
   - Don't use *than* after *different;* use *from.*
   - Don't use *between* with three or more.

   A few date from this century:

   - Don't use *hopefully* for *I hope,* as in *Hopefully, it won't rain.*
   - Don't use *which* for *that* in a RESTRICTIVE CLAUSE, as in *a car* ***which*** *I sold.*

Few of these rules have any foundation in history, and fewer still in the reliable habits of the best writers. By confounding these three quite different kinds of rules, grammarians have misled countless teachers and their students into believing that splitting an infinitive is an error as egregious as a double negative, and that both are almost on a par with scrambled syntax.

We will concentrate on that third class of rules—the trivia of usage, because only they vex educated writers. They are the rules that most of us remember from high school and whose "violation" pop-grammarians endlessly rehearse as evidence for the Decline of Western Values. But since grammarians have for centuries been accusing the best writers of violating these same rules, we have to conclude that for centuries the best writers have chosen to ignore both the rules and grammarians. Which is lucky for the grammarians, because if writers did obey all their rules, grammarians would have to keep inventing new ones, or find another line of work.

The fact is that some educated and careful writers honor every rule, but most careful writers choose to observe fewer, and their readers notice fewer still. A few writers know all the rules, but know also that they need observe only certain ones, and that other rules they can observe or ignore, as they choose.

Observing Rules Thoughtfully

But what exactly do you do if you want not only to write well but to write "correctly"?

The Worst (i.e., Safest) Case Policy

You could choose the worst-case policy: Follow all the rules all the time because somewhere, sometime, some reader might criticize you for something—for beginning a sentence with *and* or ending it with *up*. And so you scrutinize every sentence for "errors" until you learn the rules so well that you obey them without thought.

But if you follow all the rules all the time, you surrender a measure of stylistic choice. Worse, you may find yourself so obsessed with rules that you tie yourself—and your writing—into knots. And sooner or later, you will try to impose those rules—real or not—on others. After all, what good is learning a rule if all you can do is obey it?

A More Thoughtful (i.e., Riskier) Approach

The alternative to blind obedience is selective observance. But which rules must you observe, which can you ignore, and which do you observe or ignore, as you choose? And then if you do decide to ignore some trivial rule, how do you deal with those whose passion for good grammar seems to endow them with the ability to identify in a split infinitive signs of social and moral decay?

If you want to avoid being labeled "permissive," or worse "without standards," but if you also decline to submit mindlessly to whatever "rule"someone can dredge up from memories of ninth grade English, you have to know more about the rules than do the rule-mongers. For example, some teachers and editors like to abuse those who begin a sentence with *and* or *but*. For matters of this kind, it is useful to consult the most conservative guide to correct English (the standard for the most linguistically conservative Americans): H. W. Fowler's *A Dictionary of Modern English Usage* (first edition, Oxford University Press, 1926; second edition, 1965). The second edition was edited by Sir Ernest Gowers, who to Fowler's original entry on *and* added this observation:

> That it is a solecism to begin a sentence with *and* is a faintly lingering superstition. (p. 29)

To the original entry for *but,* Gowers added "see *and.*" (For more examples of rules exploded, see Fowler's entries on Fetishes, Illiteracies, Superstitions, and Sturdy Indefensibles. A reliable summary of American authorities is Roy H. Copperud, *American Usage and Style: The Consensus* [Van Nostrand Reinhold, New York, 1980].)

To be sure, even the best writers commit an occasional error. We all have occasionally slipped up on the number for a verb distant from its subject, and when someone points it out, we gratefully correct it. But the standard for "good" grammar is defined not by random errors but by the *consensus* of usage established by the habitual choices of writers who are considered competent by careful readers.

Here's the point: If vast numbers of otherwise careful writers choose to begin a sentence with *but* and the vast majority of educated, careful readers don't notice, then regardless of what any editor says, beginning a sentence with *but* can be neither a grammatical error nor a violation of "good" usage.

DISTINGUISHING KINDS OF RULES

On the basis of those two principles—how the best writers unselfconsciously and *predictably* write, and how their best readers read—we can identify one set of rules quite easily: those whose violation marks someone as unschooled:

- Don't use double negatives: *The committee had hardly no time to meet.*
- Don't use objective forms of pronouns in subjects: *Him and me are ready.*
- Don't use nonstandard verb forms: *They knowed what we wanted.*
- Don't let your verbs disagree with your subjects: *She don't understand.*

But these are rules that educated writers don't *choose* to obey; they obey them unthinkingly, as they should.

It's the other rules that cause the anxiety, and we can sort them into two groups: Folklore and Options.

1. *Folklore.* When you violate these "rules," few educated readers notice, much less care. So these are not rules at all, but folklore that you can choose to ignore, unless you are writing for someone who can exact from you whatever kind of writing that person idiosyncratically prefers.
2. *Options.* When you ignore these rules, few readers notice. But many careful readers will notice when you observe them, because when you do, you signal special formality or at least discriminating taste. So you can choose to observe these rules or not, depending on the stylistic effects you want to achieve among different groups of readers.

FOLKLORE

These rules include those whose observance we ignore, and whose violation we ignore as well. I decided what to include in this category based on reading a good deal of prose that was carefully written and intended to be read just as carefully. The quotations that illustrate "violations" of these nonrules are from writers who are of substantial intellectual and scholarly stature or who, on matters of usage, are reliable archconservatives (occasionally they are both). Some of these "rules" may be new to you, but even if you have not yet had one inflicted on you, chances are that eventually, you will.

1. "Don't begin sentences with *and* or *but.*" Allegedly, not this, a passage violating the "rule" twice (check marks will hereafter indicate sentences that are either acceptable or preferred in comparison to another):

   ✓ **But,** it will be asked, is tact not an individual gift, therefore highly variable in its choices? **And** if that is so, what guidance can a manual offer, other than that of its author's prejudices—mere impressionism?

   —Wilson Follett, *Modern American Usage: A Guide,* edited and completed by Jacques Barzun et al.

Most highly regarded writers choose to begin sentences with *and* or *but,* some more than once a page.

Some writers now even think that they should not begin a sentence with *because.* They would criticize this:

✓ **Because** we have access to so much historical fact, today we know a good deal about changes within the humanities which were not apparent to those of any age much before our own and which the individual scholar must constantly reflect on.

—Walter Ong, S.J., "The Expanding Humanities and the Individual Scholar," *Publication of the Modern Language Association*

This proscription appears in no handbook, but it is gaining popular currency. It must stem from advice intended to avoid sentence FRAGMENTS like this one:

The application was rejected. **Because** the deadline had passed.

The introductory *because* is correct when we attach it to a MAIN CLAUSE and punctuate the two as a single PUNCTUATED SENTENCE:

✓ Because the deadline has passed, the application was rejected.

A recent variation on this theme is the suspicion that neither should we begin a sentence with a preposition:

✓ **In** the morning, everyone left.

This bit of folklore probably results from overgeneralizing the "rule" about not *ending* a sentence with a preposition. Neither is a "rule" with any substance whatsoever.

2. "Use the RELATIVE PRONOUN *that*—not *which*—for restrictive clauses." Allegedly, not this:

✓ Next is a typical situation **which** a practiced writer corrects "for style" virtually by reflex action.

—Jacques Barzun, *Simple and Direct,* p. 69.

Yet on just the previous page, Barzun himself had written,

> Us[e] *that* with defining clauses except when stylistic reasons interpose.

(No reasons interposed here.) A rule has no force when a writer as prestigious as Jacques Barzun can assert it on one page and on the next unselfconsciously violate it and it is never caught, not by his editors, or by his proofreaders, not even by Barzun himself.

This "rule" first appeared in 1906 in Henry and Francis Fowler's *The King's English* (Oxford University Press; reprinted as an Oxford University Press paperback, 1973). The Fowlers invented the rule, because they thought that the random variation between *which* and *that* in restrictive clauses was messy. So they simply announced that writers henceforth should (with some exceptions) limit *which* to nonrestrictive clauses.

A nonrestrictive clause, you may recall, describes a noun that a reader can identify unambiguously without the help of a modifying clause. In this position, *which* enjoys the support of historical and contemporary usage:

✓ ABCO ended its bankruptcy, **which** it had filed in 1992, last week.

A company can have only one bankruptcy at a time, so any reader unambiguously identifies that bankruptcy as the only one in question. The clause is called nonrestrictive, because in the mind of the reader, that clause cannot "restrict" the meaning of the noun phrase any more than it already is. The writer therefore puts a comma before and after the modifying clause and begins that clause with *which.*

But, according to the Fowlers, we should use only *that* to introduce a *restrictive* clause, a clause necessary for the reader to identify the particular noun it modifies:

✓ ABCO developed a product **that** [*not* **which**] made millions.

Since ABCO probably has developed many products and the reader does not know the particular one referred to, that one product is singled out by the identifying clause, *that made millions,* from an indefinite set of others. In this case, the writer does *not* put a comma before the modifying clause, and, at least according to the Fowlers, should begin the clause not with *which* but with *that.*

In fact, this "rule" did not then and does not now enjoy the support of either historical or contemporary usage.

Francis died in 1918, but Henry continued the family tradition with *A Dictionary of Modern English Usage.* In that landmark reference work, he devoted more than a page to discussing the finer points of choosing between *which* and *that,* and then, a bit wistfully perhaps, added this:

> Some there are who follow this principle now; but it would be idle to pretend that it is the practice either of most or of the best writers. (p. 635)

That melancholy observation must have been judged still relevant to our own usage, because it was retained in the second edition. (For another example of this usage, see the passage by Walter Ong on p. 23.)

Having said all that, I confess I try to follow Fowler's advice, not because I think that a restrictive *which* is an error, but because *that* is less obtrusive a word. I do choose a *which* when it is within a few words of a *that* to avoid repeating it:

✓ We all have that one principle *which* we will not compromise.

3. "Use *fewer* with nouns you count, *less* with nouns you can't." Allegedly not this:

✓ I can remember no **less** than five occasions when the correspondence columns of *The Times* rocked with volleys of letters. . . .

—Noel Gilroy Annan, Lord Annan.
"The Life of the Mind in British Universities Today,"
American Council of Learned Societies Newsletter

No one uses *fewer* with uncountable mass nouns (*fewer sand*) but educated writers often use *less* with countable plural nouns (*less resources*).

A few other words are commonly used in ways proscribed by many conservative critics. Most careful writers use *since* to refer not just to a point in time (*We've been here* **since** *Friday*) but also with a meaning close to "We take for granted the truth of what follows *since*":

> ✓ **Since** we agree, we need not discuss it further.

Careful writers use *while* in the same way. They do not restrict it to its temporal sense (*We'll wait* **while** *you eat*), but use it as well with a meaning close to "What I state in this clause is true, but what I assert in the next qualifies it":

> ✓ **While** we agree on the problems, we disagree about solutions.

On the other hand, the occasional advice to avoid *as* as a causal conjunction is sound, because as a signal of causation it is weak:

> **As** the expenses are minor, we need not discuss them.

Use *since* instead.

On the most formal of occasions, you might choose to observe all of these rules. In ordinary contexts, though, these "rules" are ignored by most careful writers, which is to say that they are not rules at all. If you adopt the worst-case approach and observe them all, all the time—well, private virtues are their own reward.

OPTIONS THAT SIGNAL FORMALITY

These rules complement the Real Rules: Few readers notice when you violate them, but when you choose to observe them, careful readers will assume that you are either being grammatically fastidious or signaling special formality.

1. "Do not split infinitives."

   Purists would condemn Dwight MacDonald, a linguistic archconservative, for this:

   > ✓ One wonders why Dr. Gove and his editors did not think of labeling *knowed* as substandard right where it occurs, and one suspects that they wanted **to *slightly* conceal** the fact or at any rate to put off its exposure as long as decently possible.
   >
   > —"The String Untuned," *The New Yorker*

   They would require

   > One suspects that they wanted **to conceal** the fact ***slightly***. . . .

The split infinitive is now so common among the best writers that when they avoid splitting one, they invite careful readers to think that they are being formal, whether those writers choose to or not.

2. "Use *shall* as the first person simple future, *will* for second and third person simple future; use *will* to mean strong intention in the first person, *shall* for second and third person."

   Purists would condemn F. L. Lucas, a highly regarded writer on matters of style, for this, preferring *shall.*

   ✓ **I will** end with two remarks by two wise old women of the civilized eighteenth century.

   —"What Is Style?" *Holiday*

   They would be right, but only if readers had some reason to expect special formality.

3. "Use *whom* as the OBJECT of a verb or preposition."

   Purists would condemn William Zinsser for this:

   ✓ Soon after you confront this matter of preserving your identity, another question will occur to you: "**Who** am I writing for?"

   —*On Writing Well*

   They would insist on

   . . . another question will occur to you: "**For whom** am I writing?"

   Most readers take *whom* to be a small but distinct flag of self-conscious correctness. And when a writer chooses it incorrectly, that choice is probably a sign of anxiety.

   An actual rule: If you do use *who* or *whom,* decide whether it is a subject or an object *of its own clause.* Use *who* if it is a subject, *whom* if an object. Not this:

   The committee must decide **whom** should be promoted.

   In that sentence, *whom* is subject of the verb *should be promoted,* so should be *who.* This self-conscious use of *whom* probably arises from the same impulse that motivates the incorrect choice of the nominative case in *between you and I.* Though the *I* there has been common in conversation since at least the middle of the eighteenth century, it still rankles a good many purists.

4. "Do not end a sentence with a preposition."
   Purists would condemn Sir Ernest Gowers for this:

✓ The peculiarities of legal English are often used as a stick to beat the official **with.**

—*The Complete Plain Words*

and insist on this:

. . . a stick **with** which to beat the official.

The first is correct; the second formal. (And again see the Father Ong example on p. 23.) And when you choose to move a preposition away from the end of a sentence, you make that sentence even more formal if the preposition carries with it an obligatory *whom.* Compare:

✓ The man I spoke **with** was the man I had written **to.**

The man **who** I spoke **with** was the man **who** I had written **to.**

✓ The man **with whom** I had spoken was the man **to whom** I had written.

We should recognize, however, that a final preposition can make a sentence seem weak (see pp. 146–47, 216). George Orwell may have chosen to end this next sentence with a preposition to make a point about English grammar, but I suspect it just turned up there (and note the *which* toward the end).

[The defense of the English language] has nothing to do with archaism, with the salvaging of obsolete words and turns of speech, or with the setting up of a "standard English" which must never be departed **from.**

—George Orwell, "Politics and the English Language"

This would have been less awkward and more emphatically concise:

We do not defend the English language just to preserve archaisms or to create a "standard English" whose rules we must always obey.

5. "Contrary-to-fact statements require the subjunctive."
   Purists would correct this, written by H. W. Fowler himself:

✓ Another suffix that is not a living one, but is sometimes treated as if it **was,** is *-al.*

—*A Dictionary of Modern English Usage*

They would insist on this:

✓ Another suffix that is not a living one, but is sometimes treated as if it **were,** is *-al.*

As the subjunctive sinks into the sunset of linguistic history, it casts over a sentence a faintly archaic and therefore formal glow.

To express subjunctives, we usually use just the simple past tense:

✓ If we **knew** what to do, we **would** do it.

The problem is the forms of *be:* Strictly construed, the subjunctive demands *were,* but it is being displaced by *was:*

✓ If this **were** 1941, a loaf of bread would cost 20 cents.

✓ If this **was** 1941, a loaf of bread would cost 20 cents.

Certainly, when readers expect the most formal English, the prudent writer so chooses, but the emphasis is on *choice.*

6. "Use the singular with *none* and *any.*"

   Historically *none* and *any* were originally singular and so took singular verbs, but today most writers use them as plurals. Therefore, if you use them as singular, some readers are likely to notice. The second is slightly more formal than the first:

   ✓ **None** of the reasons **are** sufficient to end the project.

   ✓ **None** of the reasons **is** sufficient to end the project.

If you are careful about the way you choose to use another small group of words, you can distinguish yourself in the eyes of some very exacting readers who believe that most writers today use these words carelessly. For example, these days, relatively few writers distinguish *flaunt* from *flout.* So if you choose to use either word correctly, those readers who think the difference is worth preserving will take note that at least someone still knows that *flaunt* means to display oneself or something in a deliberately conspicuous way and that *flout* means to ignore a rule or standard scornfully. So when you flout a rule in a particularly public and scornful way, you flaunt your flouting it. Here are some others:

> *aggravate,* meaning 'to make worse.' It does not mean simply to 'annoy' or 'irritate.'
>
> *anticipate,* meaning 'to plan ahead in order to prepare for a contingency.' It does not mean just 'expect.'
>
> *anxious,* meaning 'uneasy and worried.' It does not mean 'eager.'
>
> *blackmail,* meaning 'to extort by threatening to reveal damaging information.' It does not mean simply 'extort by any kind of threat.'
>
> *cohort,* meaning 'a group of people who attend on someone.' It does not mean a single accompanying person, much less 'consort'—the spouse of a royal person.
>
> *continuous,* meaning 'without interruption.' It does not mean 'continual,' which means an activity extending over a period of time possibly with interruptions.
>
> *disinterested,* meaning 'neutral.' It does not mean 'not interested.'
>
> *enormity,* meaning something 'monstrously evil.' It does not mean just 'huge.'
>
> *fortuitous,* meaning 'by chance.' It does not mean 'fortunate.'
>
> *fulsome,* meaning 'sickeningly excessive.' It does not mean just 'a lot.'
>
> *notorious,* meaning 'well known for bad behavior.' It does not mean simply 'famous.'
>
> *comprise,* meaning 'to include all parts in a single unit.' It does not mean on the one hand parts constituting a whole nor on the other the looser meaning of a whole merely 'including' a few parts from among many.

When parts make up a whole, they *constitute* it. Thus these words constitute this sentence. On the other hand, the whole comprises all of its parts. Thus this sentence comprises its words. The ACTIVE form of each verb is almost synonymous with the other's PASSIVE:

ACTIVE		PASSIVE
Words **constitute** a sentence.	=	Words **are comprised by** a sentence.
A sentence **comprises** its words.	=	A sentence **is constituted by** its words.

And then, of course, there are the words *consist* and *compose.*

A whole **consists** of its parts.	=	A whole is **composed** out of its parts.

Though only a relatively few people care about these distinctions these days, they are often readers whose judgment we respect in larger matters. Since it takes only a few minutes to learn how to use these words in ways that testify to your own precision, it may be worth your time to do so, especially if you also think that such distinctions are useful and therefore worth preserving.

On the other hand, you win no distinction for correctly distinguishing *imply* and *infer, principal* and *principle, accept* and *except, affect* and *effect, proceed* and *precede, discrete* and *discreet.* That's just what's expected of educated writers. Most educated readers also notice when a plural Latinate noun is incorrectly used as a singular:

Singular:	*datum*	*criterion*	*medium*	*stratum*	*phenomenon*
Plural:	*data*	*criteria*	*media*	*strata*	*phenomena*

Hobgoblin

Some items have become the object of particularly zealous abuse. There is no explaining why these particular items should excite such passion, but they appear to have become the flags around which those most dedicated to linguistic purity have agreed to rally. None of these "errors" interferes with clarity or concision. But because they arouse such intense animus, every writer should both know their special status and understand that judgments about them are capricious, with no foundation in logic, history, or linguistic efficiency.

1. "Never use *like* for *as* or *as if.*" Not this:

    These operations failed **like** the earlier ones did.

    But this:

    ✓ These operations failed **as** the earlier ones did.

    Like evolved into a SUBORDINATING CONJUNCTION in the eighteenth century when writers began to drop *as* from the phrase *like as,* leaving just *like* to serve as the conjunction. This elision of one element of two is a common linguistic change. We might note that the editor of the second edition of Fowler deleted *like* for *as* from the original list of Illiteracies and moved it into the category of Sturdy Indefensibles.

2. "Use *hopefully* only when the subject of the sentence in fact feels hopeful." Not this:

    ✓ **Hopefully,** the matter will be resolved soon.

    But this:

    ✓ **Hopefully, I want** the matter to be resolved soon.

    This "rule" is so entrenched in the thinking of some that it is impossible to convince them by evidence alone that the rule has no basis in logic or grammar. In fact, at the beginning of a sentence, as every native speaker knows, *hopefully* does refer to the feelings of the speaker. It self-evidently means 'I am hopeful' in

    ✓ **Hopefully,** it will not rain tomorrow.

    It parallels other introductory words such as *candidly, frankly, sadly,* and *happily:*

    ✓ **Candidly,** there is little chance of success.

    ✓ **Seriously,** you must be careful.

    No one condemns this analogous use of *seriously* to describe the speaker's attitude.

3. "Never use *finalize* to mean 'finish,' 'complete,' or 'end.'"

But *finalize* does not mean what those words mean. *Finalize* means 'to clean up the last few small details,' a sense captured by no other word. Some think *finalize* smacks of the bureaucratic mind, an understandable objection. But we ought not believe the word is bad because *-ize* is ugly. If we did, we would also have to reject *nationalize, synthesize, rationalize,* along with hundreds of other common words.

4. "Never never use *irregardless* for *regardless.*" The word blends *irrespective* and *regardless,* but that doesn't legitimize it (or should we say, make it legitimate?).
5. "Never use *impact* as a verb, as in *The survey* ***impacted*** *our strategy.* Use it only as a noun, as in *The survey had an* ***impact*** *on our strategy.*"

   Impact has been used as a verb since the seventeenth century, but on some people, historical evidence has no impact.
6. "Do not modify absolute words such as *perfect, unique, final,* or *complete* with *very, more, quite,* and so on," a rule that would condemn this familiar sentence:

   ✓ We the People of the United States, in order to form a **more perfect** union. . . .

A Special Problem: Pronouns and Sexism

We expect literate writers to make their verbs agree with their subjects:

✓ There **are** several **reasons** for this.

We also expect their pronouns to agree with their antecedents. Not this:

> Early **efforts** to oppose the hydrogen bomb failed because **it** was not coordinated with political communities. **No one** wanted to expose **themselves** to anti-Communist hysteria unless **they** had the support of others.

But this:

✓ Early **efforts** to oppose the hydrogen bomb failed because **they** were not coordinated with political communities. **No one** wanted to expose **himself** to anti-Communist hysteria unless **he** had the support of others.

You must use a singular pronoun to refer to a singular referent:

✓ Early **efforts** to oppose the hydrogen bomb failed because **they** were. . . .

But there are two problems. First, do you use a singular or plural pronoun to refer to a singular noun that is plural in meaning: *group, committee, staff, administration,* and so on? Some writers use a singular pronoun when the group acts as a single entity:

✓ The **committee** has met but has not yet made **its** decision.

But they use a plural pronoun when members of the group act individually:

✓ The **faculty** received the memo, but not all of **them** have read it.

These days the plural is sometimes used in both senses.

Second, what personal pronoun should you use to refer to the indefinite pronouns *someone, everyone, no one* and to singular nouns that do not indicate gender: *teacher, doctor, person, student?* Casual usage invites the plural:

Everyone realizes what a soft life **they** had when **they** get a real job.

When **a person** is on drugs, it is hard to help **them.**

In both cases, more formal usage requires a singular pronoun:

✓ **Everyone** realizes what a soft life **he** had when **he** gets a real job.

✓ When a **person** is on drugs, it is hard to help **him.**

But observe the formal rule, and you raise the thorny problem of sexist language.

Common sense demands that we write in ways that do not gratuitously offend our readers. And we give up nothing when we substitute *police officer* for *policeman* and *synthetic* for *man-made,* and we stop reinforcing stereotypes. (Those who ask whether we should also substitute *person-in-the-moon* for *man-in-the-moon* are being merely tendentious.)

But if we reject *he* as a generic pronoun because it is sexist and *they* because in careful writing it is considered ungrammatical, we are left with either a clumsily intrusive *he or she,* a substantially worse *he/she,* or the worst, *s/he*:

> If a writer does not consider the ethnic background of **his** or **her** readers, **s/he** may respond in ways the writer would not expect to words that to **him** or **her** are innocent of ethnic bias.

So we rewrite. We can begin by substituting plurals for singulars:

✓ When **writers** do not consider the ethnicity of **their** readers. . . .

But to the careful ear, plurals seem less precise than singulars. So we try again. When appropriate, we can substitute a second person *you* or a first person *we* (though some readers object to the royal *we*):

✓ If **we** do not consider the ethnic background of **our** readers, **they** may respond in ways **we** would not expect to words that to **us** are innocent of ethnic bias.

We can also drop people altogether, but that leads to fuzzy abstraction, a problem that, as we shall see, this book aims to eliminate:

> **Failure to consider** ethnic background may lead to an **unexpected response** to words considered innocent of ethnic bias.

Finally, we can alternately use *he* and *she,* as I have done. But that is not a perfect solution, because to some readers, *she* is as intrusive as *he/she.* A reviewer in the *New York Times* wondered what to make of an author whom the reviewer charged with attempting to

> right history's wrongs to women by referring to random examples as "she," as in "Ask a particle physicist what happens when a

quark is knocked out of a proton, and she will tell you. . . .," which strikes this reader as oddly patronizing to women.

We might wonder how it strikes a woman who happens to be a particle physicist.

For years, writers of English will have a problem with the singular generic pronoun, and to some readers, any solution will seem awkward. I suspect that we will eventually accept *they* as a singular:

> No one should turn in **their** writing unedited.

There is precedent: Our second person singular pronoun was once *thou*. But in the fifteenth century, English speakers began to replace it with *you,* originally strictly plural. The same thing could happen with *they.* If that happens, some will predictably claim that the English language has surrendered all pretensions to precision.

PRECISION

We must, however, think about this matter of precision precisely: We must be grammatically correct. But if we define correctness by the standards of both truth and folklore, we risk overlooking what is important—the choices that make prose wordy and confusing or clear and precise. We are not precise when we merely get straight all the *which*es and *that*s, mend every split infinitive, eradicate every *finalize* and *hopefully.* Many who obsess on such details seem oblivious to the more serious matter of imprecision in substantive thought and expression, and it is that kind of imprecise thinking and writing that allows obtuse prose to become the national standard, prose like this next passage that actually appeared in print. Its grammar is as impeccable as its style is impenetrable:

> Too precise a specification of information processing requirements incurs the risk of overestimation resulting in unused capacity or inefficient use of costly resources or of underestimation leading to ineffectiveness or other inefficiencies. Too little precision in specifying needed information processing capacity gives no guidance with respect to the means for the procurement of the needed resources.

All that means is

✓ When you specify too precisely the resources that you need to process information, you may overestimate. If you do, you risk having more capacity than you need or using costly resources inefficiently. But if you do not specify what you need precisely enough, you may fail to guide others in how to procure those resources.

How you revise the one into the other is the object of the next several lessons.

Summing Up

The finer points of correct English are unpredictable, so I can offer no principles that will help you remember them all, much less decide whether any particular point of usage is Real, Optional, or Folklore. Indeed, if "correctness" did submit to principle, it would be no social issue, because most "errors" of usage occur when someone smooths out the idiosyncrasies of Standard English for principled, if unintended, reasons. But, of course, it is the very idiosyncrasy of such rules that makes them so useful. Their unpredictability guarantees that they can be mastered only by those born into the right social world or by those willing to learn such rules as the price of admission.

Actually, I think that those of us who choose to observe all the rules all the time do so not because we think that we are protecting the integrity of the language or the quality of our culture, but because we want to assert a style of our own. Some of us are self-consciously straightforward and plain speaking; others take pleasure in a bit of elegance, in a touch of self-consciously fastidious "class." The *shalls* and *whoms*, the aggressively unsplit infinitives, the subjunctive verbs: they are the private choices that let many of us publicly display our refined sense of linguistic decorum and social conservatism. It is an impulse that we ought not scorn, but only so long as it is informed and thoughtful, and only so long as those who choose to follow all the rules include in their concern the more important matter to which we now turn—the choices that define clear and graceful English prose.

Part Two

Clarity

Everything that can be thought at all can be thought clearly.
Everything that can be said can be said clearly.

Ludwig Wittgenstein

Lesson Three

Clarity 1: Actions

Whatever is translatable in other and simpler words of the same language, without loss of sense or dignity, is bad.
SAMUEL TAYLOR COLERIDGE

It takes less time to learn to write nobly than to learn to write lightly and straightforwardly.
FRIEDRICH WILHELM NIETZCHE

I am unlikely to trust a sentence that comes easily.
WILLIAM GASS

Words and deeds are quite different modes of the divine energy. Words are also actions, and actions are a kind of words.
RALPH WALDO EMERSON

Suit the action to the word, the word to the action.
WILLIAM SHAKESPEARE, *HAMLET,* 3.2

Action is eloquence.
WILLIAM SHAKESPEARE, *CORIOLANUS,* 3.2

MAKING JUDGMENTS

As readers, we have words enough to praise writing that we like: *clear, direct, concise, flowing, readable,* and more than enough to abuse writing we do not: *unclear, indirect, wordy, confusing, abstract, awkward, turgid, disjointed, complex, obscure*—words that we might use to distinguish these two sentences:

1a. The cause of our educational system's failure at teaching basic skills to all children is not understanding the influence of their cultural background on learning.

✓ 1b. Our educational system has failed to teach all children basic skills because we do not understand how their cultural background influences the way they learn.

Most of us would call (1a) indirect and unclear, (1b) clearer, more readable. Saying that, we seem to describe those sentences directly. But we are in fact describing not those sentences, but how they make us *feel.* If we say that (1a) is "less clear" than (1b), we are really saying that *we* have a harder time understanding it. If we say that (1a) is "awkward," we are saying that, reading it, *we* feel uncomfortable.

How our readers feel about what we write is crucial, of course. But if we want to understand not only *what* they feel, but *why* they feel as they do, we need another vocabulary, one less impressionistic than "less clear" and "awkward," one that lets us explain what it is *in* (1a) that makes us want to say that it is unclear, what it is *in* (1b) that makes us want to say it is more readable.

Some measures of clarity, for example, have you (or your computer) calculate ratios of syllables to words to sentences. According to such schemes, when those ratios exceed some number, readers are supposed to find a sentence difficult. If you counted every syllable in every sentence you wrote, though, you'd spend more time counting than writing. But even if your computer can figure those ratios for you, it can't explain how (1a) and (1b) differ, because (1a) has the same number of syllables and words as (1b). And finally, even if a number could tell you which sentence needed work, it couldn't tell you how to fix it.

Telling stories

We respond to (1a) and (1b) differently, not because of their numbers, but because of how those sentences use SUBJECTS and VERBS to tell the *same* story in *different* ways.

Every story needs two things: CHARACTERS and ACTIONS. This story is flawed:

> 2a. Once upon a time, there was Little Red Riding Hood, Grandma, the Woodsman, and Wolf. The end.

Interesting characters, but not much action. Here's some action:

> 2b. Once upon a time, a walk through the woods happened, when a jump out from behind a tree caused fright.

Lots of action, but no characters. This one has both:

> 2c. Once upon a time, a walk through the woods by Little Red Riding Hood to Grandma's house was occurring, when Wolf's jump out from behind a tree caused fright in her.

Something still wrong. What you expect—indeed what you *want*—is this:

> ✓ 2d. Once upon a time, Little Red Riding Hood was walking through the woods to Grandma's house, when Wolf jumped out from behind a tree and frightened her.

Academic writing may seem distant from fairy tales (some of us occasionally think otherwise). But deep down inside, behind all of the scholarly abstraction, all writing has a story to tell, even when a sentence seems analytic, like this one:

> 3a. The Federalists' argument that the destabilization of government was the result of popular democracy was based on their belief in the tendency of factions to further their self-interest at the expense of the common good.

That sentence becomes clearer when we bring to its surface the story about what the characters—Federalists, factions, and popular democracies—are *doing:*

✓ 3b. The Federalists argued that popular democracy destabilized government, because they believed that factions tended to further their self-interest at the expense of the common good.

In (3a), the language seems complex and impersonal; (3b) seems clearer, more direct. These two sentences differ in the same way that the sentences about Little Red Riding Hood differ, and in the same way that sentences (1a) and (1b) differ: They differ in the way each tells essentially the same story about the same characters, but uses its subjects and verbs to tell that story in different ways.

The Narrative Style

We can see how sentences can do that if we start with a sentence that seems clear, then change it into one that is not.

✓ 4a. Although the governor knew that the cities needed more money for schools, she vetoed a bigger education budget to encourage the cities to increase their local taxes.

This sentence seems reasonably clear because we know who the main characters are and what they are doing. The characters are the governor and the cities (a legislature is implied). The governor is the source or AGENT of three connected actions:

1. The governor **knew** something,
2. [yet] she **vetoed** a bigger education budget,
3. [because] she wanted to **encourage** the cities to do something.

The cities are involved in two actions:

4. The cities **need** money,
5. [so] they [should] **increase** their local taxes.

Each of those characters plays the same role in its sentence: They are subjects. And each of their five actions—*knew, vetoed, encourage, need, increase*—is the same part of speech: They are verbs. That's important.

Exercise 3.1

Stop now and write a different version of that story, but instead of using those five verbs to express actions, use their corresponding NOUN forms. Two of those nouns differ from their corresponding verbs:

to know	→	knowledge
to encourage	→	encouragement

The other three nouns are identical to their corresponding verbs:

to need	→	the need
to veto	→	the veto
to increase	→	the increase

Here is one version. Yours may differ:

4b. Despite her **knowledge** of the **need** by cities for more money, the governor executed a **veto** of a bigger education budget to give **encouragement** to cities for an **increase** in local taxes.

At some level, this sentence tells the same story as (4a). But in clarity, the stories differ as much as the two versions of Little Red Riding Hood. How do they differ? It has to do with the way the two versions of the same story use their subjects to name characters and their verbs to express actions.

Look again at the Little Red Riding Hood sentences. First, compare their underlined subjects and bold-faced verbs:

✓ 5a. Once upon a time, <u>Little Red Riding Hood</u> **was walking** through the woods on the way to Grandma's house, when <u>Wolf</u> **jumped** out from behind a tree and **frightened** her.

5b. Once upon a time, <u>a walk through the woods by Little Red Riding Hood to Grandma's house</u> **happened,** when <u>Wolf's jump out from behind a tree</u> **caused** fright in her.

In (5a), the subjects of the verbs *walk, jump,* and *frighten* are the main characters in the story: *Little Red Riding Hood, Wolf.*

But in (5b), the subjects of the two verbs—*happened* and *caused*—are not characters but abstractions: *a walk through the woods* and *Wolf's jump out.*

Second, compare the actions in (5a) and (5b). They are boldfaced.

✓ 5a. Once upon a time, Little Red Riding Hood **was walking** through the woods on the way to Grandma's house, when Wolf **jumped** out from behind a tree and **frightened** her.

5b. Once upon a time, a **walk** through the woods by Little Red Riding Hood to Grandma's house happened, when Wolf's **jump** out from behind a tree caused **fright** in her.

In (5a), the actions are all verbs: *was walking, jumped, frightened.* In (5b), on the other hand, the actions are not verbs, but abstract nouns: *walk, jump,* and *fright.*

Now make the same comparisons between those more academic sentences about the Federalists and factions, (6a) and (6b) below. We find the same pattern of differences (subjects are underlined; verbs are boldfaced; actions are italicized):

6a. <u>The Federalists' *argument* that the *destabilization* of government **was** a consequence of popular democracy</u> **was based** on their *belief* in the *tendency* of factions to ***further*** their self-interest at the expense of the common good.

✓ 6b. <u>The Federalists</u> ***argued*** that <u>popular democracy</u> ***destabilized*** government, because <u>they</u> ***believed*** that <u>factions</u> ***tended*** to ***further*** their self-interest at the expense of the common good.

Sentences (6a) and (6b) differ in the same way as (5a) and (5b).

- In the clearer sentence, (6b), all of the subjects are characters and all of the specific actions are verbs:

SUBJECTS	VERBS
Federalists	argued
popular democracy	destabilized
they	believed
factions	tended to further

- But in the less clear sentence, (6a), the subjects are abstractions and two of the verbs have little meaning:

SUBJECTS	**VERBS**
destabilization	was
argument	was based

And the important actions are not in verbs but in nouns: *argue → argument, destabilize → destabilization, believe → belief, tend → tendency.*

Do the same kind of analysis on the sentence that you created for Exercise 3.1.

Here's the point: Readers feel they are reading clear prose when you meet two expectations:

1. You use subjects to name your central characters.
2. You express their most important actions as verbs.

In the rest of this lesson, we first look briefly at how our judgments are influenced by characters and subjects, then in more detail at how those judgments are influenced by actions and verbs. In the next lesson, we'll revisit characters and subjects.

CHARACTERS AND SUBJECTS

To readers, the most important characters are "agents" or "doers," characters who initiate actions or are the source of conditions expressed by specific verbs and adjectives. Look at how sentences (7a) and (7b) represent agents (agents are boldfaced, subjects underlined, verbs italicized):

7a. <u>**Our** lack of data</u> *prevented* evaluation of **state** actions in targeting funds to **areas** in need of assistance.

✓ 7b. Because <u>**we**</u> *lacked* data, <u>**we**</u> *could not evaluate* whether <u>the **state**</u> *had targeted* funds to <u>**areas** that</u> *needed* assistance.

In (7a), the less clear sentence, there are three characters: *we* in the form of *our, state,* and *areas.* Where do those characters appear? None of them is the subject of a verb; the subject of the verb *prevented* in (7a) is an abstraction, *lack:*

Our **lack** *of data*$_{\text{subject}}$ prevented$_{\text{verb}}$. . . .

If the characters in (7a) are not in subjects, where are they in the sentence?

- *Our* is a modifier of *lack:* ***our*** *lack.*
- *State* is a modifier of *action:* ***state*** *action.*
- *Areas* is the PREPOSITIONAL OBJECT: *to* ***areas***

Now look at where those same characters appear in (7b):

✓ 7b. Because **we** lacked data, **we** could not evaluate whether the **state** had targeted funds to **areas** that needed assistance.

In the clearer sentence, these characters are consistently subjects:

- *We* is the subject of the verbs *lacked* and *could not evaluate:*

  Because **we** *lacked* . . . **we** *could* not *evaluate*. . . .

- *The state* is subject of the verb *had targeted:*

  the state *had targeted*. . . .

- *Area* is the object of *to* (***to*** *areas*), but also the subject of *needed:*

  areas **that** *needed* assistance.

Sentence (7a), the less clear sentence, consistently departs from our first principle: Its author did *not* make characters subjects of verbs, and so readers judge it to be less clear than (7b). Sentence (7b), on the other hand, does observe that principle: It makes characters subjects of verbs, and so readers judge it to be clearer.

> ***Here's the point (again):*** When you consistently write sentences whose subjects are characters, your readers will judge your prose to be clearer than if you had not.

But that's only half the story; the other half has to do with verbs.

VERBS AND ACTIONS

As we use the word here, *action* covers movement, mental process, relationships, conditions, literal or figurative. Just as your sentences will seem clearer if you use characters as subjects, so will your sentences seem clearer if you express actions in verbs. Look at how sentences (7a) and (7b) express the actions their characters perform. In (7a), actions (bold faced) are not verbs (italicized), but nouns:

> 7a. Our **lack**$_{\text{noun}}$ of data *prevented* **evaluation**$_{\text{noun}}$ of state **action**$_{\text{noun}}$ in **targeting**$_{\text{noun}}$ funds to areas in **need**$_{\text{noun}}$ of **assistance**$_{\text{noun}}$.

In the clearer sentence (7b), on the other hand, the actions are almost all verbs:

> ✓ 7b. Because we ***lacked***$_{\text{verb}}$ data, we could not ***evaluate***$_{\text{verb}}$ whether the state had ***targeted***$_{\text{verb}}$ funds to areas that ***needed***$_{\text{verb}}$ **assistance**$_{\text{noun}}$.

These two sentences differ not in some abstract ratio of syllables/words, but in whether their subjects and verbs name characters and actions.

Verb → Noun = Nominalization

If our readers think that we have written in ways that seem complex, impersonal, or abstract, we have almost certainly used too many abstract nouns, particularly nouns derived from verbs and ADJECTIVES, nouns typically ending in *-tion, -ment, -ence,* and so on. Such nouns have a technical name: NOMINALIZATIONS. The word illustrates its own meaning: When we nominalize the verb *nominalize,* we create the nominalization *nominalization.*

VERB	→	NOMINALIZATION	ADJECTIVE	→	NOMINALIZATION
discover	→	discovery	careless	→	carelessness
resist	→	resistance	different	→	difference
react	→	reaction	proficient	→	proficiency

We can also nominalize a verb by adding *-ing* (making it a GERUND):

She *flies* → her *flying* We *sang* → our *singing*

Some nominalizations are identical to their corresponding verb:

hope → hope result → result repair → repair charge → charge

✓ We **request**$_{\text{verb}}$ that when you **return**$_{\text{verb}}$, you **review**$_{\text{verb}}$ the data.
Our **request**$_{\text{noun}}$ is that on your **return**$_{\text{noun}}$ you do a **review**$_{\text{noun}}$ of the data.

The frequent use of nominalizations instead of verbs results in the frustration of reader expectations. Their expectation is of the appearance of characters as subjects and their actions as verbs. Increased frustration results from dropping characters from sentences altogether. That feeling no doubt occurred in your reading of this:

Once upon a time, a walking through the woods occurred, when a jump out from behind a tree caused surprise.

Dropping Little Red Riding Hood and the Wolf from the story became a possibility subsequent to the nominalization of the verb *walk* into the nominalization *walking,* the verb *jump* into the nominalization *jump,* and the verb *surprise* into the nominalization *surprise.*

Actions in Adjectives

Actions occasionally hide out in adjectives, as well. These adjectives usually appear after a form of *be:*

The results *are* **indicative** that the data *are* **representative** of the population.

✓ The results **indicate** that the data **represent** the population.

Some examples:

applicable → apply	deserving of → deserve	dubious → doubt
fearful of → fear	hopeful → hope	indicative → indicate
reflective → reflect	representative → represent	suggestive → suggest

Exercise 3.2

Analyze the subject/character and verb/action patterns in this pair of sentences in the same way we analyzed the other pairs of sentences:

8a. There is public opposition to nuclear power plants near population centers because of a widespread belief in their threat to human health.

✓ 8b. The public opposes nuclear power plants near population centers because it believes that they threaten human health.

Reformulating Some Ninth Grade Definitions

Most of what you've read here contradicts what most of us learned about subjects and verbs in the ninth grade. Then, most of us learned that the order of S–V–O was fixed, and so were their definitions: subjects *are* characters (then called "doers"), verbs *are* actions, objects *are* "receivers."

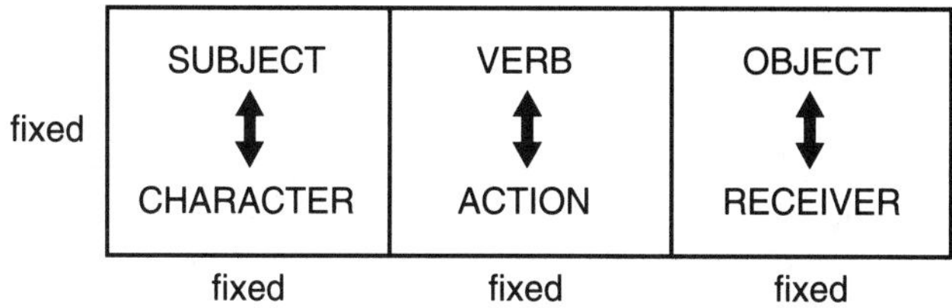

That happens to be true in a sentence like this:

subject	verb	object
We	analyzed	the problem.
doer	action	receiver

But it is not true for this almost synonymous sentence:

subject	verb	complement		modifier	object
The problem	was	the object	of	our	analysis.
receiver				doer	action

So instead of that ninth grade model of a sentence, a model in which not only word order but definitions of subject and verb are fixed, versatile writers learn a new one. It is a model of sentences that makes ideas like "doer" and "action" only *contingently* connected to subject and verb, and that gives you the freedom to put those characters and actions where you choose:

fixed	SUBJECT	VERB	COMPLEMENT
variable	CHARACTER	ACTION	———

But that choice is not wholly independent of the desires of our readers, because while we may move characters and actions around, our readers would prefer that we keep most of them in subjects and verbs.

Here's the point: Subjects *may be* characters and verbs *may be* actions. But those are *not* fixed relationships.

- By turning verbs into nouns, we can move actions into different positions.
- We can move characters into different positions in a sentence, even drop them altogether.
- We can even turn characters into verbs: ***chair*** *a meeting,* ***pilot*** *a plane,* ***guard*** *a prisoner.*

But while writers are free to move these elements of a story in and out of different grammatical positions, readers generally prefer sentences whose parts fit those traditional ninth grade school definitions: subjects *as* characters, actions *as* verbs. That's the kind of prose that readers call clear and direct.

Exercise 3.3

Here are several verbs, adjectives, and nominalizations. If you are feeling at all uncertain about the differences, spend a few minutes turning the verbs and adjectives into nominalizations and nominalizations into adjectives and verbs. Recall that some verbs and nominalizations have the same form:

✓ Poverty predictably **causes** social problems.
Poverty is a predictable **cause** of social problems.

analysis	*believe*	*attempt*	*conclusion*	*emphasize*	*evaluate*
suggest	*approach*	*comparison*	*define*	*discuss*	*explanation*
expression	*failure*	*acquisition*	*appeal*	*appearance*	*description*
decrease	*improve*	*increase*	*accuracy*	*careful*	*clear*
intelligence	*important*	*precise*	*relevant*	*decide*	*explicit*

Exercise 3.4

Now make up two or three sentences using in each of them two or three of these verbs and adjectives. Then rewrite those sentences you just created by using the corresponding nominalizations to express the same idea. In some cases, you change an adjective to an adverb. For example, picking *suggest, discuss,* and *careful,* you first write:

✓ I **suggest** that we **discuss** the issue **carefully.**

Then rewrite that sentence into its nominalized form:

My **suggestion** is that our **discussion** of the issue be done with **care.**

It may seem odd to ask you to make a clear sentence unclear. But only when you see how a sentence can be less clear than it is will you understand why it seemed clear in the first place.

Exercise 3.5

Exchange with other students some of the nominalized sentences that you made up to see whether you can revise theirs and they can revise yours back to the originals.

Exercise 3.6

Now do the reverse. Make up some sentences using two or three nominalizations in each; then try to express the same idea using corresponding verbs, adjectives, and adverbs. This is harder.

Exercise 3.7

Revise any paragraph in Lesson One (or in any text that you think is clearly written) by substituting nominalizations for the important verbs. For example, the preceding sentence could be rewritten

> Do a **revision** of any paragraph in Lesson One (or any text whose **writing** is, in your **thinking,** characterized by **clarity**) by substituting nominalizations for verbs of **importance.**

Then exchange your passage with someone else's to see if you can return each other's revision to the original.

FROM DIAGNOSIS TO ANALYSIS TO REVISION

These two principles about characters as subjects and actions as verbs help you analyze and explain why readers judge a sentence to be clear or unclear. But just as important, those principles also suggest how you can revise it. (Again, note the emphasis on *revise.* Only after you have thoroughly assimilated them as habits of revision can these principles become part of your habits of drafting.)

Three Steps: Diagnosis, Analysis, Revision

1. Diagnosis: If you want to predict whether a reader might think your prose is unclear, hard to read, do this:
   a. Ignoring short introductory phrases, underline the first seven or eight words in each of your sentences.
   b. Look for three characteristics:

- Sentences begin not with characters, but with abstract nouns.
- Sentences take more than six or seven words to get to a verb.
- Verbs represent actions that are less specific than the abstractions around them.

2. Analysis: If you find such sentences, do this:
   a. Find or invent a cast of characters.
   b. Find nominalizations that name the actions those characters perform.
3. Revision: Once you locate the characters and their actions, do this:
   a. Change the nominalizations into verbs and adjectives.
   b. Make the characters the subjects of those new verbs.
   c. Rewrite the sentence with conjunctions like *because, if, when, although.*

Exercise 3.8

A paragraph in the last few pages is quite nominalized. Find and revise it.

SOME TYPICAL PATTERNS AND THEIR REVISIONS

A few common patterns of nominalizations are easy to spot and revise.

1. A nominalization follows a verb with little specific meaning. In these cases, the subject is probably already a character:

   The agency *conducted* an **investigation** into the matter.

   - Change the nominalization to a verb.
   - Replace the empty verb with your new verb.

   ✓ The agency **investigated** the matter.

2. A nominalization follows *there is* or *there are,*

   There is no **need** for further **study** of this problem.

- Change the nominalization to a verb.
- Find a new subject.

✓ *The engineering staff* **need** not **study** this problem further.

3. The nominalization is the subject of an empty verb:

   The **intention** of the IRS *is* to audit the records.

   - Change the nominalization to a verb.
   - Find a character to be its subject:

   ✓ *The IRS* **intends** to audit the records.

4. Two or three nominalizations in a row are joined by prepositions:

   There was first a **review** *of* the **evolution** *of* the dorsal fin.

   - Turn the first nominalization into a verb.
   - Either leave the second alone,
   - Or turn it into a verb in a CLAUSE beginning with *how* or *why:*

   ✓ First, she **reviewed** the **evolution** of the dorsal fin.
   ✓ First, she **reviewed** *how* the dorsal fin **evolved.**

5. Often, one nominalization appears in a subject and a second in the COMPLEMENT of a verb or phrase like *be, seems, has the result of,* etc.:

   Their **increase** in revenues was a result of their **expansion** of outlets.

You have to revise these sentences more extensively:

- Identify the nominalizations in the two halves:

Subject:	Their **increase** in revenues
Connecting verb or phrase:	was a result of
Complement:	their **expansion** of outlets.

- Make nominalizations verbs: *increase* → *increase, expansion* → *expand.*

- Find subjects for those verbs: **they** *increase,* **they** *expand.*
- Link the new clauses with a word that expresses their logical connection.

That connection will typically be some kind of causal relationship:

- To express simple cause: *because, since, when*
- To express conditional cause: *if, provided that, so long as*
- To contradict expected causes: *though, although, unless*

Their **increase** in revenues	→ ✓	They **increased** revenues
was the result of	→	**because**
their **expansion** in outlets.	→	they **expanded** outlets.

Exercise 3.9

These pairs contrast in nominal and verbal styles. Identify which is which: Circle nominalizations, and underline verbs.

1a. Some have argued that carbon dioxide in the atmosphere will almost certainly elevate global temperature.

1b. There has been speculation by educators as to the positive effect of a good family environment on educational achievement.

2a. Smoking during pregnancy may lead to fetal injury.

2b. When we write concisely, readers understand more easily.

3a. AIDS researchers have identified the AIDS virus but have failed to develop a vaccine that will immunize those at risk.

3b. Attempts by economists at formulating principles for the definition of full employment have achieved some success.

4a. Complaints by editorial writers about voter apathy should also provide suggestions about dispelling it.

4b. Although many critics have claimed that when children watch television they tend to become less able readers, no one has yet demonstrated that to be true.

5a. The loss of market share to Japan by domestic auto makers resulted in the loss of employment of hundreds of thousands of workers and a decline in domestic auto production.

5b. If educators could discover ways to use computer-assisted instruction, our schools could teach more complex subjects and students could learn them faster.

6a. We need to know which areas of our national forests are being logged most extensively so that we can save virgin stands at greatest risk.

6b. There is a need for an analysis of the intensity of library use to provide a reliable base for the projection of needed new resources.

7a. Professional athletes often discover that they are unprepared for life after stardom because their teams protect them from the problems that the rest of us adjust to every day.

7b. Many colleges have reached the realization that continued increases in tuition are no longer possible because of strong resistance from parents to the high cost of higher education.

8a. In this article, we examine how buyers influence advertising and how advertising agencies respond to those influences when they create a strategy that appeals to consumers.

8b. This study is a review of responses to rhetorical patterns and of judgments of textual well-formedness by readers with prior knowledge of a subject before reading.

Exercise 3.10

Return to the previous exercise and change the original verbal sentence in each pair into a nominalized sentence. Use the paired nominal version as a pattern for your revision. For example, if the nominalized sentence in the pair begins with *There,* begin your revised sentence with *There:*

Sentence to revise: 1a. Some have **argued** that carbon dioxide in the atmosphere will almost certainly elevate global temperature.

Model: 1b. **There** has been speculation by educators as to the positive effect of a good family environment on educational achievement.

You write: 1c. **There** have been **arguments** by some as to. . . .

Exercise 3.11

Now do the reverse. Revise the original nominalized sentences into corresponding verbal sentences. Use the paired verbal version as a pattern. For example, if the verbal sentence in the pair begins with a *when,* begin your revised sentence with *when:*

Sentence to revise: 2a. **Smoking** during pregnancy may lead to fetal injury.

Model: 2b. **When** we write concisely, readers understand more easily.

Your revision: 2a. **When** pregnant women **smoke**. . . .

Exercise 3.12

Revise these next sentences so that the nominalizations are verbs and characters are the subjects of those verbs. In 1 through 5, characters are italicized and nominalizations are boldfaced.

1. *Lincoln's* **hope** was for the peaceful **preservation** of the Union, but *the South's* **attack** on Fort Sumter marked the **beginning** of the war.
2. **Attempts** were made on the part of *President Nixon's aides* to assert *his* **immunity** from a Supreme Court subpoena.
3. There were **predictions** by *members of the Administration* that the *nominee* would receive quick *committee* **approval.**
4. The *author's* **analysis** of our data omits any **citation** of sources that would provide **support** for *his* criticism of our argument.
5. *The health industry's* **ability** to exert cost **controls** could lead to the *public's* **decision** that *congressional* **action** is not needed.

In sentences 6 through 10, only the agents are boldfaced.

6. A **papal** appeal was made to the **industrialized nations of the world** for assistance to **those in Somalia** facing the threat of starvation.
7. Attempts at explanations for increases in **voter** participation in this year's elections were offered by **several candidates.**
8. The agreement by the **participants** on the program was based on the assumption that there was a promise of **federal** funds.
9. There was no independent **business-sector** study of the cause of the sudden increase in the trade surplus.
10. Agreement as to the need for revisions in the terms of the treaty was reached by **the two sides.**

In 11 through 15, only the nominalizations are boldfaced.

11. There was **uncertainty** in the White House about Iraqi **intentions** in regard to **withdrawal** from Kuwait's borders.
12. There must be thorough **preparation** of the specimen sections by the laboratory personnel.
13. Any **contradictions** among data in any result requires an **explanation** of the reasons for the **inconsistencies.**
14. The board's **rejection** of our proposal was a **disappointment** but not a **surprise** because of our **expectation** that a **decision** had already been made to delay any new initiatives.
15. Their **performance** of the music was marked by great **enthusiasm** but lacked historical **accuracy.**

Some Happy Consequences

We began with these two principles:

- Central characters as subjects.
- Actions as verbs.

When we revise sentences to observe those principles, we make other useful changes:

1. You may have been told to avoid too many prepositional phrases. It's not clear how many is "too many," but whenever you use nominalizations, you have to add prepositional phrases to keep the characters in the sentence. That's just the way the language works. You can eliminate most prepositions by using verbs:

   A revision **of** the program will result **in** increases **in** efficiency **in** servicing clients.

   ✓ If we revise the program, we can serve clients more efficiently.

2. You may have been told to write more concretely. Your sentences will seem more concrete if you name characters in subjects and actions in verbs. Compare:

   There was an affirmative **decision** for program **expansion.**

   ✓ *The Director* **decided** to **expand** the program.

3. You may have been told to order your ideas logically. When you string nominalizations through prepositional phrases, you can distort the logical sequence of your story. This next sequence of actions distorts the chronological sequence. (Actions are boldfaced, the numbers refer to the sequence in which the actions actually occur.) Compare:

   Decisions[4] in regard to **administration**[5] of medication despite **inability**[2] of an irrational patient **appearing**[1] in Trauma Centers to provide legal **consent**[3] rest with the attending physician alone.

   ✓ When a patient **appears**[1] in a Trauma Center and **behaves**[2] so irrationally that he cannot legally **consent**[3] to treatment, only the attending physician can **decide**[4] whether to **administer**[5] medication.

   When you use subjects to name characters and verbs to name their actions, you are more likely to match the logical grammar of your sentences to the chronological sequence of your story.

4. You may have been told to clarify logical relationships. When you nominalize verbs, you often have to use diffuse connectors like *as a result of* and *in regard to.* But when

you use verbs, you must link the new clauses with more precise SUBORDINATING CONJUNCTIONS like *because, although,* and *if:*

> Our effective presentation of our needs **resulted in** our success in acquiring federal funds, **despite** lobbying efforts by others.
>
> ✓ **Although** other agencies lobbied Congress, we acquired federal funds **because** we presented our needs more effectively.

> ***Here's the point:*** When you observe these two principles—characters as subjects and actions as verbs—you help your readers in many ways: They have to read fewer words, the words will be concrete, the sequence of actions coherent, and their logical connections clear.

A Common Problem and Its Solution

At this point you can probably identify problems in the writing of others but have a harder time recognizing them in your own. It's entirely predictable.

Most of you recognize this experience: You write something you think is clear, but when you get it back from a reader, you are told that your ideas are confusing, your organization hard to follow. You wonder whether your critic is just being difficult, but you bite your tongue and try to fix what you are certain should have been clear to anyone who can read prose more complex than stories about My Dog Spot. When that happens to me, I almost always realize—eventually—that my critics were, in fact, right, that they recognized what was unclear better than I did.

How can we be right about other people's writing, and so often so wrong about our own? The answer lies in this paradoxical fact: We judge the writing of others more accurately than we do our own because we usually know less about their subject than they do. And we misjudge the clarity of our own writing, because we know more about our subject than do our readers.

This explains why you are your own worst editor: Who knows more about your subject than you do (or should)? In fact, as you reread your own writing, you usually aren't reading; you're just reminding yourself of what you wanted to mean when you wrote it. But since your readers lack your knowledge, they are likely to respond in ways that you cannot predict. This also explains why two readers can disagree about the quality of the same passage: Someone who understands its content is more likely to think the passage is clearly written than someone who knows less. Both are right.

Since you can never read as your readers do, you have to look at your own writing in ways that sidestep your understanding of it, and to do that, you need a way to diagnose your prose that is almost formulaic:

1. The quickest method is to underline the first seven or eight words of every sentence. If you don't see a character as subject or a verb as an action, you have a candidate for revision:

    Our analysis of the results of the experiment *did not provide* an explanation of its failure, because our data collection lacked the precision needed.

2. A method more demanding but more reliable is to look at the subject of *every* verb in *every* clause.

    Our analysis of the results of the experiment *did not provide* an explanation of its failure, because our data collection *lacked* the precision needed.

3. The most demanding method is to start by looking for *any* nominalization that you can turn into a verb.

    Our **analysis** of the results of the experiment did not provide an **explanation** of its **failure,** because our data **collection** lacked the **precision** needed.

Get the characters into subjects and actions into verbs, and you get a clearer, more concise sentence:

✓ When we **analyzed** the results of the experiment, we could not **explain** why it **failed,** because we did not **collect** data **precisely.**

Again, don't think about these principles as you draft. Apply them only after you have something, anything drafted. You can locate specific passages most likely to need this kind of revision if you can recall where in your drafting you were least confident, where you were struggling with complex ideas. That kind of uncertainty is likely to reveal itself in confused and confusing abstraction.

Useful Nominalizations

I have urged you to avoid nominalizations, so I will now seem to contradict myself by saying that, in fact, you cannot write well without them (the next lesson will expand on this idea). The trick is to know which nominalizations to keep and which to turn into verbs. Keep these:

1. The nominalization is in a subject that refers to a previous sentence:

   ✓ **These arguments** all depend on a single unproven claim.

   ✓ **This decision** can lead to positive outcomes.

   These nominalizations link sentences into a more cohesive flow.

2. A succinct nominalization can replace an awkward *The fact that:*

   The fact that she acknowledged the problem impressed me.

   ✓ **Her acknowledgment of the problem** impressed me.

   But then, why not

   ✓ When she **acknowledged** the problem, she **impressed** me.

3. A nominalization saves a word when it names what would be the object of the verb:

   I accepted **what she requested.**

   ✓ I accepted her **request.**

   This kind of nominalization feels more concrete than an abstract nominalization. Contrast *request* above with this next sense of *request,* one that is more of an action:

Her **request** for assistance was a surprise to us.

✓ When she **requested** assistance, she surprised us.

4. A nominalization at the end of the first sentence of a paragraph, especially after a *there is/are* construction, can introduce a topic that we intend to develop in the sentences that follow:

✓ *There is* no **need,** then, for argument about the **existence,** the **inevitability,** and the **desirability** of **change** [in language]. *There is* **need,** however, for argument about the **existence** of such a thing as good English and correct English. Let us not hesitate to assert that "The pencil was laying on the table" and "He don't know nothing" are at present incorrect no matter how many know-nothings say them.

—Theodore M. Bernstein, *The Careful Writer*

Of course, Bernstein might have revised those first two sentences into this:

✓ While we need not debate whether language changes in ways that are inevitable and desirable, we do argue that some English is correct and good.

5. Some nominalizations refer to a concept so familiar that the concept itself is almost a character.

✓ Few problems have so divided us as **abortion on demand.**

✓ The Equal Rights **Amendment** was an issue in past **elections.**

✓ **Taxation** without **representation** was not central to the **Revolution.**

These nominalizations name familiar concepts: *abortion on demand, amendment, election, taxation, representation, Revolution.* We always compress some familiar concepts into nouns so that we don't have to spell them out repeatedly in subjects and verbs: *freedom, death, love, life.* Without such abstract words, we would find it at least difficult to write about subjects that have preoccupied us for millennia. We have to develop an eye for the nominalization that expresses one of these ideas and the nominalization that hides a significant action:

> There is a **demand** for a **repeal** of the **entertainment tax.**
>
> ✓ We **demand** that the government **repeal** the **entertainment tax.**

We'll take up this matter in more detail in the next lesson.

Exercise 3.13

Revise these sentences. At the end of each is a hint. For example,

> Congress's reduction of the deficit resulted in the decline of interest rates. (because)
>
> ✓ Interest rates declined **because** Congress reduced the deficit.

1. The use of models in teaching prose style does not invariably result in improvements of clarity and directness. (although)
2. Precision in plotting the location of fragments of the vase enhances the possibility of accurate reconstruction. (when)
3. Any departures from the established procedures may cause delays and even termination of the program. (if)
4. A student's lack of socialization into a field may lead to writing problems because of her insufficient knowledge about the construction of arguments by professionals in that field. (When. . . , ... , because . . . .)
5. The successful implementation of a new curriculum depends on the cooperation of faculty with students in setting achievable goals within a reasonable time frame. (In order to. . . , ...)
6. Our evaluation of the outcomes of the programs placed emphasis on objective measures despite our recognition of the low level of rater agreement. (When. . . , ... , even though. . . .)

Exercise 3.14

On any page in the Preface, find five nominalizations and decide whether they should be changed or left as they are.

Exercise 3.15

Look through your old papers for the kinds of problems you have found here. Revise them, then bring the originals to class to exchange with other students who will have done the same thing. Revise each other's prose; then compare your revisions of your own writing with someone else's revision of your writing. Whose do you like better?

Exercise 3.16

Find some professional writing and revise specific verbs into nouns. Then exchange your revisions with someone else, revise each other's passages, then compare your revision with the original.

Clarity, Not Simplemindedness

To the degree that you can match actions to verbs and characters to subjects, your readers will think that you write clearly. But you must also avoid a prose style that sounds as if it were written by a ninth grader. This was written by a student aspiring to academic sophistication:

> After Czar Alexander II's emancipation of Russian serfs in 1861, many freed peasants chose to live on communes for purposes of cooperation in agricultural production as well as for social stability. Despite some communes' attempts at economic and social equalization through the strategy of imposing low economic status on the peasants, which resulted in their reduction to near poverty, a centuries-long history of social distinctions even among serfs prevented social equalization.

In his struggle to follow our principles, he revised that paragraph into sentences that sounded as if they could have been written by a junior high school student:

> In 1861, Czar Alexander II emancipated the Russian serfs. Many of them chose to live on agricultural communes. There they thought they could cooperate with one another in agricultural production. They could also create a stable social structure. The leaders of some of these communes tried to equalize the peasants economically and socially. As one strategy, they tried to impose on all a low economic status that reduced them to near poverty. However, the communes failed to equalize them socially. This happened because even serfs had made social distinctions among themselves for centuries.

In Lessons Nine and Ten we look at ways to revise a series of too-short, too-simple sentences into a style that is readable but still complex enough to communicate complex ideas. Applying those principles to his primer-style passage, he revised again:

> ✓ After the Russian serfs were emancipated by Czar Alexander II in 1861, many chose to live on agricultural communes, hoping they could cooperate in working the land and establish a stable social structure. At first, those who led some of the communes tried to equalize the new peasants socially and economically by imposing on them a low economic status, a strategy that reduced them to near poverty. But the communes failed to equalize them socially because the serfs had for centuries been observing their own social distinctions.

The first two sentences are long but clear, because the writer consistently aligned major characters with subjects and actions with verbs. Admittedly, you cannot do this with every subject and every verb. But to the degree that you can, your readers will think that you write clearly.

SUMMING UP

The System of Clarity

We can represent our principles systematically. As we read, we have to integrate two levels of sentence structure. One level is a predictable and relatively fixed grammatical sequence:

fixed	SUBJECT	VERB	COMPLEMENT

The other level of structure is its story, a level of meaning whose elements have no fixed order, but do appear in one that our readers *expect:*

variable	CHARACTER	ACTION	———

We can graphically represent the conjunction of these principles.

fixed	SUBJECT	VERB	COMPLEMENT
variable	CHARACTER	ACTION	———

Readers expect to see characters not just *in* a subject, as in these two:

> The **President**'s veto of the bill$_{\text{subject}}$ infuriated Congress.
>
> The veto of the bill by the **President**$_{\text{subject}}$ infuriated Congress.

Readers prefer to see the character *as* the subject, like this:

✓ When the **President**$_{\text{subject}}$ vetoed the bill, he$_{\text{subject}}$ infuriated Congress.

They also expect to see verbs express important actions that involve those characters. To the degree that you fail to meet those expectations, to that degree you make your readers work harder and encourage them to judge you an unclear, complex, difficult-to-read writer. So keep these principles in mind as you revise:

1. When appropriate, express actions and conditions in verbs:

   The **intention** of the committee is **improvement** of morale.

   ✓ The committee **intends** to **improve** morale.

2. When appropriate, make subjects of verbs the agents of actions.

   A decision by **the Dean** in regard to the funding by **the Department** of the program is necessary for there to be adequate **staff** preparation.

   ✓ If **the staff** is to prepare adequately, **the Dean** must decide whether **the Department** will fund the program.

Don't revise nominalizations that do the following:

1. Refer to a previous sentence:

   ✓ **These arguments** all depend on a single unproven claim.

2. Sum up an awkward "The fact that":

   The fact that she strenuously objected impressed me.

   ✓ **Her strenuous objections** impressed me.

3. Name what would be the object of a verb:

   I do not know **what she intends.**

   ✓ I do not know her **intentions.**

4. Refer to a familiar and often repeated concept:

   ✓ The Equal Rights **Amendment** was an issue in past **elections.**

5. Occur after *there is/are* introducing a topic that you develop in the next few sentences:

   ✓ *There are* three ways to explain our **successes.** First, we. . . .

Lesson Four

Clarity 2: Characters

I have never had a thought which I could not set down in words, with ever more distinctiveness than that which I conceived it.
EDGAR ALLAN POE

There is no artifice as good and desirable as simplicity.
ST. FRANCIS DE SALES

Affected simplicity is refined imposture.
LA ROCHEFOUCAULD

When character is lost, all is lost.
ANONYMOUS

THE IMPORTANCE OF CHARACTERS

As we saw in the last lesson, we get close to a style that readers judge clear and direct when we consistently express crucial ACTIONS in VERBS. Compare the directness of (1a) with the wordiness of (1b):

✓ 1a. The CIA **feared** the president would **recommend** that Congress should **reduce** its budget.

1b. The CIA had **fears** that the president would make a **recommendation** to Congress for a **reduction** in its budget.

But to your readers, more important than NOMINALIZATIONS alone is how you use CHARACTERS, because when your readers can see characters in most of your SUBJECTS, they can tolerate nominalizations better. Compare (1b) and (1c). Although (1b) has as many nominalizations as (1c), it is clearer than (1c):

1c. The **fear** of the CIA was that a **recommendation** from the president would go to Congress for a **reduction** in its budget.

Readers find (1c) less clear than (1b) because in (1c) the main characters—*the CIA, the president,* and *Congress*—have been changed from subjects of verbs into PREPOSITIONAL OBJECTS: *of the CIA, from the President, to Congress.* But even (1c) is clearer than (1d) below, because (1d) has no characters at all:

1d. There were fears that there would be a recommendation for a reduction in the budget.

Here's the point: The "best" place for the important characters in your story is in the subject of a verb, especially when an important character is the AGENT of the action expressed by the verb. You risk giving your readers problems when you either move characters away from subjects, or worse, delete them entirely.

To revise such sentences, you have to know three things:

1. When you have not put characters where your readers like to see them.
2. Where you should look for characters.
3. What you should do when you find them.

Finding and Relocating Characters

Once you have a draft, do this:

1. First, look at the way your sentences begin: Your readers are likely to have a problem if they don't see a character as a subject in the first six or seven words (ignoring short introductory phrases).
2. Next, locate your characters. Start by looking for characters in POSSESSIVE PRONOUNS that modify a nominalization and in objects of prepositions, particularly *by* and *of.*

   The Federalists' argument that the destabilization *of* **government** was the result *of* **popular democracy** was based on **their** belief in the tendency *of* **factions** to further **their** self-interest at the expense of the common good.

3. Then skim the passage for nominalizations and convert them to verbs with the characters as subjects:

The Federalists' **argument**	→	*The Federalists* **argued**
their **belief**	→	*they* **believed**
destabilization of government was the result	→	*popular democracy* **destabilized** government
tendency of factions to further	→	*factions* **tended** to further

4. Finally, the hardest task: You have to reassemble these propositions into a complete sentence. As you do this, keep in the front of your mind the words *if, although, because, that, when, how,* and *why,* words we use most often to stitch a new sentence together:

✓ The Federalists argued **that** popular democracy destabilized government, **because** they believed **that** factions tended to further their self-interest at the expense of the common good.

Note that sometimes characters hide out in ADJECTIVES:

> Medieval **theological** debates often addressed issues that to modern **philosophical** thought are considered trivial.

When you find a character in an adjective, you can revise in the same way:

> ✓ Medieval **theologians** often debated issues that **philosophers** today consider trivial.

RECONSTRUCTING MISSING CHARACTERS

Readers have their biggest problem when they see no characters at all:

> A decision was made in favor of conducting a study of the disagreements.

We typically write sentences like this in the context of other sentences that do name characters because we assume that a reader can infer characters from the context. That assumption is often a mistake, because readers usually need more help than we think they need. If you are revising your own prose, you rarely can get too specific:

> ✓ **We** decided that **I** should study why **they** disagreed.

We often omit characters in the first place to make general rather than specific statements, so when we revise, we face the problem of creating characters and then deciding what to call them. Unfortunately, English offers few good choices. This sentence lacks characters:

> Multivariate strategies are of more use in understanding factors that contribute to psychiatric disorder than strategies based on the assumption that the presence or absence of psychopathology is dependent on a single major gene or on strategies in which a single biological variable is studied.

When we revise, do we use *one* or *we,* or name some generic "doer?"

✓ If **one/we/researchers** are to understand what causes psychiatric disorder, **one/we/they** should use multivariate strategies rather than assume that a single major gene is responsible for psychopathology or adopt a strategy in which **one/we/they** study only a single biological variable.

Most readers feel that *one* is stiff, but *we* may be ambiguous because it can refer just to the writer, to a group that includes the writer but not the reader, to just reader and writer, or to people in general. And *they* may be ambiguous when a sentence has several plural nouns. As a consequence, when a writer wants to avoid nominalizations but also wants to avoid these pronouns, she can slip into PASSIVE verbs (boldfaced):

To understand what makes patients vulnerable to psychiatric disorders, multivariate strategies **should be used** rather than strategies in which it **is assumed** that a major gene causes psychopathology or only a single biological variable **is studied.**

In extreme cases, characters are so remote from the surface of a sentence that you just have to start over:

There are good reasons to account for the lack of evidence.

✓ **I** can explain why **I** have not found any evidence.

This general problem has no pat solution. The only certain principle is that the more distant and abstract your characters seem, the less likely your readers will admire your prose.

A Major Complication: Abstractions as Characters

So far, we have been thinking about characters as if they were always flesh-and-blood people. I now have to complicate matters by defining character in a different and more complex way, because we can also tell stories about abstractions; indeed, the central characters of some stories are nominalizations. Here's a story about "freedom of speech."

✓ No right is more fundamental than *freedom of speech. Free speech* was the weapon used by the far left in the 1960s to protest against

> the Vietnam War, and *it* is now the weapon of the far right when conservatives claim the federal government is conspiring with the United Nations to take over the country. *The doctrine of free speech* has been embraced by all sides of all questions to guard against those who would silence their unpopular views. *As a distinct concept, it* originated in. . . .

The phrase *free speech* does not refer to any flesh-and-blood character, but we turn it into a *virtual* character when we use it as the subject in a series of sentences and assign to it actions such as *was used, has been embraced,* and *originated.*

So for our purposes from now on, *a character is whatever entity that you can tell a story about,* and you can tell a story about whatever you can make the subject of a sentence. Though typically, that's a flesh-and-blood character, you can also tell stories about abstractions like *free speech.*

When those abstract concepts are as familiar to your readers as *free speech* is to most of us, they respond to those words almost as they would to real characters. But when your readers are not familiar with them, they may find it difficult to distinguish those abstractions from others in the same sentence, and when that happens, the passage may seem to collapse into a muddle of abstractions and prepositional phrases.

For example, if you are unfamiliar with "intention" as a philosophical concept, you may find it difficult under the best of circumstances to understand a story whose main characters are two strange characters called "Prospective Intention" and "Immediate Intention." But you will find that story even more difficult to the degree that you have to cope with yet more nominalizations. Here is a story about those two virtual characters, Prospective and Immediate Intention. To a reader not familiar with such stories, this passage will seem difficult because those characters (boldfaced) are embedded in a field of other nominalizations (italicized).

> The *argument* is this. The cognitive component of **intention** exhibits a high degree of *complexity.* **Intention** is temporally divisible into two: **prospective intention** and **immediate intention.** The cognitive *function* of prospective **intention** is the *representation* of a subject's similar past *actions,* his current situation, and his course of *future actions.* That is, the cognitive component of prospective **intention** is a *plan.* The cognitive *function* of immedi-

ate **intention** is the *monitoring* and *guidance* of ongoing bodily *movement.*

—Myles Brand, *Intending and Acting*

If we revise the peripheral nominalizations into verbs and introduce a few flesh-and-blood characters to accompany the abstract characters, the passage becomes clearer, especially to someone unfamiliar with such stories (the characters are italicized):

✓ *I* argue this about **intention. It** has a complex cognitive component of two temporal kinds: **prospective intention** and **immediate intention. Prospective intention** lets *us* represent how *we* have acted in the past, how *we* act in the present, and how *we* will act in the future. That is, *we* use the cognitive component of **prospective intention** to help *us* plan. **Immediate intention** lets *us* monitor and guide our bodies as *we* move them.

I have, of course, changed the writer's voice into my own, a presumptuousness he might well reject. But have I made him say something he did not mean? Some argue that any change in form changes content, but I doubt that it always does. In this case, only the author could say.

Here's the point: Most readers prefer flesh-and-blood characters as subjects. But when you write about concepts, you can treat them almost as if they were real characters by making them the subjects of verbs that seem to indicate an action:

Intention **has** a complex cognitive component.

Prospective intention **lets** us represent. . . .

Immediate intention **lets** us monitor and guide. . . .

When your readers are familiar with these abstractions, they have no serious problem understanding the sentences in which they appear. But when readers are not familiar with them, then you have to avoid using a lot of other nominalizations with them. If you do, your readers may well think your prose is a jumble of abstractions.

An Overview: Two Principles

All this must seem complicated, but there are in fact just two principles that you need to keep straight in order to understand, analyze, and revise either your own prose or that of others.

1. Two of the terms used in Lesson Three and in this one refer to grammar: *subject* and *verb.*

   Subject and *verb* refer to positions and relationships in the *grammatical* structure of a sentence. Subjects are usually first; verbs second:

   Clinton$_{\text{subject}}$ + defeated$_{\text{verb}}$ + **Bush**$_{\text{object.}}$

2. Two other terms refer to meaning: *character* and *action.*

   Character and *action* refer to your story. In most stories, a particular kind of character, an *agent* performs an action directed toward a goal:

   Clinton$_{\text{agent}}$ → defeated$_{\text{action}}$ → **Bush**$_{\text{goal.}}$

You understand style best when you think of a sentence as having these two "levels" of organization or structure simultaneously:

1. a fixed level of grammatical structure involving subjects and objects
2. a variable level of meaning involving characters and actions

fixed	SUBJECT	VERB	COMPLEMENT
variable	CHARACTER	ACTION	———

To the degree that you can match characters to subjects and actions to verbs, your readers will judge you to be a clear and direct writer. To the degree that you depart from it, particularly when you move characters out of the subject position and actions into it, your readers may find your writing increasingly difficult.

Exercise 4.1

Before you revise these next sentences, practice diagnosing them. Look at the first six or seven words of every sentence. Then revise them so that each has a specific character as subject of a specific verb. You may have to invent characters. Use *we, I,* or any other word that seems appropriate.

1. The existence of differences in interpretation about the meaning of the discovery of America has led to a reassessment of Columbus's place in Western history.
2. A solution to the UFO problem is impossible without a better understanding about the possibility of extraterrestrial life.
3. Tracing the transitions in a book or a well-written article will provide assistance in efforts at improving coherence in prose.
4. Decisions about forcibly administering medication in an emergency room setting despite the inability of an irrational patient to provide legal consent is an on-scene medical decision.
5. Resistance has been growing against building new mental health facilities in residential areas because of a distrust founded on the belief that the few examples of improper management are typical. There is a need for a modification of these perceptions.
6. With the decline in network television viewing in favor of cable and rental cassettes, awareness is growing at the networks of changes in tastes and viewing habits, resulting in a need to change programming accordingly.
7. Of concern is the increasing cost of protecting museum artifacts. Their mere storage is a contributing factor to deterioration, to say nothing of the effects of their display. The concept of conservation means that higher expenditures are necessary to ensure the availability of skills and equipment to ensure their preservation for future generations.
8. Recent assertions about failures to present information with fairness are accurate in regard to journalism in the Middle East today. A comparison of press coverage

from different countries reveals many inaccuracies in reporting by politically biased newspapers. The omission of facts and the slanting of stories show the failure of the press to carry out its mission with objectivity. As a result, lack of knowledge has resulted in a public opinion based more on emotion than on reason.

PASSIVES AND CHARACTERS

The Standard Advice

Nominalizations encourage an indirect, impersonal style, a kind of writing devoid of characters, because as we've seen, once a verb is nominalized, we can drop the characters associated with it.

✓ **We** *expected* that **we** would *recruit* **the staff** quickly.

Our *expectation* was that **our** *recruitment* of **the staff** would be quick.

The *expectation* was for quick *recruitment.*

But if writers fall into this kind of style because their cast of mind is impersonal and aloof, they typically adopt another feature of style that lets them drop even more characters: Instead of writing in the ACTIVE voice (not *tense*), they choose the passive.

When we write in the active voice, we typically name in the subject of a sentence the agent of an action, and in the OBJECT of the verb we name the goal or receiver of that action:

	subject	verb	object
Active:	I	found	the money.
	agent	action	goal

This sequence is reversed in a sentence in the passive voice:

	subject	(*be* + past participle)	prepositional phrase
Passive:	The money	was found	[by me.]
	goal	action	agent

In that construction, the subject expresses the goal of the action, a form of *be* precedes a PAST PARTICIPLE form, and the agent of the action appears optionally after the verb in a *by*-phrase.

Here's what happens when we go from active-verbal to passive-nominalized:

✓ Active-verbal:	We **investigated** why the employment office **interviewed** so few minority applicants.
Active-nominalized:	We began an **investigation** into why the employment office did so few **interviews** of minority applicants.
Passive-nominalized:	An **investigation** *was begun* into why so few **interviews** *were done.*

When we combine nominalizations with passives, we create that kind of prose that readers variously call *sociologicalese, educationese, legalese, bureaucratese*—the kind of prose written by those who confuse authority and objectivity with polysyllabic abstraction and remote impersonality, a style in which no one does anything, least of all claims responsibility.

Like some other terms we've looked at, though, the terms *active* and *passive* can be confusing, because we use them not only to name particular grammatical constructions but also to describe our stylistic impressions. We often call a sentence passive if it *feels* flaccid. Both of these sentences are in the active voice:

> The success of the project depends on cost control.
>
> The project will succeed if we can control costs.

But if that first sentence has no passive verbs in the grammatical sense of the term, it certainly feels less active than the second. It's a good idea to keep distinct the grammatical and impressionistic meanings of *active* and *passive.*

More Complicated Advice: Choosing between Active and Passive

Unreflective critics of style relentlessly urge us to avoid the passive, because it requires an extra word and because it encourages impersonality. In general, that's not bad advice, but like so many other bits of standard advice, it is often wrong: Often, the passive is the better choice.

To choose active or passive, you have to answer three questions:

1. Must your readers know who is acting?
2. Would the active or passive better help your readers move from one sentence to the next?
3. Would the active or passive encourage your readers to focus on a logically consistent and appropriate string of subjects?

1. Must your readers know who is acting?

   Often, we don't say who is responsible for an action, because we don't know or because our readers don't care. For example, the passive is the natural choice in these:

   ✓ The president **was rumored** to have considered resigning.

   ✓ Those who **are found** guilty can **be fined.**

   ✓ Valuable records should always **be kept** in a fireproof safe.

   If we do not know who rumored, we cannot say. And since we all know who finds criminals guilty, who fines them, and who should keep records in a safe, our readers wouldn't wonder. On those grounds, this next passive sentence would be more economical than its active version:

   Once *those who publicize things* **publicized** the design, *others* quickly **adopted** it.

   ✓ Once the design **was publicized,** it **was** widely **adopted.**

   Some writers, of course, deliberately avoid naming names when they don't want their readers to know who was responsible for an action with bad consequences, especially when that person is the writer. In this next sentence, we might predict the passive, for reasons having less to do with style, more with avoiding responsibility:

   Because the safety inspection **was** not **monitored,** the mechanism **was left** unaligned, a fact that **was known** several months before it **was decided** to reveal that information.

Here's the point: Choose the passive when you don't know who did it, your readers don't care who did it, or you don't want them to know who did it.

2. Would the active or passive better help your readers move from one sentence to the next?

When we read, we depend on the beginning of a sentence to locate us in a context of what we know before we follow the sentence to what it tells us that is new. A sentence can confuse us if it starts with new and unexpected information.

For example, in the second sentence of (2a), the subject (boldfaced) communicates new and complex information, while its object names a concept from the previous sentence, a concept that is therefore familiar to the reader:

2a. We must decide whether to focus on improving education in the sciences alone or to attempt to raise the level of education across the whole curriculum. [**The weight given to two factors, industrial competitiveness and the value we attach to the liberal arts,**]$_{\text{new information}}$ *will influence*$_{\text{active verb}}$ [this decision]$_{\text{familiar information}}$.

That second sentence is in the active voice, but it would be more readable in the passive, because the familiar information would then be first and the new and complex information last:

✓ 2b. We must decide whether to focus on improving education in the sciences alone or to attempt to raise the level of education across the whole curriculum. [This decision]$_{\text{familiar information}}$ *will be influenced*$_{\text{passive verb}}$ by [**the weight we give to two factors, industrial competitiveness and the value we attach to the liberal arts**]$_{\text{new information}}$.

Here's the point: Readers have a problem with sentences that begin with long, complex subjects that express unfamiliar information. You can use a passive verb to shift that long and complex bundle of information to the end of its sentence, especially if it also lets you move to its beginning a unit of information that is shorter and more familiar.

3. Would the active or passive encourage your readers to focus on a logically consistent and appropriate string of subjects?

   This third consideration is more complex: It is whether the subjects in a sequence of sentences focus your readers' attention on a *consistent* and *appropriate* sequence of concepts.

   Look at the subjects in this next paragraph about energy. In the first version, the subjects (boldfaced) of the verbs (italicized) seem to have been chosen almost at random:

> **It** *was found*$_{\text{passive}}$ that **data about resources allocated to the states** *were not obtained*$_{\text{passive}}$. **This action** *is needed*$_{\text{passive}}$ so that **it** *can be determined*$_{\text{passive}}$ how **resources** *can be redirected*$_{\text{passive}}$ when conditions change. **Sufficient support** *must be provided*$_{\text{passive}}$ to the agency so that **data on fuel consumption** *may be gathered*$_{\text{passive}}$ on a regular basis.

We can revise this to help the reader if we choose active and passive verbs in order to create a sequence of subjects that consistently focuses on characters that the reader already knows:

✓ **We** *found*$_{\text{active}}$ that **the Department of Energy** *did not obtain*$_{\text{active}}$ data about resources that **federal offices** *were allocating*$_{\text{active}}$ to the states. **The agency** *needs*$_{\text{active}}$ these data so that **it** *can determine*$_{\text{active}}$ how to *redirect*$_{\text{active}}$ resources when conditions change. **The energy secretary** *must be provided*$_{\text{passive}}$ with support so that **his office** *can gather*$_{\text{active}}$ data on fuel consumption on a regular basis.

Note the passive in the last sentence:

✓ The energy secretary **must be provided** with support. . . .

That passive focuses the reader on a consistent point of view by creating a consistent sequence of subjects.

Here's the point: If in a series of active or passive sentences, you find yourself shifting almost randomly from one subject to another, try rewriting those sentences in the passive or active to make them consistent. If you need a passive verb—choose the passive.

But if a series of subjects is consistent, it should also be appropriate. Almost all stories have more than one character, and we can tell almost any story from any character's point of view:

> Once upon a time, Little Red Riding Hood was walking to Gramma's house.
>
> Once upon a time, Wolf was loitering in the woods.
>
> Once upon a time, Grandma was wondering where lunch was.
>
> Once upon a time, the Woodsman was chopping down a tree.

Writers always have to *choose* whose story they want to tell, and that choice has consequences on how readers determine who or what the main character is supposed to be. The writer of this next passage reports the end of World War II from the point of view of the Allies. In so doing, he used a series of active verbs (italicized):

✓ By early 1945, **the Allies** *had* essentially *defeated* the Axis nations; all that remained was a bloody climax. **American, French, and British forces** *had breached* German borders and *were bombing* Germany and Japan around the clock. But **they** *had* not yet so *devastated* either country as to destroy its ability to resist.

But if the writer had wanted the reader to understand history from the point of view of Germany and Japan, he should have used passive verbs:

✓ By early 1945, **the Axis nations** *had been* essentially *defeated;* all that remained was a bloody climax. **German borders** *had been breached,* and **both Germany and Japan** *were being bombed* around the clock. **Neither country,** though, *had been so devastated* that **it** could not resist.

AN EXCEPTION TO THE PRINCIPLE: There is another use for the passive, one that paradoxically emphasizes the agent of an action when that agent appears in the *by*-phrase at the *end* of a passive sentence. As we'll see in Lessons Five and Seven, the end of a sentence has a particular function: to introduce new information that the reader has not seen before. So the *first* time you name a new character, put that character at the end of the sentence, if you can. If that means using a passive verb, use the passive verb. If that agent becomes a main character in the rest of your story, then it should be the subject of most of your sentences thereafter.

✓ All of these issues became even more confused when they were analyzed by **another committee, one appointed a year earlier.** This committee looked into the matter of. . . .

Here's the point: First decide whom from among your characters you want your readers to recognize as main characters. Then choose either the active or passive verb to make those characters the subjects of your sentences.

We revisit this principle in Lesson Five.

Exercise 4.2

In the following, change as many active verbs as you can into passives, and passives into actives. Which sentences improve? Which do not? (In the first five, the active verbs that can be made passive are italicized, the already passive verbs are boldfaced.)

1. Independence **is gained** by those on welfare when skills **are taught** that the marketplace *values*.

2. In this textbook students **are trained** to perceive rhythm not as a series of individual notes but as a larger movement that *creates* a sense of musical architecture.
3. When fewer goods **are made** available to consumers while prices **are being raised** by inflation, the rate of inflation **will be accelerated** when consumers *hoard* goods that they most *need.*
4. The heat-resistant tiles **had to be redesigned** and **replaced** because their surfaces **had been bombarded** by micrometeorites.
5. The different planes of the painting **are** immediately **noticed,** because their clashing colors **are set** against a background of subtle shades of gray that **are laid** on in thin layers that **cannot be noticed** unless the surface **is examined** closely.
6. Before Ann Richards was elected governor of Texas, she was attacked as a liberal Democrat with a background in which drugs may have been used, but her campaign was conducted in a way in which negative advertising was also used.
7. In this article, it is argued that the Vietnam War was fought to extend influence in Southeast Asia and was not ended until it was made clear that the United States could not defeat North Vietnam unless atomic weapons were used.
8. Science education cannot be improved to a level sufficient to ensure that American industry will be supplied with skilled workers and researchers until more money is provided to primary and secondary schools.
9. The tone in the first part of Bierce's "An Occurrence at Owl Creek Bridge" is presented in a dispassionate way. In the first paragraph, two sentinels are described in detail, but the line, "It did not appear to be the duty of these two men to know what was occurring at the center of the bridge" takes emotion away from them. In paragraph 2, a description is given of the surroundings and spectators, but no feeling is betrayed because the language used is neutral and unemotional. This entire section is presented as devoid of emotion even though it is filled with details.

Exercise 4.3

Revise any paragraph in Lesson One so that all the active verbs are passive. Then exchange your paragraphs with someone and see if you can each rewrite your revisions back into the original.

The "Objective" Passive

In one social context, the passive has been given a special role: In the sciences, it allegedly contributes to an objective point of view. Here is an example:

> Based on the writers' verbal intelligence, prior knowledge and essay scores, their essays **were analyzed** for structure and **evaluated** for richness of concepts. The subjects **were** then **divided** into a high- or low-ability group. Half of each group **was** randomly **assigned** to a treatment group or to a placebo group.

In fact, despite the widespread belief that we should choose the passive in order to avoid using *I* or *we* in academic writing, particularly in scientific writing, many highly regarded writers use *I* and *we* regularly. These next passages all come from the introductions of articles in respected journals:

✓ This paper is concerned with two problems. How can **we** best handle, in a transformational grammar certain restrictions that. . . . To illustrate, **we** may cite. . . . **we** shall show. . . .

✓ Since the pituitary-adrenal axis is activated during the acute phase response, **we** have investigated the potential role. . . . Specifically, **we** have studied the effects of interleukin-1. . . .

✓ Any study of tensions presupposes some acquaintance with certain findings of child psychology. **We** may begin by inquiring whether. . . . **We** should next proceed to investigate.

Here are the first few words from several consecutive sentences in an article from *Science,* a journal of considerable prestige:

✓ **We** examine. . . . **We** compare. . . . **We** have used. . . . Each has been weighted. . . . **We** merely take. . . . They are subject. . . . **We** use. . . . Efron and Morris (3) describe. . . . **We** observed. . . . **We** might find. . . .

—John P. Gilbert, Bucknam McPeek, and Frederick Mosteller, "Statistics and Ethics in Surgery and Anesthesia," *Science*

To be sure, some writers and editors resolutely avoid the first person everywhere. But they are wrong to claim that academic writing must always be in the impersonally objective third person, because the passive does not make the science objective. It only makes the sentences reporting it seem so.

Metadiscourse: Writing about Writing

When academic writers do use the first person, however, they use it systematically. Look at the verbs in the passages above. There are two kinds:

- One kind refers to the most general sort of activities: *study, investigate, examine, observe, use.*
- The other kind refers not to the subject matter or the research, but to the writer's own writing and thinking: *handle, cite, show, inquire.*

When writers refer to their own acts of thinking and writing or to their readers' acts of reading and understanding, we call that language *metadiscourse,* discourse about discourse. We need some metadiscourse in everything we write because it helps us to explain ourselves and to manage how our readers follow and understand us.

Some kinds of metadiscourse:

- Rhetorical actions: *explain, show, argue, claim, deny, suggest, contrast, add, expand, summarize*
- Parts of our discourse: *first, second, third; to begin, finally*
- Logical connections: *therefore, however, consequently, if so*
- Hedges and emphatics to our beliefs: *it seems, perhaps, undoubtedly*
- Guides for our readers: *consider now, recall, imagine*

Writers use metadiscourse most often in introductions, where they announce their intentions: *We* ***claim*** *that. . .*, *We* ***shall show****. . .*, *We* ***begin*** *by. . .* If they use metadiscourse at the beginning, they are likely to use it again at the end, when they summarize: *We have* ***suggested****. . .*, *I have* ***shown****. . .*, *We have not* ***claimed****. . .*

On the other hand, academic and scholarly writers rarely use the first person to describe *particular* actions that they performed in their research. We rarely find passages like this:

✓ To determine if monokines elicited an adrenal steroidogenic response, **I** added a monocyte-conditioned medium and preparations of. . . .

More likely is the passive verb of the original sentence and its technical subject:

✓ To determine if monokines elicited a response, *preparations* . . . **were added**. . . .

But when the writer cast that sentence in the passive, he dangled his modifier. You dangle a modifier when the implied subject of an introductory phrase differs from the specific subject of the clause you attach it to. The implied subject of the infinitive verb *determine* is *I* or *we: I determine* or *we determine.* But that implied subject *I* or *we* differs from the explicit subject of the clause it attaches to—*preparations.* And thus does a modifier dangle.

Writers of scientific prose use this pattern so often, however, that in their world it has become standard usage. When editors with stern views about correct grammar reject both first person subjects and dangling modifiers, they put their authors into a predicament where they are damned if they do and damned if they don't.

Here's the point: The first person *I* and *we* appear in much scholarly prose. Some critics nevertheless frown on its use, particularly the expressions *I think. . . .*, *I feel. . . .*, *I believe. . . .*, because those words usually introduce the expression of mere baseless opinion. But when you have performed—or are performing—a specific action, don't avoid the first person just because you think it is generally prohibited.

As a small historical footnote, we might note that this impersonal "scientific" style is a modern development. In his "New Theory of Light and Colors" (1672), Sir Isaac Newton wrote this charming first-person account of an early experiment:

> I procured a triangular glass prism, to try therewith the celebrated phenomena of colors. And for that purpose, having darkened my laboratory, and made a small hole in my window shade, to let in a convenient quantity of the sun's light, I placed my prism at the entrance, that the light might be thereby refracted to the opposite wall. It was at first a very pleasing diversion to view the vivid and intense colors produced thereby.

Exercise 4.4

Sentences (1) through (4) below are all passive, but two of them could be active because those passive verbs are metadiscourse verbs that frequently take first-person subjects. Change the verbs that should be changed. But when you have finished doing that, go through each sentence again and revise into verbs any nominalizations that you think are hiding important actions.

1. It is concluded that instability of the image is caused by a deterioration of the optical system.
2. The model has been subjected to statistical analysis.
3. Failure to export sufficient crude oil for hard currency is proposed here as the cause of the collapse of the Soviet economy.
4. The creation of a database is being considered, but no estimate has been made in regard to the potential of its usefulness.

Sentences (5) through (8) are active, but two of their verbs should be passive because they are not metadiscourse verbs. Revise in other ways that you think appropriate.

5. In Section IV, I argue that the indigenous culture engaged in overcultivation of the land at the base of the mesa leading to its exhaustion as a viable food-producing area.

6. Our intention in this book is to help readers achieve an understanding not only of the differences in grammar between Arabic and English but also the differences in worldview as reflected by Arabic vocabulary.
7. To make an evaluation of changes in the flow rate, I made a comparison of the original flow rate on the basis of figures I had compiled with figures that Jordan had collected in a study of the diversion patterns of slow-growth swamps.
8. We performed the tissue rejection study on the basis of methods developed with our discovery of increases in dermal sloughing as a result of cellular regeneration.

Exercise 4.5

Revise these passages. Change passives into actives only where you think doing so will improve the sentence. If necessary, invent a rhetorical situation to account for your choice of active or passive.

1. Your figures were reanalyzed to determine their accuracy. Results will be announced when it is judged appropriate.
2. Home mortgage loans now are made for 30 years. With the price of housing at inflated levels, those loans cannot be paid off in any shorter period of time.
3. The author's impassioned narrative style is abandoned and in its place a cautious treatment of theories of conspiracy is presented. But the moment the narrative line is picked up again, he invests his prose with the same vigor and force.
4. Many arguments were advanced against Darwinian evolution in the nineteenth century because basic assumptions about our place in the world were challenged by it. No longer were we defined as privileged creatures but rather as a product of natural forces.
5. For many years federal regulations concerning the use of wiretapping have been ignored. Only recently have tighter restrictions been imposed on the circumstances that warrant it.

In these sentences, change passives to actives and edit nominalizations into a more direct agent-action style. Invent agents where necessary.

6. It is my belief that the social significance of smoking receives its clearest explication through an analysis of peer interaction among adolescents. In particular, studies should be made of the manner in which relational interactive behavior is conditioned by social class.
7. These directives are written in a style of maximum simplicity as a result of an attempt at more effective communication with employees with limited reading skills who have been hired in accordance with recently imposed guidelines.
8. The ability of the human brain to arrive at solutions of human problems has been undervalued, because studies have not been done that would be considered to have scientific reliability.

Exercise 4.6

What follows is a slightly altered version of a letter from the chancellor of a major state university to parents of students. Why is the first part so impersonal? The next more personal? Change the first part so that whoever performed the actions referred to are specific subjects of verbs. Then change the second part so that no specific character appears. How do they differ? Revise passives into actives and nominalize where necessary.

> As you probably have heard, the U of X campus has been the scene of a number of incidents of racial and sexual harassment over the last several weeks. The fact that similar incidents have occurred on campuses around the country does not make them any less offensive when they take place here. Of the 10 to 12 incidents that have been reported since early October, most have involved graffiti or spoken insults. In only two cases was any physical contact made, and in neither case was anyone injured.
>
> U of X is committed to providing its students with an environment where they can live, work, and study without fear of being taunted or harassed because of their race, gender, religion, or ethnicity. I have made it clear that bigotry and intolerance will not be

permitted and that U of X's commitment to diversity is unequivocal. We are also taking steps to improve security in campus housing. We at U of X are proud of this university's tradition of diversity. . . .

NOUN + NOUN + NOUN

One more point of style can distort the coincidence that readers expect between the syntax of an idea and the grammar of a sentence: the long COMPOUND NOUN phrase.

> **Early childhood thought disorder misdiagnosis** often results from unfamiliarity with recent **research literature** describing such conditions. This paper is a review of seven recent studies in which are findings of particular relevance to **pre-adolescent hyperactivity diagnosis** and to **treatment modalities** involving **medication maintenance level evaluation procedures.**

Some grammarians insist that we should never use one noun to modify another, but that would rule out such common phrases as *stone wall, student committee, space shuttle,* and a good many technical terms that technical writers need.

But we should reject a long series of nouns when it is ambiguous and especially when the series includes unnecessary nominalizations and the phrase is not very familiar to our intended readers. (We will always debate what counts as "unnecessary," of course.)

> ***Here's the point:*** Whenever you write a string of nouns that you haven't seen before, try disassembling them. Start from the last and reverse their order, linking them with prepositional phrases. If one of the nouns is a nominalization, rewrite it into a full verb.

Here is the first compound in the example passage revised:

1	2	3	4	5
early	childhood	thought	disorder	misdiagnosis
misdiagnose	disordered	thought	in early	childhood
5	4	3	1	2

Now we can see the ambiguity: What's early, the childhood, the disorder, or the diagnosis? Next we reassemble them:

✓ Physicians misdiagnose disordered thought in young children because they are unfamiliar with recent literature on the subject.

Exercise 4.7

Finish rewriting that passage about misdiagnosing disordered thought. Then turn the compound noun phrases in (1) through (4) into prepositional phrases.

1. The plant safety standards committee discussed recent air quality regulation announcements.
2. Diabetic patient blood pressure reduction may be brought about by renal depressor medication.
3. The main goal of this article is to describe text comprehension processes and recall protocol production.
4. On the basis of these principles, we may now attempt to formulate narrative information extraction rules.

In these next sentences, unpack compound nouns and edit by placing characters and actions in subjects and verbs. Invent characters as needed.

5. This paper is an investigation into information processing behavior involved in computer human cognition simulation games.
6. Enforcement of guidelines for new automobile tire durability must be a Federal Trade Commission responsibility.
7. The Social Security program is a monthly income floor guarantee for individuals whose benefit package potential is based on a determination of lifelong contribution schedule.
8. Based on training needs assessment reviews and on office site visits, there was the identification of concepts and issues that can be used in our creation of an initial staff questionnaire instrument.

9. Corporate organization under state law supervision has resulted in federal government failures in regard to the effective implementation of accident reduction measures.

The Professional Voice

Every group demands that its members demonstrate they accept its values by learning its voice and vocabulary. The aspiring physicist must learn not only to think like a physicist but to sound like one as well. Too often, though, writers think that they sound professional only when they write in ways that are complex and abstract. Or they fall into that style because they read so much of it. But when they complicate substantive complexity with an unfriendly prose style, they make it difficult, if not impossible, for the merely well-educated layperson to understand issues with considerable social significance. And that erodes the trust that we must have in one another if we are to live in a civil society where information and expert knowledge are now the means to power and control.

It is true that some high-level scholarship will never be clear to merely intelligent lay readers—but less often than many scholars believe. Here is an excerpt from Talcott Parsons, a social scientist who was as influential in shaping the way sociologists think as he was notorious for the opacity of his prose.

> Apart from theoretical conceptualization there would appear to be no method of selecting among the indefinite number of varying kinds of factual observation which can be made about a concrete phenomenon or field so that the various descriptive statements about it articulate into a coherent whole, which constitutes an "adequate," a "determinate" description. Adequacy in description is secured insofar as determinate and verifiable answers can be given to all the scientifically important questions involved. What questions are important is largely determined by the logical structure of the generalized conceptual scheme which, implicitly or explicitly, is employed.

We can make that clearer to moderately well-educated readers:

> When scientists lack a theory, they cannot select from everything they could say about a subject only that which they can fit into a

> coherent whole that would be "adequate" or "determinate." Scientists describe something "adequately" only when they can verify answers to questions they think are important, and they decide what questions are important on the basis of their implicit or explicit theories.

And even that could be more concise:

> Whatever you describe, you need a theory to fit its parts into a whole. You need a theory not only to verify answers, but even to decide what questions to ask.

The clearer version omits Parsons's nuances. But the ordinary mind surely misses them in the original as his excruciating style numbs all but the most masochistically dedicated reader.

Here's the point: Whether we are readers or writers, teachers or editors, all of us must understand three things about a style that seems complex:

- Such a style may be necessary to express complex ideas precisely
- Such a style may gratuitously complicate already complex ideas
- Such a style may gratuitously complicate simple ideas.

As readers, our task is to discriminate among these kinds of complexity so that we can know when a passage is needlessly complex and, if not condemn it, at least not blame ourselves for failing to understand it. As writers, our task is to recognize when we have committed that gratuitous complexity and, if we have, to revise it into something more accesible.

It is important to be clear on another point: These principles of analysis and revision are *not* offered as a way to reduce your prose to a kind of Dick-and-Jane primer style intended for those who do not read much or well. To be sure, when applied relentlessly, these principles can help you reach marginal readers. But mature readers would consider every revision we've offered here to be both clear and mature. To be sure, experts have their own technical language, much of which consists of necessary abstractions. But even experts can baffle their colleagues when they write in ways that needlessly complicate already complex ideas.

In short, if we are responsible writers, we owe a civil duty to our intended readers: Without compromising the intrinsic complexity of our thought, we are obliged not to impose on them gratuitous complexity, and nothing complicates prose more surely than gratuitous nominalizations.

Summing Up

1. Though there are exceptions, we judge prose clear when subjects of sentences are agents of actions and those actions are verbs.

fixed	SUBJECT	VERB	COMPLEMENT
variable	CHARACTER	ACTION	———

2. When you tell stories in which abstract nominalizations function as main characters, use as few other nominalizations as you can:

   A **nominalization** is a **transformation** of a verb into a noun, often resulting in **displacement** of characters from subjects by nouns.

   ✓ When a **nominalization** *transforms* an action verb into a noun, that noun often *displaces* characters from subjects.

3. Don't hesitate to use a passive if the agent of an action is obvious:

   The voters reelected the president with 54 percent of the vote.

   ✓ The president **was reelected** with 54 percent of the vote.

4. Do not hesitate to use a passive if it lets you replace a long subject with a short one:

   Research that demonstrated the soundness of our reasoning and the need for action **supported** this decision.

✓ *This decision* **was supported by** research that demonstrated the soundness of our reasoning and the need for action.

5. Don't hesitate to use a passive if the passive gives you a coherent and appropriate sequence of subjects:

✓ By early 1945, **the Axis nations** had been essentially defeated; all that remained was a bloody climax. **The German borders** had been breached, and **both Germany and Japan** were being bombed around the clock. **Neither country,** though, had been so devastated that **it** could not resist.

6. Don't avoid an active verb if it is a metadiscourse verb:

The terms of the analysis must first **be defined.**

✓ We must first **define** the terms of the analysis.

7. When convenient, rewrite long compound noun phrases:

We discussed the board candidate review meetings schedule.

✓ We discussed the schedule of meetings to review candidates for the board.

Lesson Five

Cohesion and Coherence

If he would inform, he must advance regularly from Things known to things unknown, distinctly without Confusion, and the lower he begins the better. It is a common Fault in Writers, to allow their Readers too much knowledge: They begin with that which should be the Middle, and skipping backwards and forwards, 'tis impossible for any one but he who is perfect in the Subject before, to understand their Work, and such an one has no Occasion to read it.

BENJAMIN FRANKLIN

The two capital secrets in the art of prose composition are these: first, the philosophy of transition and connection; or the art by which one step in an evolution of thought is made to arise out of another: all fluent and effective composition depends on the connections; secondly, the way in which sentences are made to modify each other; for the most powerful effects in written eloquence arise out of this reverberation, as it were, from each other in a rapid succession of sentences.

THOMAS DE QUINCY

"Begin at the beginning," the King said, gravely, "and go on till you come to the end; then stop."

LEWIS CARROLL

LOCAL VERSUS GLOBAL CLARITY

So far, we've looked at style as if we could write clearly just by mapping CHARACTERS and ACTIONS onto SUBJECTS and VERBS to mirror what's "out there" in the world. But effective writing depends on more than the local clarity of individual sentences.

- Your readers must feel that they can move easily from one sentence to the next, that each sentence "coheres" with the one before and after.
- They must feel that sentences are not just individually clear but constitute a unified passage focused on a coherent set of ideas.

The problem with global cohesion and coherence, however, is that neither quality is directly "in" what you write. Like all other characteristics of prose, it is created by your readers out of what you put before them. But so powerful is their desire—and ability—to impose their own sense of order on what they read, that you can count on your readers to go more than halfway toward creating a coherent experience for themselves. They will infer logical connections that you do not state; they will impose a shape on parts that you do not explicitly relate. Sometimes they will even make more sense out of your text than it might deserve.

But to do that, your readers need *some* cues, *some* signals of the coherence in your own mind. The object of this lesson is to explain those features of style that help readers feel they are reading prose that is not just clear, but both flowing (cohesive) and well-formed (coherent). We'll deal with cohesion first, then with coherence.

COHESION: A SENSE OF FLOW FROM OLD TO NEW

Compare these two passages. Which do you like better?

1a. The means by which Asian products have successfully competed with your products in Western Pacific markets will constitute the objective of the first phase of this study. The labor costs of competitors and their ability to introduce new products quickly are the first issues to be examined. A plan that will demonstrate how your industry can take advantage of unexpected market opportunities, particularly on the Pacific Rim, will be developed from this study.

✓ 1b. In the first phase of this study, we will examine how Asian products have successfully competed with your products in Western Pacific markets. The study will first examine labor costs of competitors and their ability to introduce new products quickly. We will develop from this study a plan that will demonstrate how your industry can take advantage of unexpected market opportunities, particularly on the Pacific Rim.

Most readers feel that (1b) is more readable than (1a), but they describe their responses differently from the way they describe the nominalized and passive passages in Lessons Three and Four. Instead of calling (1a) *wordy* or *abstract* or *impersonal,* most readers say it is *disjointed, unfocused, lacking flow.* They describe (1b) as *flowing, connected,* and *more focused.* This is a new language of impressions that calls for a new vocabulary of analysis.

Something Old, Something New, and in that Order

In Lesson Four, we devoted a few pages (80–86) to qualifying that widely repeated advice, "Avoid PASSIVES." If we followed the standard advice, we would choose the ACTIVE verb in (a) over the PASSIVE verb in (b):

2a. The collapse of a dead star into a point perhaps no larger than a marble **creates** a black hole.

2b. A black hole **is created by** the collapse of a dead star into a point perhaps no larger than a marble.

But we also saw that, in certain contexts, the passive has its uses, including helping a reader sense the flow and cohesion of a passage. From a reader's point of view, which of those two sentences, the active (2a) or the passive (2b), fits between these next two sentences, (1) and (3), better?

[1]Some astonishing questions about the nature of the universe have been raised by scientists exploring black holes in space. 2a/b[ ]. [3]So much matter compressed into so little volume changes the fabric of space around it in puzzling ways.

Try first the active sentence, then the passive:

> [1]Some astonishing questions about the nature of the universe have been raised by scientists exploring black holes in space. [2a]The collapse of a dead star into a point perhaps no larger than a marble creates a black hole. [3]So much matter compressed into so little volume changes the fabric of space around it in puzzling ways.

✓ [1]Some astonishing questions about the nature of the universe have been raised by scientists exploring black holes in space. [2b]A black hole is created by the collapse of a dead star into a point perhaps no larger than a marble. [3]So much matter compressed into so little volume changes the fabric of space around it in puzzling ways.

Our sense of "flow" should tell us that this passage calls for the passive.

The reason is clear: In the last words of sentence (1), readers are introduced to an important new character—black holes:

> [1]Some astonishing questions about the nature of the universe have been raised by scientists exploring **black holes in space.**

Follow that sentence with the active version, (2a):

> [1]. . . universe have been raised by scientists exploring **black holes in space.** [2a]The collapse of a dead star into a point perhaps no larger than a marble creates a **black hole.**

In sentence (2a), the first concept that the reader hits is collapsed stars and marbles, information that *to the reader* must seem to come out of nowhere. The first familiar information that a reader would recognize, *black hole,* doesn't appear until the end of that sentence.

But now after sentence (1) try the passive sentence, (2b):

✓ [1]. . . exploring [**black holes in space.** [2b]**A black hole**] is created-$_{\text{passive}}$ by the collapse of a dead star into a point perhaps no larger than a marble. [3]So much matter compressed into so little volume. . . .

Readers now move from sentence (1) to (2b) more easily because they *begin* (2b) with *a black hole,* a familiar concept that helps them connect (2b) to the end of (1).

Note too that by using the passive, we have now located at the end of sentence (2b) words that the reader can easily recall when beginning sentence (3), thereby making sentences (2b) and (3) cohere better:

✓ [1]. . . black holes in space. [2a]A black hole is created by the collapse of a dead star into [**a point perhaps no larger than a marble.** [3]**So much matter compressed into so little volume**] changes the fabric. . . .

That's all cohesion is: our feeling that we can connect each sentence in a series to the one before and to the one after. How writers help readers create that sense of flow is the problem—and the challenge—of English prose.

> ***Here's the point:*** With every *sequence* of sentences that we write, we have to find the best trade-off between the principles that make individual sentences clear and the principles that give a passage of sentences a sense of a cohesive flow. *But in that compromise, we always give priority to those features of style that help readers create a sense of cohesion.* Readers may understand individual sentences just fine, but if they cannot see how they "hang together," those individually clear sentences will add up to no coherently cumulative meaning.

The First Principle of Cohesion: Old-to-New

We can now formulate two more strategies of writing and revision; they are mirror images of each other:

1. Begin sentences with ideas that your readers will readily recognize, ideas that they have just read or that you *know* will not surprise them in that context.
2. End sentences with information that your readers cannot anticipate or with information that they would find difficult to understand, such as detailed lists, new technical words, complex conditions (the topic of Lesson Seven).

It is easier to see those two principles at work—or not—in the writing of others than in your own. You will always be your own worst editor because by the time you write a final draft, everything you have written will seem old—to *you.* But your readers must think that some of it is new (why else read it?). So even though we all find it difficult to distinguish old information from new, we must try, because we have to begin our sentences from our readers' point of view—with what they know, either from information that we provided in previous sentences or from knowledge they bring with them and would not be surprised to see in that context. Readers build that sense of cohesion when they regularly start sentences in familiar territory.

Factitious Cohesion

I've described here what we might call "organic cohesion." Readers feel that texts are organically cohesive when they can move easily from one individual sentence to the next, never noticing how consistently the information in each sentence carries them from old to new. Some writers, though, try to fake cohesion by lacing a text with conjunctions like *thus, therefore, however,* and so on, regardless of whether those conjunctions signal real logical connections. Here is one such passage:

> Because the press is the major medium of interaction between the president and the people, how it portrays him influences his popularity. **Therefore,** it should report on the president objectively. Both reporters and the president are human, **however,** subject to error and favoritism. **Also,** people act differently in public than they do in private. **Hence,** to understand a person, it is important to know the whole person, his environment, upbringing, and education. **Indeed,** from the correspondence with his family, we can learn much about Harry S. Truman, our thirty-third president.

Here's the point: Words like *furthermore, hence,* and *but* help readers see real connections among ideas, but when you use them more than two or three times a page, look closely. If the logic of your ideas is sound, your readers probably don't need those words. You may in fact be trying to impose a factitious cohesion on a passage that is intrinsically incoherent.

Exercise 5.1

Revise this passage to improve its flow.

The Hart Queen is one of the best skis for beginning skiers. A thin layer of tempered ash from hardwood forests of Kentucky makes up its inner core. Therefore, two innovations for strength and flexibility are built into its outer construction. Also, two sheets of ten-gauge steel reinforce a layer of ash for increased strength. A wrapping of fiberglass thus surrounds the two steel sheets for increased flexibility. In fact, most conventional bindings can be used with the Queen. The Salomon Double is the best, however. A cushion of foam and insulation firmly cradles the foot and ankle, yet freedom of movement is still permitted.

Coherence: A Sense of Focus

Cohesion, however, is only the first step toward helping your readers create a sense of the whole. Your writing must also seem *coherent,* a quality different from cohesion. This next passage has great cohesive "flow," because we move from one sentence to the next without a hitch:

> Saner, Wisconsin, is the snowmobile capital of the world. The buzzing of snowmobile engines fills the air, and their tanklike tracks crisscross the snow. The snow reminds me of Mom's mashed potatoes, covered with furrows I would draw with my fork. Mom's mashed potatoes usually made me sick, that's why I was playing with them. I like to make a hole in the middle of the potatoes and fill it with melted butter. This behavior has been the subject of long chats between me and my analyst.

While this passage may be cohesive, it is incoherent. Each sentence connects to the one before and after, but as a whole it does not "hang together," it has no "focus," because each sentence begins with a different topic—first with Saner, then snowmobiles, then snow, then Mom's mashed potatoes, finally with behavior. As a consequence, those sentences scatter our attention across a seemingly random set of concepts. (The passage was created by six different writers, one of whom wrote the first sentence, with the other five sequentially adding one sentence to fit just the preceding sentence.)

To help readers feel a passage is coherent, you have to understand not just how readers link pairs of sentences, but how they make sequences of sentences seem to coalesce into a whole. How easily your readers can do that depends largely on how each sentence in a unified passage *begins*. (Paradoxically, it also depends on how the first sentence in that passage *ends*. But more about that in Lesson Seven.)

THE TOPIC OF A SENTENCE

The first thing that readers want to know in a sentence is what it is "about," its *topic*. We ordinarily name the topic of a sentence in its subject:

> And therefore, politically speaking, in Eastern states since 1980, **acid rain** has become a serious concern.

That sentence is in some sense about politics, the East, and 1980, but its real topic, what it is centrally "about," is its subject/topic, *acid rain*. Readers judge a *whole passage* coherent to the degree that they can see two things in a string of sentences:

- They can recognize the topics of individual sentences quickly.
- They can see how a *sequence* of concise topics makes consecutive sense.

Compare (1a) and (1b) again, this time noting how the two passages express their topic/subjects. In (1b) the topic/subject of every CLAUSE, are boldfaced.

> 1a. **The means by which Asian manufacturers have successfully competed with your products in Western Pacific markets** will constitute the objective of the first phase of this study. **The labor costs of competitors and their ability to introduce new products quickly** are the first issues to be examined. **A plan that will demonstrate how your industry can take advantage of unexpected market opportunities, particularly on the Pacific Rim,** will be developed from this study.

> ✓ 1b. In the first phase of this study, **we** will examine how **Asian manufacturers** have successfully competed with your products in Western Pacific markets. **The study** will first examine labor costs of competitors and their ability to introduce new products quickly. **We** will develop from this study **a plan that** will demonstrate how **your industry** can take advantage of unexpected market opportunities, particularly on the Pacific Rim.

The subject/topics in (1a) are long, complex, and abstract; the subject/topics of (1b) are short, concise, and more concrete.

More importantly, in (1a) readers are unlikely to see any focused connection among the topics *as a set;* in (1b), on the other hand, the set of topics is more focused and more coherent. This is a matter that deserves some attention because it is complex, but also because it is important in how readers read.

Subjects, Topics, and Grammar

For 500 years, English teachers have defined *subject* in two ways:

1. The subject of a sentence is the "doer" of the action.
2. The subject of a sentence is "what the sentence is about."

In Lessons Three and Four, we saw why that first definition is unreliable:

> [Our analysis of the data]$_{\text{subject}}$ led to our discovery of a new principle.

The "doer" is not the subject, *analysis,* but its modifier, *our.* Revised:

✓ When **we** analyzed the data, **we** discovered a new principle.

But if that definition about "doers" is not true for all sentences, it implies some good advice: In prose that we judge to be clear, subjects usually are in fact "doers"—that is, characters who are AGENTS of actions.

Subjects, Topics, and Psychology

Also flawed but useful is that second schoolbook definition: A subject is what a sentence is "about." In this sense, "about" does not mean gist or summary, but the first explicit main idea that we read in a sentence and that the rest of the sentence "comments" on. In this sense, the idea of topic describes part of the "psychological geography" of a sentence, a place near its beginning where readers expect to see the concept that the rest of the sentence will say something about. That place is usually the subject of each clause, and that subject is usually a NOUN. This next sentence is "about" its topic, *international cooperation,* a phrase that in this case is also its subject:

> **International cooperation** is still the goal of most countries.

But in many sentences, subjects do not announce what their sentences are "about."

- The subject of this next sentence is *it,* but the sentence is "about" its topic, *claims,* the OBJECT of *for.*

  It is impossible for **these claims** to be proved to our satisfaction.

- The subject of this next sentence is *I,* but the sentence is "about" its topic, *questions,* the object of *for.*

  As for **these questions,** *I* believe there should be more research.

- The subject of this next sentence is *it,* but the sentence is "about" its topic, *proposals,* the subject of a SUBORDINATE CLAUSE.

  It is likely that **these proposals** will be accepted.

- The subject of this next sentence is *no one,* but it is about its topic, *results,* a direct object shifted to the front of its sentence for special emphasis.

  Results such as these *no one* could have predicted.

So when we use the term "topic" to mean what a sentence is "about," we mean not its grammatical subject but its *psychological subject.* The topic is *usually* its grammatical subject, but not always. If the topic is not the subject of a sentence, however, it will usually be one of its first few words—or at least readers prefer that it should be, because only then can they easily assemble out of a sequence of sentences the general topic of a whole passage, what the whole passage is about.

THE IMPORTANCE OF SEQUENCES OF TOPICS

Compare the coherence of these substantively identical passages (Topics in both are boldfaced.):

1a. **The particular ideas toward the beginning of sentences** define what a passage is "about" for a reader, so a **sense of coherence** depends on topics. **Moving through a paragraph from a cumulatively coherent point of view** is made possible by a sequence of topics that seem to constitute this coherent sequence of topicalized ideas. **A seeming absence of context for each sentence** is one consequence of making random shifts in topics. **Feelings of dislocation, disorientation, and lack of focus** will occur when that happens.

✓ 1b. **Topics** are crucial for readers because **they** depend on topics to focus their attention on particular ideas toward the beginning of sentences so that **they** can understand what a whole passage is "about." If **readers** feel that a sequence of topics is coherent, then **they** will feel they are moving through a paragraph from a cumulatively coherent point of view. But if through that paragraph **readers** feel that **topics** seem to shift randomly, then **they** have to begin each sentence out of context, from no coherent point of view. When that happens, **readers** feel dislocated, disoriented, out of focus.

Most readers feel the first is "unfocused," "disorganized." The second seems "focused," more "coherent."

To understand why they feel that way, compare the string of topics in both passages. Note that in (1b), I have picked out a topic not just for each sentence, but for each clause (I abbreviate topics in [1a]):

Passage (1a)	✓ Passage (1b)
The particular ideas toward. . . .	Topics, they, they
a sense of coherence. . . .	readers, they
Moving through a paragraph. . . .	readers, topics
A seeming absence of context. . . .	readers, topics, they
Feelings of dislocation. . . .	readers

- In (1a), the string of topics is inconsistent, scattered, and diffuse because the subjects are long and complex.
- In (1b), the string of topics constitutes a consistent set because those topics are concise and clearly focus our attention on some variation of just two concepts: *topics* and *readers*.

Here's the point: Readers impose a sense of coherence on a passage when they can see two things:

1. They can identify the topics of individual sentences quickly and easily.
2. They can see how a string of topics "hangs together" as a logical set.

This does not mean that you must begin every sentence with the same topic in the same place. It means only that *to your readers,* your string of topics must seem to constitute a related set.

Predictably, this principle of reading suggests principles of diagnosis and revision:

1. Diagnosis:
   a. Underline the first five or six words of every sentence; then read what you have underlined straight through.
   b. If you do not quickly see what you think is a series of concise topics of your sentences, your readers are likely to have a hard time finding them.
   c. If you do see your topics, but you can see few or no connections among them, your readers are unlikely to see any either.
   d. Even if *you* can see connections, think hard about how likely your readers will.
2. Revision:
   a. Decide globally what a passage is "about" by imagining a title for it consisting of no more than three or four nouns. Those nouns will provide most of your topics.
   b. In most of your sentences, signal those topics by making them the subjects of your sentences.
   c. Locate most of those subjects close to the beginning of your sentences, not obscured by long introductory phrases.

The System of Systems

These principles about old and new and a consistent topic string reinforce the points we made about characters and actions: In fact, we can integrate these insights into an expanded model of sentences that we began to develop in Lessons Three and Four (I'll fill in the empty box in Lesson Seven).

fixed	TOPIC		
variable	OLD, FAMILIAR		NEW, UNFAMILIAR

fixed	SUBJECT	VERB	COMPLEMENT
variable	CHARACTER	ACTION	———

To the degree that you can begin your sentences with information that is familiar to your readers, with concepts that are concise and easy to understand, to that degree your readers will think you write clearly. No two units of information are shorter and simpler than a character as a concise subject and a specific action as a concise verb.

Again, do not take this principle to mean that you must restrict your topics in a passage to just one or two. The point is only to see your strings of topics as your readers will. If you are certain that they will recognize how your topics constitute a coherent set, then use as many different ones as you need. On the other hand, if your readers cannot see how even three topics would constitute a coherent set, then just three could confuse them. The point is to focus your readers' attention on a set of topics that *they* feel constitute a coherent set.

At this point, some of you may be recalling advice about avoiding monotony—"don't begin sentences with the same subjects." From your reader's point of view, bad advice. Readers judge your prose to be monotonous for reasons more serious than repeated topics. They will think it monotonous if you write one short sentence after another or string one long sentence after another, or if you pack your sentences with nominalizations and passives.

Exercise 5.2

Revise these passages to give them consistent topic strings. First determine the characters, then their actions. Then start each sentence with a character, and let the sentence take you where it wants to go. In (1), words that could be consistent subject/topics are boldfaced.

1. **Vegetation** covers the earth, except for those areas continuously covered with ice or utterly scorched by continual heat. Richly fertilized plains and river valleys are places where **plants** grow most richly, but also at the edge of perpetual snow in high mountains. The ocean and its edges as well as in and around lakes and swamps are densely **vegetated.** The cracks of busy city sidewalks have **plants** in them as well as in seemingly

barren cliffs. Before humans existed, the earth was covered with **vegetation,** and the earth will have **vegetation** long after evolutionary history swallows us up.

2. The power to create and communicate a new message to fit a new experience is not a competence animals have in their natural states. Their genetic code limits the number and kind of messages that they can communicate. Information about distance, direction, source, and richness of pollen in flowers constitutes the only information that can be communicated by bees, for example. A limited repertoire of messages delivered in the same way, for generation after generation, is characteristic of animals of the same species, in all significant respects.
3. The importance of language skills in children's problem-solving ability was stressed by Jones (1985) in his paper on children's thinking. Improvement in nonverbal problem solving occurred as a result of improvements in language skills. The use of previously acquired language habits for problem articulation and activation of knowledge previously learned through language was the cause of better performance. Therefore, systematic practice in the verbal formulation of nonlinguistic problems prior to attempts at their solution might be an avenue for exploration in the enhancement of problem solving in general.

Exercise 5.3

Distort the topic strings in any paragraph in this book. Then exchange your revision with someone who did the same and try to revise each other's revisions back to the original.

Exercise 5.4

Find an old paper of yours and analyze its topic strings. Or exchange old papers with someone and critique each other's topics.

THE DIFFICULT CRAFT OF OPENING A SENTENCE WELL

It's hard to begin a sentence well. In its first few words you have to juggle several elements that can delay readers from getting to its topic, that element that is crucial to whether they will judge your text to be coherent. Here are some traits of prose that prevent readers from achieving that sense of coherence:

Throat-clearing

We often start a sentence with the kind of METADISCOURSE that connects that sentence to the previous one, with a transition such as *and, but, therefore:*

> And therefore. . . .

We then add a second kind of metadiscourse that expresses an attitude toward what is coming, words and phrases such as *fortunately, perhaps, allegedly, it is important to note, for the most part, politically speaking:*

> And therefore, **politically speaking**. . . .

Then we might indicate time, place, or manner: *by May, in Europe, in order to complete the project.*

> And therefore, politically speaking, **in Eastern states since 1980**. . . .

Only then do we get to the topic:

> And, therefore, politically speaking, in Eastern states since 1980, **acid rain** has become a serious problem.

This kind of windup is sometimes called "throat-clearing." It keeps us from getting to the part of a sentence that is crucial in our reader's understanding not just what an individual sentence is "about," but what the whole passage is about. When you find a sentence with several words before its topic, revise:

✓ Since 1980, **acid rain** in Eastern states has become a serious political problem.

Sometimes this kind of long windup is all metadiscourse. This next passage appeared in a college curriculum review that some readers thought quite good—at least those who were willing to slog through it. But it went largely unread because its style was so thick with metadiscourse that few of us could get past the first few pages. I have italicized metadiscourse and boldfaced the appropriate character/topic—programs.

> *We think it useful to provide some relatively detailed illustration of* the varied ways "corporate curricular personalities" organize themselves in **programs.** *We choose to feature as a central device in our presentation what are called* "introductory," "survey," or "foundational" courses. *It is important, however, to recognize* the diversity of what occurs in **programs** after the different initial survey courses. *But what is also suggested is that if one talks about* a **program** *simply in terms of* the intellectual strategies or techniques engaged in, when these *are understood in a general way, it becomes* difficult to distinguish many **programs** from others.

Get rid of the metadiscourse and make the central character—curricula and programs—the topic, and readers have a more readable passage:

✓ We can understand how **curricula** organize themselves into programs through their "introductory," "survey," or "foundational" courses. After these courses, **programs** seem to offer diverse curricula, but **they** are actually alike because **they** employ similar intellectual strategies and become hard to distinguish.

Opening Nominalizations

When you revise nominalizations, especially those that begin sentences, you usually can bring topics into sharper focus:

> Our lack of data prevented evaluation of state actions in targeting funds to areas in need of assistance.

✓ Because **we** lacked data, **we** could not evaluate whether the state had targeted funds to areas that needed assistance.

Choosing Active/Passive

As we saw with the "black holes in space" example (p. 102), the passive can switch a long complex subject full of new information with a short one expressing familiar information. In fact, that's the main reason for the passive—to improve focus on topics.

During the early years of our nation, we were fortunate to have been governed so well. *A series of brilliant and virtuous presidents committed to democracy yet confident in their own worth* conducted **its affairs.**

✓ During the early years of our nation, we were fortunate to have been governed so well. **Its affairs** were conducted by *a series of brilliant and virtuous presidents committed to democracy yet confident in their own worth.*

TWO QUALIFICATIONS

Having asserted the principle of coherent topics strings so strongly, I must now qualify it twice.

To be sure, readers can feel that your prose is monotonous if you pursue the same topic relentlessly. The writer of this next passage mistook advice about consistent topics not as a diagnostic principle, but as an inviolable rule:

"Moral climate" is created when an objectivized moral standard for treating people is accepted by others. Moral climate results from norms of behavior which are accepted by society whereby if people conform they are socially approved of, or if they don't they are shunned. In this light, moral climate acts as a reason to refrain from saying or doing things that the community does not support. A moral climate encourages individuals to conform to a moral standard and apply that standard to their own circumstances.

Here's the point: If you find that through several consecutive sentences you have used *exactly* the same words for the same topic in the same position, your readers may in fact feel that you have created a topic string that is too consistent. If so, revise: Use pronouns, move the topic into a prepositional phrase, paraphrase the topic. Be cautious though: most writers change topics too often.

A second qualification: Readers judge the clearest topic to be a short noun phrase that appears early in a sentence, usually as its subject. But readers decide what a passage is "about" not on the basis of a single word or two. They perceive that sense of aboutness in verbs and adjectives as well. Most readers would judge this paragraph to be out of focus because its sentences do not open from any consistent point of view:

> In recent years, **many strides in identifying Alzeheimer's disease** have been made in psychiatric medicine. Not too long ago, **senility in an older patient who seemed to be losing touch with reality** was often confused with Alzheimer's. In the past few years, however, **blood chemistry and genetic clues** have become tools to diagnose this condition. There is **the risk of human tragedy of another kind,** however, as a result of the increasing accuracy of these procedures: Long before the appearance of any of its overt symptoms, **physicians** may be able to predict Alzheimer's. At that point, **an otherwise apparently healthy person** could be devastated by such an early and accurate diagnosis.

In this next revised paragraph, the sentences that follow the first one open with concepts that readers would recognize, words that paraphrase the central concept of this passage—*identifying Alzheimer's disease.* But notice how this central topic is expressed in ways other than in just nouns in subjects:

> ✓ In recent years, **psychiatric medicine** has made strides in identifying Alzheimer's disease. Not too long ago, when a **physician examined an older patient who seemed out of touch with reality,** she had to guess whether that person had Alzheimer's or was senile, an entirely different syndrome. In the past few years, however, **new and more reliable tests** have focused on blood chemistry and genetic clues. In **the accuracy of these new tests,** however, lies the risk of human tragedy of another kind: **Physicians may be able to predict Alzheimer's** long before its overt appearance, **but such an early and accurate diagnosis** could psychologically devastate an otherwise healthy person.

In this revised passage, I expressed its topic, kinds of tests, in subject noun phrases: *new and more reliable tests, the accuracy of these new tests,* and *such an early and accurate diagnosis.* But I also expressed it in the object of a preposition: *in the accuracy of these new tests,* and in whole clauses: *a physician examined an older patient who seemed out of touch with reality, physicians may be able to predict Alzheimer's,* clauses that all mean or imply "test."

We need a new term to cover all these words that run through a series of sentences as the central concepts of the whole passage. We can call all the words that reappear in a passage THEMES. These word-themes are like musical themes that run through a symphony or opera, and thereby impose a kind of unity on it. In prose, these themes are the central concepts that appear in a passage, a section, or a whole. When these words appear toward the beginning of a sentence in subjects and focus the reader's attention on a specific set of concepts, we call them topics. When they appear elsewhere, we can call them themes. It's not a crucial distinction, but it is a useful one.

Here's the point: Readers prefer that writers consistently locate words that suggest what a whole passage is "about" early in a sentence, in its topic positions. That usually means as a noun in a subject. But they can also recognize that old information distributed through adjectives, verbs, and objects, so long as they are also close to the beginning of a sentence.

Exercise 5.5

Revise these passages so that they have more consistent topic strings. Before you begin, decide who the main characters should be, and then make those main characters the subject of as many sentences as you can. In the first example, I have boldfaced topics so that you can see how inconsistent they are.

1. **Some potential threats** exist in the modern mass communications media, though there are many significant advantages. If **a powerful minority** should happen to control it, **public opinion** could be manipulated through biased reporting. And while **a wide knowledge of public affairs** is a great advantage that results from national coverage, **divisiveness and factionalism** can be accentuated by connecting otherwise isolated, local conflicts into a single larger conflict as a result of show-

ing that **conflicts about the same issues** are occurring in different places. It will always be true, of course, that **human nature** produces differences of opinion, but **the threat of faction and division** may be reinforced when **national coverage** publicizes uninformed opinions. According to some, **education** can suppress faction when **the true nature of conflicts** reaches the public through the media, but **history** has shown that as **much coverage** is given to people who encourage conflict as to people who try to remove conflict.

2. Some sort of palace revolt or popular revolution plagued seven out of eight reigns of the Romanov line after Peter the Great. In 1722, achievement by merit was made the basis of succession when the principle of heredity was terminated by Peter. This resulted in many tsars not appointing a successor before dying, including Peter. Ivan VI was less than two months old when appointed by Czarina Anna, but Elizabeth, daughter of Peter the Great, defeated Anna and ascended to the throne in 1741. Succession not dependent upon authority resulted in the boyars' regularly disputing who was to become sovereign. Male primogeniture became the law in 1797 when Paul I codified the law of succession. But conspirators strangled him, one of whom was probably his son, Alexander I.
3. Many issues other than science, domestic politics in particular, faced Truman when he was considering the Oppenheimer committee's recommendation to stop the hydrogen bomb project. A Sino-Soviet bloc had been proclaimed by Russia and China, so the Cold War was becoming an issue. Support for Truman's foreign policy was shrinking among Republican leaders in Congress. And the first Russian atom bomb test made the public demand a strong response from him. Truman's conclusion that he could not afford letting the public think that Russia had been allowed to be first in developing the most powerful weapon yet was inevitable. In retrospect, the risk in the Oppenheimer recommendation was worth taking according to some historians, but the political issues that Truman had to face were too powerful to ignore.

Exercise 5.6

Revise the "moral climate" passage. First, cut redundancy. Then revise topics so that the passage does not repeat exactly the same topic in the same position in every sentence.

SUMMING UP

In this complex lesson, there are just two simple principles:

1. Arrange your sentences so that readers move from old information to new. Do that and they will feel they are reading prose that is *cohesive.*
2. Arrange sentences so that readers see a consistent *set* of topics, a consistent topic *string* through a passage of sentences. Do that and they will feel they are reading prose that is *coherent.*

We can represent these principles in a simple model.

fixed	TOPIC	
variable	OLD, FAMILIAR	NEW, UNFAMILIAR

fixed	SUBJECT	VERB	COMPLEMENT
variable	CHARACTER	ACTION	———

There are just two principles here:

1. Open sentences with ideas that you have already mentioned or with knowledge that you can assume you and your reader share.

> The number of dead in the Civil War exceeded **all other wars in American history.** A reason for the lingering animosity between North and South today is **the memory of this terrible carnage.**

✓ **Of all the wars in American history,** none has exceeded the Civil War in the number of dead. **The memory of this terrible carnage** is one reason for the animosity between North and South today.

2. Through a series of sentences that you want your readers to understand as a coherent, focused passage, keep your topics short and reasonably consistent:

✓ In the first phase of this study, **we** will examine how Asian companies compete with American companies in the Pacific region. **We** will examine in particular labor costs and their ability to introduce new products quickly. **We** will develop from this study **a plan** that will show American industry how to restructure its facilities.

Lesson Six

Point of View

That which the fool does in the end the wise man does in the beginning.
R. C. TRENCH

The beginning is half of the whole.
PLATO

Nothing is new except arrangement.
WILL DURANT

Let it not be said that I have said nothing new. The arrangement of the material is new.
BLAISE PASCAL

Style and structure are the essence of a book; great ideas are hogwash.
VLADIMIR NABOKOV

The Ethics of Prose

In these pages, I have self-consciously avoided describing writing simply as good or bad. I have called some passages unclear or out of focus, and matched them with passages that seem to me clearer, more concise, and flowing. I have avoided flat judgments because sometimes writing that we call good is not clear and direct: We don't want our readers to know that we don't know what we're talking about; and sometimes even when we do know what we're talking about, we don't want anyone else to know. And sometimes we want to seem to be clear, but at the same time to be indirect.

So "good" has two meanings. Assassins who do their jobs efficiently may do a good job, but their jobs are not good. In the same way, writing can be good if it gets a job done, but if the job is ethically contemptible, then the writing may be very bad indeed just because it is so good. In other words writing has an ethical dimension that is worth some time exploring.

Intended Unclarity

Here is the text of a letter from a natural gas utility notifying its customers that it was raising their rates (The TOPIC/SUBJECT in every CLAUSE, MAIN or SUBORDINATE, is boldfaced):

> **The Illinois Commerce Commission** has authorized a restructuring of our rates together with an increase in Service Charge revenues effective with service rendered on and after November 12, 1990. **This** is the first increase in rates for Peoples Gas in over six years. **The restructuring of rates** is consistent with the policy of the Public Utilities Act that **rates for service to various classes of utility customers** be based upon the cost of providing that service. **The new rates** move revenues from every class of customer closer to the cost actually incurred to provide gas service. **This bill** covers a period in which proration of Service Charges is occurring. **Proration** means that **part of the bill** is based on the former **Service Charges, which** are identified on your bill as "Old Rate," and **part of the bill** is based on newly authorized **Service charges,** which are identified on your bill as "New Rate."

Even educated readers would not judge this notice to be immediately clear. In effect, it says simply "Starting this month, you have to pay us more." The writer mentions one character, Peoples Gas, only once, in the third person, and not as a topic/AGENT/subject:

> increase in rates for **Peoples Gas** in over six years. . . .

And it mentions the reader only three times, again in the third person, and never as a topic/agent/subject:

> for services to various classes of **utility customers**
>
> move revenues from every class of **customer**
>
> **your** bill. . . .

Had the company wanted to make clear who the real "doer" was, it could have begun like this:

> As authorized by the Illinois Commerce Commission, **we** will charge you more for service after November 12, 1990. **We** have not charged you more in over six years. But under the Public Utilities Act, **we** can. . . .

Exercise 6.1

Go on revising this notice, using *we* as a topic/agent/subject wherever you can. Then revise it a second time so that the topic/agent/subject is *you.* For example:

> As the Illinois Commerce Commission has authorized, **you** will have to pay us higher Service Charges after November 12, 1990. **You** have not had to pay higher rates in. . . .

Would the company resist sending either revision? Why? What ethical issues does the original raise? Was it "good" writing?

Artful Misdirection

I have emphasized how important it is to put characters in subjects, but almost every story has several characters, any one of which *could* be made a topic, even those who are not agents; that's what the passive is for. So the idea of topic is not given in the nature of things. We must therefore choose *which* characters to topicalize, even, as we have seen, whether to topicalize flesh-and-blood characters at all (look again at the story about Prospective and Immediate Intention [p. 76]).

What is worth some attention are the subtly different effects that we can create by finding verbs that let us shift into the subject/topic position different characters that serve different purposes. Children learn how quickly. Even four-year-olds understand the difference between

> **I** bumped into Tom, dropped the glass, and spilled the juice.
>
> **Tom and me** bumped, **the glass** dropped, and **the juice** spilled.

And they grow into adults who know the difference between

> **You** make me lonely when **you** don't tell me what **you** think.
>
> **I** feel lonely when **I** can't share **our** thoughts.

Sometimes there is more at stake than personal relationships. A few years ago, the California attorney general's office accused the Sears Company of overcharging for automobile repairs. In response, Sears ran newspaper advertisements that included these two sentences:

> With over two million automotive customers serviced last year in California alone, mistakes may have occurred. However, Sears wants you to know that we would never intentionally violate the trust customers have shown in our company for 105 years.

In the first sentence, the writer could have avoided mentioning Sears as the party that made the mistakes by using the PASSIVE voice saying that mistakes "were made," but that would have encouraged readers to wonder "By whom?" Instead, its writers found another VERB that gave the mistakes a life of their own: mistakes just *may have* "occurred." In the second sentence, however, the writer explicitly names in the subject Sears as the responsible agent, because in that sentence Sears wants to advertise its own good actions.

If we revise the first sentence so that it explicitly refers to Sears and the second so that it hides Sears, we get a rhetorical effect that would have made the Sears' public relations department blanch:

> When we at Sears serviced over two million automotive customers last year in California, we made some mistakes. However, you should know that no intentional violation of 105 years of trust occurred.

Exercise 6.2

Several years ago, the Government Accounting Office sponsored a study that inquired into why fewer than half the automobile owners who received recall letters complied. That study found that many car owners did not bring their cars in because they could not understand the letters or were not particularly moved by them. I actually received the following. It illustrates how writers can meet legal obligations and ignore ethical ones.

> [1]A defect which involves the possible failure of a frame support plate may exist on your vehicle. [2]This plate (front suspension pivot bar support plate) connects a portion of the front suspension to the vehicle frame, and [3]its failure could affect vehicle directional control, particularly during heavy brake application. [4]In addition, your vehicle may require adjustment service to the hood secondary catch system. [5]The secondary catch may be misaligned so that the hood may not be adequately restrained to prevent hood fly-up in the event the primary latch is inadvertently left unengaged. [6]Sudden hood fly-up beyond the secondary catch while driving could impair driver visibility. [7]In certain circumstances, occurrence of either of the above conditions could result in vehicle crash without prior warning.

Look at the topics of the sentences; they are concise and fairly consistent.

[1]a defect	[2]this plate	[3]its failure	[4]your vehicle
[5]the secondary catch	[6]sudden hood fly-up	[7]occurrence of . . . conditions	

The topics of this story, its main characters, are car parts and impersonal events. The author—probably a committee—NOMINALIZED verbs that might make me anxious and made most other verbs passive. Then they deleted most references to me and to themselves, thereby creating a story not about me or themselves, but about my car.

Revise this letter, topicalizing *you* as often as you can. Certainly one of the sentences will read,

✓ If **you** brake hard and the plate fails, **you** will. . . .

Why would the company have been reluctant to send out that version? What ethical issues are involved here? Are they different from those in the gas company notice? Is the original "good" writing? Which of these, if either, is closer to the "truth":

> If the plate fails, you could crash.
>
> If the plate fails, your car could crash.

Subtle Effects

The examples so far all seem motivated by ethically questionable motives. Sometimes, though, these kinds of manipulations of topic strings have motives entirely benign. One of the intentions of this book is to help you diagnose and revise not only your own writing but, when necessary, the writing of others. And nowhere is this matter of choosing the right character to topicalize, to tell your story about, more important than in the way you work with the writing of others. Here are three versions of the "same" story. How do they differ?

1. When you wrote this paragraph, you did not make clear what you meant, and so you don't get your point across. You are also wordy. Finally, you fail to support your claim, because you don't present any evidence.
2. The meaning of this paragraph is not clear, and so it does not get its point across. It is also wordy. Finally, it doesn't present any evidence to support its claims.
3. After reading this paragraph, I could not understand it as well as I need to. I also felt I was reading too many words. Finally, I looked for but could not find evidence that would help me accept these claims.

Exercise 6.3

That first passage is about the writer, the second about the writing, the third about the reader. Do they mean essentially "the same thing?" If you were the object of the criticism, which would make you feel worst? Which is least bad? Is any one of them closest to the "truth?" Revise this next paragraph twice. Make one version a story about the text, the other about the reader.

When you introduced your paper, you failed to describe the problem or question that you address later. Then when you started the body of the paper, you gave no hint how you related the first paragraph of the body to the introduction. You mentioned not a single concept from the introduction in that first paragraph of the body. Finally, you did not organize this paper, because you just present one point after another. You never explain why you deal with each point in the order you do or how you connect each paragraph to the next.

Exercise 6.4

This passage tells the story of women in the classroom.

> [W]omen are more interested than are the men in talking in class to support friends, and in spirited shared discussion; they also feel more at ease with teachers who do not impose their views on others. Women are seemingly more concerned than are the men with the teaching-learning process and attend more to the personal experiences of other students. . . . [Women] consider the openness and supportiveness of the instructor the salient factor in determining whether they feel comfortable about talking in class and give more importance than do men to the teacher's attempts to insure that class members feel good about each other.
>
> From Cheris Kramarae and Paula A. Treichler, "Power Relationships in the Classroom," in *Gender in the Classroom: Power and Pedagogy.*

Revise it so that it says "the same thing" but tells a story about men. That is, begin,

> Men are less interested than women. . . .

What is the consequence? How does this change the story? So what if it does?

Exercise 6.5

At the beginning of this passage from his essay, "Stranger in the Village," James Baldwin makes the cathedral at Chartres the topic and metaphorical agency. Here is his first sentence (subjects are boldfaced, verbs are italicized):

> **The cathedral at Chartres,** I have said, *says* something to the people of this village which **it** *cannot say* to me, but it is important to understand that **this cathedral** *says* something to me which **it** *cannot say* to them.

But in the second sentence, he switches the topic/subjects to the villagers and then to himself:

> Perhaps **they** *are struck* by the power of the spires, the glory of the windows; but **they** *have known* God, after all, longer than **I** *have known* him, and in a different way, and **I** *am terrified*. . . .

Revise this passage so that you change the sequence of topics in a variety of ways. Here is one new version:

> **I** have said that **I** hear something from the cathedral at Chartres that **the people** of this village do not hear, but it is important to understand that. . . .

How do they differ? What are the consequences? Here is the whole passage:

> The cathedral at Chartres, I have said, says something to the people of this village which it cannot say to me, but it is important to understand that this cathedral says something to me which it cannot say to them. Perhaps they are struck by the power of the spires, the glory of the windows; but they have known God, after all, longer than I have known him, and in a different way, and I am terrified by the slippery bottomless well to be found in the crypt, down which heretics were hurled to death, and by the obscene, inescapable gargoyles jutting out of the stone and seeming to say that God and the devil can never be divorced. I doubt that the villagers think of the devil when they face a cathedral because they have never been identified with the devil. But I must accept the status which myth, if nothing else, gives me in the West before I can hope to change the myth.

Exercise 6.6

Revise Lincoln's Gettysburg Address so that the topics are not human characters, but abstractions. The first sentence might be, "Fourscore and seven years ago, **this continent** was the place where **a new nation** was brought forth by our fathers. . . ." How do the new topics change the impact of the speech?

An Extended Analysis

Along with our Constitution, the most celebrated nonfictional prose texts in American culture are the Declaration of Independence, Abraham Lincoln's Gettysburg Address, and his Second Inaugural Address. These last three have not only the power of great thought, but the eloquence of great literature. In previous editions of this book, I have written about the Gettysburg Address and the Declaration of Independence. Here I would like to explore the style of the Second Inaugural.

Lincoln delivered this speech in March of 1865, a few weeks before the end of the Civil War. He knew that the North would win, but he was worried that as the victor, it would claim the right to punish the South both for slavery and for the war's terrible carnage. As history has demonstrated, he was right to worry. Anticipating that outcome, Lincoln tried to reunite the country in words that every American recognizes:

> With malice toward none; with charity for all; with firmness in the right, as God gives us to see the right, let us strive on to finish the work we are in; to bind up the nation's wounds. . . .

We do not memorize the opening sentences, however, because we are stirred by neither their thought nor their language:

> Fellow-countrymen: At this second appearing to take the oath of the presidential office, there is less occasion for an extended address than there was at the first. Then a statement, somewhat in detail, of a course to be pursued, seemed fitting and proper. Now, at the expiration of four years, during which public declarations have been constantly called forth on every point and phase of the great contest which still absorbs the attention and engrosses the energies of the nation, little that is new could be presented. The progress of our arms, upon which all else chiefly depends, is as well known to the public as to myself; and it is, I trust, reasonably satisfactory and encouraging to all. With high hope for the future, no prediction in regard to it is ventured.

In fact, were that paragraph written by someone other than Lincoln, we might say that it is at best pedestrian. He could have written this just as easily:

> Fellow-countrymen: As **I** appear here for the second time to take the oath of the presidential office, **I** have less occasion to address you at length than I did at the first. Then **I** thought it fitting and proper that **I** state in detail the course to be pursued. . . .

In fact, that is close to the style of his First Inaugural Address:

> Fellow-citizens of the United States: In compliance with a custom as old as the government itself, **I** appear before you to address you briefly, and to take in your presence the oath prescribed by the Constitution of the United States to be taken by the President "before he enters on the execution of his office." **I** do not consider it necessary at present for me to discuss those matters of administration. . . .

Or he could have written this:

> Fellow-countrymen: As **we** meet together for this second taking of the oath of the presidential office, **we** have less need for an extended address than **we** had at the first. Then **we** felt a statement, stating in detail, the course **we** would pursue, fitting and proper. . . .

And that is close to the style of the Gettysburg Address:

> Now **we** are engaged in a great Civil War, testing whether that nation, or any nation so conceived and so dedicated, can long endure. **We** are met on a great battlefield of that war. **We** have come to dedicate a portion of that field, as a final resting place for those who here gave their lives that that nation might live. It is altogether fitting and proper that **we** should do this.

In fact, Lincoln seems so intent on creating an impersonal and distant tone, that in the last sentence of his opening paragraph, he DANGLED a MODIFIER:

> With high hope for the future, no prediction in regard to it is ventured.

Either Lincoln's power of expression slipped, or something else is going on. Here is the rest of the speech. As you read it, note his subject/topics (italicized).

On the occasion corresponding to this four years ago, *all thoughts* were anxiously directed to an impending civil war. *All* dreaded it—*all* sought to avert it. While *the inaugural address* was being delivered from this place, devoted altogether to saving the Union without war, *insurgent agents* were in the city seeking to destroy it without war—seeking to dissolve the Union, and divide effects, by negotiation. *Both parties* deprecated war, but *one of them* would make war rather than let the nation survive; and *the other* would accept war rather than let it perish. And *the war* came.

One eighth of the whole population were colored slaves, not distributed generally over the Union, but localized in the southern part of it. *These slaves* constituted a peculiar and powerful interest. *All* knew that this interest was, somehow, the cause of the war. *To strengthen, perpetuate, and extend this interest* was the object for which the insurgents would rend the Union, even by war; while *the government* claimed no right to do more than to restrict the territorial enlargement of it. *Neither party* expected for the war the magnitude or the duration which it has already attained. *Neither* anticipated that the cause of the conflict might cease with, or even before, the conflict itself should cease. *Each* looked for an easier triumph and a result less fundamental and astounding. *Both* read the same Bible, and pray to the same God; and *each* invokes His aid against the other. It may seem strange that *any men* should dare to ask a just God's assistance in wringing their bread from the sweat of other men's faces; but let *us* judge not, that *we* be not judged. *The prayers of both* could not be answered; *that of neither* has been answered fully. *The Almighty* has His own purposes. "*Woe* unto the world because of offences! for it must needs be that *offences* come; but *woe* to that man by whom the offence cometh." If *we* shall suppose that *American slavery* is one of those offences which in the providence of God, must needs come, but which, having continued through His appointed time, *He* now wills to remove, and that *He* gives to both North and South, this terrible war as the woe due to those by whom the offence came, shall *we* discern therein any departure from those divine attributes which *the believers in a Living God* always ascribe to Him? Fondly do *we* hope—fervently do *we* pray—that *this mighty scourge of war* may speedily pass away. Yet, if *God* wills that *it* continue until *all the wealth piled by the bondman's two hundred and fifty years of unrequited toil* shall be sunk, and until *every drop of blood drawn with the lash* shall be paid by another drawn with the sword, as was said three thousand years ago, so still it must be said, "*the judgments of the Lord*, are true and righteous altogether."

With malice toward none; with charity for all; with firmness in the right, as God gives us to see the right, let *us* strive on to finish

> the work we are in; to bind up the nation's wounds; to care for him who shall have borne the battle, and for his widow, and his orphan—to do all which may achieve and cherish a just, and a lasting peace, among ourselves, and with all nations.

The first sentence of the second paragraph continues in the same impersonal style of the introduction, both nominalized and passive:

> On the occasion corresponding to this four years ago, **all thoughts were anxiously directed** to an impending civil war.

He could have written, *everyone was anxiously thinking.* Then for two short clauses, he switches to the simplicity that most of us think characterizes his prose:

> **All** dreaded it—**all** sought to avert it.

But in the next sentence, he's back to the passive again:

> While the inaugural address **was being delivered** from this place. . . .

And then just as suddenly, he's back to the direct, subject/agent–verb/action style, this time for several consecutive sentences:

> . . . **insurgent agents** *were* in the city *seeking to destroy it* without war—*seeking to dissolve* the Union, and *divide effects,* by negotiation. **Both parties** *deprecated* war, but **one of them** *would make* war rather than let the nation survive; and **the other** *would accept* war rather than let it perish. And the **war** *came.*

After another weak sentence about where the slaves were localized, Lincoln settles into the style that we expect of him: elegantly simple and direct, agents as subjects, strong actions in verbs:

> **All** *knew.* . . .
> **the insurgents** *would rend* the Union. . . .
> **the government** *claimed* no right to do more than to restrict. . . .
> **Neither party** *expected.* . . .

> **Neither** *anticipated. . . .*
>
> **Each** *looked* for an easier triumph. . . .
>
> **Both** *read* the same Bible, and *pray* to the same God.
>
> **each** *invokes* his aid against the other.
>
> It may seem strange that **any men** should *dare to ask. . . .*
>
> but let **us** *judge* not, that **we** *be not judged.*

After these two simple and appropriately passive clauses:

> **The prayers of both** *could not be answered;* **that of neither** *has been answered* fully.

Lincoln returns to the same simple, direct style:

> **The Almighty** *has* His own purposes.
>
> "**Woe** unto the world because of offences!
>
> for . . . **offences** *come;*
>
> but **woe** to that man by whom the offence cometh."
>
> If **we** *shall suppose* that. . . .
>
> **American slavery** . . . *must needs come. . . .*
>
> **He** now *wills to remove. . . .*
>
> **He** *gives* to both North and South this terrible war. . . .
>
> *shall* **we** *discern* therein any departure from those divine attributes. . . .
>
> **the believers** in a living God always *ascribe* to Him?
>
> Fondly do **we** *hope*—fervently do **we** *pray. . . .*
>
> Yet, if **God** *wills* that
>
> **it** continue. . . .
>
> **all the wealth piled** . . . **toil** *shall be sunk,*
>
> **every drop of blood** . . . *shall be paid* by another
>
> **the judgments of the lord,** *are true. . . .*
>
> With malice toward none . . . let **us** *strive* on to finish the work. . . .

Once Lincoln gets past the first paragraph and a half, he demonstrates what we take to be his classic American style: direct, clear, honest.

With one exception.

I think that among all the sentences crafted by American writers, none has written one more cleverly constructed than than this one:

> If we shall suppose that American slavery is one of those offences which in the providence of God, must needs come, but which, having continued through His appointed time, He now wills to remove, and that He gives to both North and South this terrible war as the woe due to those by whom the offence came, shall we discern therein any departure from those divine attributes which the believers in a living God always ascribe to Him?

This sentence is at the heart of his argument that revenge would be wrong: It is not the South that is responsible for the terrible war, but God:

> **He gives** to both North and South this terrible war. . . .

Nor can the North take credit for ending slavery. God did:

> **He now wills** to remove [this offence of American slavery].

And who will end the war? Not the victorious North, but God, when He chooses:

> . . . if **God wills** that [the war] continue. . . .

That accounts for the source of the war, for ending it, and for slavery. It was the responsibility of neither North nor South, but of God.

But whence came slavery? Here is Lincoln's curiously indirect account:

> **American slavery** is one of those offences which in the providence of God, **must needs come**. . . .

Now that is an oddly written clause: When Lincoln was explaining who brought the war, who ended slavery, and who will end the war, he wrote as directly as he could that God did it or will do it. Slavery, however, seems to have a different history: Like the war at the end of the second paragraph, the offence of slavery just "came." And in contrast to other sentences with their direct agent/subject–action/verb clauses about God's role, this one is full of nominalizations:

> American **slavery** is one of those **offences** [in] the **providence** of God.

We could revise those nominalizations into verbs and assign them agents:

American **slavery**	→	Americans **enslave** Africans
one of those **offences**	→	Americans **offend** God
the **providence** of God	→	God **provides** [something]

And if we assemble these three clauses into a sentence, we get something like this:

> God **provided** that Americans **enslave** Africans, and that **offends** God.

Is it reasonable to suppose that Lincoln might have thought that such a direct statement would raise a theological issue that, at least on this occasion, he would just as soon avoid? To be sure, Lincoln did believe that God was responsible for every terrible thing that had happened. But while he had no problem saying clearly that God gave the war to both North and South, that God willed to remove slavery, that God might will the war to continue, he seems less candid about the responsibility of God in the origin of slavery.

In that line, of course, he quotes from the Bible; but whatever his source, Lincoln clearly did not want to be as direct about who caused slavery as he was about who gave us the war. And so he stylistically finessed the problem: He nominalized the part of the sentence that might have troubled his audience, an audience that was more likely to accept the idea that in the providence of God, slavery just "came," than the idea that God willed that *all* Americans (not just Southerners) should enslave Blacks.

But what does all this have to do with that impersonal, abstract, almost bureaucratic opening paragraph? Perhaps this: Lincoln believed that the enormity of the war was God's work, that the North and South were the passive but nevertheless culpable instruments of His will. The only time he referred to North or South by name, he made them indirect objects, recipients of a war willed by God. All the other subject/topic/agents are general, nonspecific: *agents, parties, one, the other, both, all, each, neither, any man.* In fact, Lincoln appears to have been deliberately vague about naming the specific agent of any action, until he reached the middle of his speech, where he made his rhetorical move of assigning agency to the only agent in the speech whom he called by name: God.

And perhaps that helps explain the impersonality of the opening paragraph. Knowing that later he would introduce God as the only moving agent, he wanted to create in the first half an indefinite, impersonal, not particularly specific blue/gray–gray/blue background in order to highlight the direct agency of God in American history. Except for the origin of slavery.

It is a great speech, especially that last sentence whose words are engraved in our national consciousness. But now even the parts that seem uninspired seem at least explicable. And when we look at the way Lincoln managed his syntax in that sentence where he explained how God directly willed (almost) everything, we see why, along with the Declaration of Independence and the Gettysburg Address, this document is rightly included among our sacred secular texts.

Exercise 6.7

What do you make of the way this sequence of sentences describes the coming and hoped passing of the war? How else could he have described its origins?

> [O]ne of them would *make* war.
>
> And the war *came.*
>
> [Slaves were *an interest that was the*] *cause of* the war.
>
> The insurgents would rend the Union . . . by war.
>
> [God] *gives* to both North and South this terrible war.
>
> [T]his mighty scourge of war may speedily *pass away.*
>
> God *wills* that [the war] *continue.*

Exercise 6.8

Lincoln was as deliberate in distancing God from slavery as the writer of the automobile recall letter was in distancing the manufacturer from its defective product, or the writer of the gas company letter was in distancing the company from its increase in rates. What kinds of ethical distinctions, if any, would you make among these three?

Summing Up

Writers of the highest skill construct passages that focus attention on the characters they want their readers to remember and that divert attention from those they want them to overlook, without their readers being aware of it:

> **You** must pay higher taxes for your children's quality education.
>
> **Only higher** taxes can provide quality education for your children.
>
> **Your children** can receive a quality education only with higher taxes.
>
> **Quality education** for your children demands higher taxes.

Which of these is the best choice would depend on the entire rhetorical context. There are no hard rules here, only rules of thumb:

1. If you want to distance your readers from an action, assign to it a character that is distant from them.
2. If you want to link your readers to an action, assign it to a character that is close to them.

The tricky part is to figure out how to represent the action in a way that lets you make the "right" character seem to be its agent.

Lesson Seven

Emphasis

In the end is my beginning.
T. S. ELIOT

The end of a matter is better than its beginning.
ECCLESIASTES 7:8

Beginning and end shake hands with each other.
GERMAN PROVERB

All's well that ends well.
WILLIAM SHAKESPEARE

One of the most difficult things is the first paragraph. I have spent many months on a first paragraph, and once I get it, the rest just comes out very easily. In the first paragraph you solve most of the problem with your book. The theme is defined, the style, the tone.
GABRIEL GARCIA MARQUEZ

Begin a sentence well, and you are likely to end it well. If you organize SUBJECT/TOPICS around a few central CHARACTERS, if you keep those subjects short and quickly join them to precise VERBS, your readers are likely feel that everything else is in the right place, too. But anyone with an ear for style recognizes that while clarity depends on how a sentence begins, how it ends determines not only clarity but the emphasis and energy that characterize strength. We'll address clarity first, then emphasis.

Clarity

Managing Syntactic Complexity

Managing the end of a sentence is just the mirror image of managing its beginning. If simplicity goes first, complexity, by default, goes last. Which of these three passages do you prefer?

1a. The suggestion by plaintiff's counsel that plaintiffs should be allowed to question the defendant to determine whether tax reform measures were passed in the mid-1980s and whether this country has experienced a collapse of the real estate market or national recession is simply bizarre.

1b. It is simply bizarre for plaintiff's counsel to suggest that plaintiffs should be allowed to question the defendant to determine whether tax reform measures were passed in the mid-1980s and whether this country has experienced a collapse of the real estate market or national recession.

1c. Plaintiff's counsel suggests that plaintiffs should be allowed to question defendant to determine whether tax reform measures were passed in the mid-1980s and whether this country has experienced a collapse of the real estate market or national recession. That suggestion is simply bizarre.

Most readers prefer (1b) or (1c) because they don't like the long complex subject in (1a). They can deal with exactly the same complex information most easily when it appears not at the beginning of a sentence as in (1a), but at the end, as in (1b), or in a sentence of its own, as in (1c).

> ***Here's the point:*** In general, readers best comprehend long complex units *after* they have read a relatively short and clear subject + verb sequence. Don't start a sentence by forcing them to slog through a list of items, a complex set of conditions, or long abstract clumps of nominalizations.

Recall that our boxes reflect that *quality* of information:

fixed	TOPIC	
variable	OLD, SHORT, SIMPLE	NEW, LONG, COMPLEX

fixed	SUBJECT	VERB	COMPLEMENT
variable	CHARACTER	ACTION	———

Since we can move long and short units of information around in a sentence, we locate those kinds of elements at the variable level, but they have default locations: simplicity first, complexity last.

Managing New Technical Terms

Readers have a problem with a second kind of complexity: It has less to do with unpacking long complicated PHRASES and CLAUSES than with the added effort they need to understand new information, regardless of its syntactic complexity. Compare these next two passages:

1a. The effects of calcium blockers in the control of cardiac irregularity can be seen through an understanding of the role of calcium in the activation of muscle groups. The regulatory proteins actin, myosin, tropomyosin, and troponin make up the sarcomere, the basic unit of muscle contraction. The thick filament is made up of ATPase, an energy-producing protein myosin, while actin, tropomyosin, and troponin make up the thin filament.

✓ 1b. When muscles contract, they need calcium. We must therefore understand how calcium influences muscle contraction in order to understand how cardiac irregularity is controlled by drugs called calcium blockers. The basic unit of muscle contraction is the sarcomere. It has two filaments, one thin and one thick, consisting of proteins that regulate contraction. Muscles contract when a protein in the thin filament, actin, interacts with another protein in the thick filament, an energy-producing or ATPase protein called myosin.

Both passages have the same technical terms, but the novice in muscle chemistry can read (1b) more easily than (1a).

They differ in two ways. First, information that is implicit in (1a) is explicit in (1b):

1a. . . . and troponin make up the sarcomere, the basic unit of muscle contraction. The thick filament is made up of. . . .

✓ 1b. The basic unit of muscle contraction is the sarcomere. It has two. . . .

In the same way, I also turned information that was indirectly stated in an ADJECTIVE in (1a) into direct statements with full subjects and verbs in (1b):

regulatory proteins → proteins that **regulate.**

But the more important way they differ is that I moved technical terms that might be unfamiliar to a reader away from the beginnings of sentences toward their ends:

2a. The effects of **calcium blockers** in the control of cardiac irregularity can be seen through an understanding of the role of **calcium** in the activation of muscle groups.

2b. When muscles contract, they need **calcium.** We must therefore understand how calcium influences muscle contraction in order to understand how cardiac irregularity is controlled by drugs called **calcium blockers.**

Here's the point: When readers see a technical term for the first time, particularly a term that they will not instantly recognize, they can best grasp that term if it appears not at the beginning of a sentence, in its topic, but at the end.

Before you conclude that these principles apply only to prose intended for rank novices in a field, I should note that writers introduce new technical terms in this way in even the most professional writing, as in this passage from the *New England Journal of Medicine:*

✓ The incubation of peripheral-blood lymphocytes with a lymphokine, interleukin-2, generates lymphoid cells that can lyse fresh, noncultured, natural-killer-cell-resistant tumor cells but not normal cells. *We term these cells* **lymphokine-activated killer (LAK) cells.**

Even experts in a field find prose difficult when it goes against the grain of the principles offered here.

Introducing Longer Units of Discourse

In fact, this principle leads to an even more important one, one that helps readers grasp the unity of a whole passage. Which of these two passages do you like better?

1a. The advantages of the equitable right of recovery exceed those of the statutory method. Strict compliance with statutory requirements is not necessary for recovery in equity. The particular facts of the controversy therefore help tailor recovery, with the result that greater or lesser amounts may be recoverable. Rents based upon the value of the property including improvements by the defendant were granted to plaintiff in a recent recovery in equity case, whereas only the value of use and occupation exclusive of improvements would have been recoverable in a statutory action.

1b. In comparison to the statutory method, a plaintiff may find certain advantages in the equitable method of recovery. In equity, the plaintiff need not strictly comply with statutory requirements. Further, because she can tailor recovery to the specific facts of the controversy, she can recover greater or lesser amounts. In a statutory action for the recovery of rents, a plaintiff can recover only the value of use and occupation exclusive of improvements to the property. However, in a recent equitable action, the plaintiff recovered rents based upon the value of the property including the defendant's improvements.

Most readers prefer (1b) for two reasons:

1. Every sentence in (1a) begins with new information that someone reading this material for the first time could not predict. In the second, the sentences begin with more familiar units of information: *plantiff* or *she,* flesh-and-blood characters. Most important, that revision puts all of the new and complex information at the ends of those sentences.
2. In (1b), the reader can better predict the key terms of the passage after reading the words *at the end of the first sentence.* Compare how the two opening sentences end:

1a. The advantages of the equitable right of recovery **exceed** those of the **statutory method.**

✓ 1b. In comparison to the statutory method, a plaintiff may find certain **advantages** in the **equitable** method of **recovery.**

At the end of (1b), the reader sees the THEMES of the passage, those other key conceptual elements that will weave through the sentences in a variety of places, particularly different versions of *advantages.*

I underline, italicize, and boldface related themes that the first sentence signals:

✓ 1b. In comparison to the statutory method, a plaintiff may find certain advantages in the *equitable* **method of recovery.** In *equity,* the plaintiff need not strictly comply with statutory requirements. Further, because she can tailor **recovery** to the specific facts of the controversy, she can **recover** greater or lesser amounts. In a *statutory* action for the **recovery** of rents, a plaintiff can **recover** only the value of use and occupation exclusive of improvements to the property. However, in an *equitable* action (*Wilson*), the plaintiff **recovered** rents based upon the value of the property with the defendant's improvements.

The word *advantages* anticipates *need not strictly comply, can tailor, recover greater or lesser amounts,* etc.; the word *equitable* anticipates *equity, equitable,* and its antonym, *statutory;* the word *recovery* anticipates *recover* and *recovery.*

Here's the point: Readers pay special attention to the last few words of a sentence that *introduces* a passage of sentences: They read those words as signaling the central concepts that will follow. You can help your readers in three ways if you pay special attention to the last few words of a sentence.

1. It is toward the end of a sentence that a reader can best understand long and complex units of information.
2. It is at the end of a sentence that a reader can best understand new information, particularly unfamiliar technical words.
3. It is at the end of an introductory sentence in particular that readers note those important concepts that your next several sentences will develop.

Exercise 7.1

Here are three opening sentences and the rest of a paragraph. Which one best sets up the ideas in that following paragraph? In this case, assume that the reader would be familiar with the characters—Russian rulers. What we have to introduce are the new concepts to be associated with those rulers. The last few words of a sentence that opens a paragraph should stress the key concepts that the rest of the paragraph develops. When you finish with that, try revising any more redundancy you find in that paragraph.

1. The next century the situation changed, because disputes over succession to the throne caused some sort of palace revolt or popular revolution in seven out of eight reigns of the Romanov line after Peter the Great.
2. The next century the situation changed, because after Peter the Great seven out of eight reigns of the Romanov line were plagued by turmoil over disputed succession to the throne.
3. Because turmoil over disputed succession to the throne plagued seven out of eight reigns of the Romanov line after Peter the Great, the situation changed in the next century.

The problems began in the year 1722, when Tsar Peter the Great passed a law of succession to the throne that brought to an end the principle of succession by heredity and required the sovereign on the throne to appoint someone to succeed him when he died. But because many of the Russian Tsars, including Peter, died before they were able to name successors, those who aspired to rule over Russia had no authority or legal power by appointment from the Tsar, and so their succession was often disputed by the boyars, who were lower level aristocrats in Russian society. There was turmoil and turbulence even when successors were appointed by Tsars, usually. In the year 1740, Ivan VI was adopted by Czarina Anna Ivanovna and named as her successor at two months of age, but his succession to the throne was challenged by Elizabeth, who was daughter of Peter the Great. In the year 1741, she defeated Anna and ascended to the throne herself instead. In the year 1797 Paul tried to eliminate these disputes over succession to the throne by codifying and instituting a new law: it stated that the oldest born in the male line would succeed to the throne. But trouble and turmoil continued to occur. Paul was strangled to death by conspirators, one of whom was probably his son, Alexander I.

On pp. 118–19 in Exercise 5.5, there are two other passages whose opening sentences could be revised.

Emphasis and Stress

But if readers look in the last part of your sentences for new and complex information, they also respond in particular to the last few words in ways that make them feel that your prose is not just clear, but strong and emphatic.

In Lessons Five and Six, we saw that among the elements that open a sentence, readers look for one that is particularly important—its *topic,* its grammatical or psychological subject (see pp. 107–109). Another important "position" in the psychological geography of a sentence is very close to its end. You can sense it when you hear your voice naturally rise and fall on the last word or two of a sentence (to a lesser extent every clause inside a sentence), stressing one syllable more strongly than you do the others. Listen to how that sentence ended:

ó-

. . . more strongly than you do the

-thers.

We'll call this climactic part of a sentence its *STRESS.* We can add this element to fill out our boxes.

fixed	TOPIC	STRESS
variable	OLD, SHORT, SIMPLE	NEW, LONG, COMPLEX

fixed	SUBJECT	VERB	COMPLEMENT
variable	CHARACTER	ACTION	———

How you manage the words that appear in that concluding stress position goes a long way toward establishing the energy that your readers hear in the voice that your writing projects.

Compare these passages. One was written to emphasize the failures of the American administration in dealing with arms control. The other is mine; it puts more blame on the then-Soviet Union. You can tell which is which if you imagine thumping your finger on the desk as you read the words at the ends of the sentences:

2a. The administration has blurred an issue central to arms control, **the issue of verification.** Irresponsible charges, innuendo and leaks have submerged **serious problems with Soviet compliance.** The objective, instead, should be not to exploit these concerns in order to further poison our relations, repudiate existing agreements, or, worse still, terminate arms control altogether, but to insist on compliance and **clarify questionable Soviet behavior.**

2b. The issue of verification—so central to arms control—has been **blurred by the administration.** Serious problems with Soviet compliance have been submerged in **irresponsible charges, innuendo and leaks.** The objective, instead, should be to clarify questionable Soviet behavior and insist on compliance—not to exploit these concerns in order to further poison our relations, repudiate existing agreements, or, **worse still, terminate arms control altogether.**

Here's the point: Readers assign special emphasis to the words they hear in their "mind's ear" under this final stress, and what they hear emphasized, they take to be rhetorically significant. So just as readers look for topics, so do they listen for stress.

Managing Endings for Emphasis

Three Tactical Revisions

You probably won't know what words you want to move to the end of a sentence for either clarity or emphasis until you read your rough first draft, preferably out loud. Then if you decide that you didn't get the right words under the right stress, you have to revise. Here are three general strategies:

1. Trim the end.

   Sociobiologists now make the provocative claim that our genes control our social behavior **in the way we act in situations we find around us every day.**

   Since *social behavior* means the way we act, we can drop everything after *behavior:*

   ✓ Sociobiologists now make the provocative claim that our genes **control our social behavior.**

2. Shift peripheral ideas to the left.

   The data offered to establish the existence of ESP do not make us believers **for the most part.**

   ✓ **For the most part,** the data offered to establish the existence of ESP do not make us believers.

   Particularly avoid ending with anticlimactic METADISCOURSE.

   Opportunities are good at the graduate level, **it must be remembered.**

   ✓ **It must be remembered** that opportunities at the graduate level are good.

3. Shift important ideas to the right.

   A more common way we manage stress is by moving rhetorically salient information to the right, closer to the end of a sentence.

   Questions relating to the ethics of withdrawing intravenous fluid are *more important* [than something else just mentioned before].

   ✓ *More important* [than something else just mentioned before] are **questions relating to the ethics of withdrawing intravenous fluid.**

Seven Syntactic Devices

There are seven syntactic devices that shift elements closer to the end of a sentence and thereby emphasize them.

1. PASSIVES (for the last time)

   The most important function of the passive is to shift elements around in a sentence to get both topics and stresses right. If the sentences following either of these next two developed the concept of *controlling genes,* readers would judge the second to be more helpful than the first, because it ends with that concept:

> ✓ Sociobiologists make the provocative claim that **our genes** *determine* our social behavior. Our genes. . . .
>
> Sociobiologists make the provocative claim that our social behavior *is determined* by **our genes.** Our genes. . . .

2. *There*

As we will point out (p. 174), some editors discourage the use of *there is/there are* constructions. But that would deprive you of a device that lets you shift information a bit closer to the end of a sentence:

> **Several syntactic devices** let you manage where in a sentence you locate units of new information.
>
> ✓ **There are** several syntactic devices that let you manage where in a sentence you locate units of new information.

This device is particularly useful at the beginning of a paragraph because it signals to your readers that you are introducing a new set of concepts that they will see developed in the sentences that follow (see p. 143).

3. *What*-Shift

This throws special emphasis on the words that follow a linking verb:

> We need *a monetary policy that will end wild fluctuations in money supply, unemployment, and high rates of inflation.*
>
> ✓ **What** we need **is** *a monetary policy that will end wild fluctuations in money supply, unemployment, and high rates of inflation.*

4. *It*-shift 1

In this pattern, you simultaneously select and emphasize a topic and throw added weight on the stress. Compare:

> In 1933 we experienced a depression that almost wrecked our democratic system of government.

✓ **It was** *in 1933* **that** we experienced a depression that almost wrecked our democratic system of government.

5. *It*-shift 2

   By using *it* as a subject, you can shift a long and complex introductory CLAUSE that would have been the subject to a position after the verb:

   That oil prices must eventually rise to a level that could be dictated by OPEC once seemed inevitable.

   ✓ **It** once seemed inevitable *that oil prices must eventually rise to a level that could be dictated by OPEC.*

   The cost to the reader of these five devices is extra words, so use them sparingly.

6. *Not only X, but Y, (as well)*

   Compare:

   We must clarify these issues and develop trust.

   ✓ We must **not only** clarify these issues, **but** develop trust **as well.**

   The added words emphasize the last element of the pair. Unless you have reason to emphasize the negative, end with the positive half of this construction:

   The point is to highlight our success, not to **emphasize our failures.**

   ✓ The objective is not to emphasize our failures but to **highlight our success.**

7. Repeated words and pronoun substitution

   This is a fine point: Sometimes a sentence will seem to end flatly because you can't avoid using a word at the end of a sentence that you used just a few words before or at the end of the previous sentence. But when you repeat that word at the end of a sentence, your voice carries less emphasis, and it drops at the end of a sentence. (If you read those last two sentences aloud, you can hear that happen.) In that case, if you use a pronoun instead of repeating the noun, the reader will at least hear emphasis on the word before that pronoun (and that sentence is a candidate for such a revision).

Sometimes a sentence will seem to end flatly because you can't avoid using a word at the end of a sentence that you used just a few words before or even at the end of the previous **one.** But when you repeat that word **there,** your voice carries less emphasis, and it **drops.** In that case, if instead of repeating the noun you use a pronoun, the reader will at least hear emphasis on the word just before **it.**

Exercise 7.2

Revise these sentences so that the concepts that deserve emphasis appear at the end. In the first five, I have boldfaced elements that I think should be stressed. Then eliminate wordiness, unnecessary NOMINALIZATION, etc.

1. **The judiciary's tendency to rewrite the Constitution** is the biggest danger to the Republic, in my opinion, at least.
2. **A new political philosophy that could affect our society well into the twenty-first century** may emerge from these studies.
3. There are **limited** opportunities for teachers to work with individual students in large American colleges and universities.
4. As used in the industry, "turnkey" means **responsibility for the satisfactory performance of a piece of equipment in addition to the manufacture and installation** of that equipment, according to everyone who understands the matter.
5. **Several upper and lower eyelid reconstruction evaluation studies** are presented with the aforementioned summary discussions for your general information.
6. Building suburban housing developments in floodplains has led to the existence of extensive and widespread flooding and economic disaster in parts of our country in recent years, it is now clear.
7. The teacher who makes an assignment of a long final term paper at the end of the semester and who then gives only a grade at the end and nothing else such as a critical comment is a common complaint among students at the college level.

8. Renting textbooks rather than buying them for basic required courses such as mathematics, foreign languages, and English, whose textbooks do not experience change from year to year, is feasible, however, economically speaking.
9. The outcome of the war was changed as a result of an event that occurred at about this same point in time, on the other hand.
10. Guidelines in the MLA style sheet and the NCTE guidelines for the non-sexist use of language should be adhered to by speakers and writers, to the best of their ability.

Exercise 7.3

Revise these passages so that their sentences begin with appropriate topics and end with appropriate emphasis.

1. The story of King Lear and his daughters was a popular one during the reign of Queen Elizabeth. At least a dozen available books offered the story to anyone wishing to read it, by the time Elizabeth died. The characters were undeveloped in most of these stories, however, making the story a simple narrative that stated an obvious moral. When he began work on *Lear,* perhaps his greatest tragedy, Shakespeare must have had several versions of this story available to him. He turned the characters into credible human beings with complex motives, however, even though they were based on the stock figures of legend.
2. Whether the date an operation intends to close down might be part of management's "duty to disclose" during contract bargaining is the issue here, it would appear. The minimization of conflict is the central rationale for the duty that management has to bargain in good faith. In order to allow the union to put forth proposals on behalf of its members, companies are obligated to disclose major changes in an operation during bargaining, though the case law is scanty on this matter.
3. Athens' catastrophic Sicilian Invasion is the most important event in Thucydides' *History of the Pelopon-*

nesian War. Three-quarters of the history is devoted to setting up the invasion because of this. Through the step-by-step decline in Athenian society that Thucydides describes, we can see how Thucydides chose to anticipate the Sicilian Invasion. The inevitability that we associate with the tragic drama is the basic reason for the need to anticipate the invasion.

This next passage will seem difficult, because it deals with a strange subject. But even if you don't understand the words, you can still make it more readable.

4. Mucosal and vascular permeability altered by a toxin elaborated by the vibrio is a current hypothesis to explain this kind of severe condition. Changes in small capillaries located near the basal surface of the epithelial cells, and the appearance of numerous microvesicles in the cytoplasm of the mucosal cells is evidence in favor of this hypothesis. Hydrodynamic transport of fluid into the interstitial tissue and then through the mucosa into the lumen of the gut is believed to depend on altered capillary permeability.

Revise this next passage so that the most important data appear consistently at the ends of their sentences.

5. Changes in revenues are as follows. An increase to $56,792 from $32,934, a net increase of approximately 73%, was realized July 1–August 31 in the Ohio and Kentucky areas. In the Indiana and Illinois areas there was in the same period a 10% increase of $15,370, from $153,281 to $168,651. However, a decrease to $190,580 from $200,102, or 5%, occurred in the Wisconsin and Minnesota regions in almost the same period of time.

Exercise 7.4

In Lesson Five, you were asked to revise a few passages according to the old/new principle (p. 112–13, 118–19). Look at your revisions again from the point of view of these two principles of cohesion and coherence. Look particularly at the opening sentences of those passages and if necessary revise them.

Exercise 7.5

Look again at the automobile recall letter in Lesson Six (p. 126). Where in those sentences are the words referring to alarming facts? Beginning? Middle? End? Why were they placed there?

Exercise 7.6

Find some famous speech or other highly charged piece of rhetoric and read it aloud, thumping your finger on the last few words of every sentence. Do the words you thump feel like the words that should be thumped? If not, revise the sentence so that you do thump on the words that should receive the most emphasis.

Summing Up

By now, we begin to see the real complexity of an ordinary English sentence. A sentence is more than its subject, verb, and **OBJECT**, certainly more than the sum of its parts. It is a system of systems whose parts we can fit together in delicate ways to achieve delicate ends—if we know how. We can match, mismatch, or metaphorically manipulate the grammatical units and their meanings.

fixed	TOPIC	STRESS
variable	OLD, SHORT, SIMPLE	NEW, LONG, COMPLEX

fixed	SUBJECT	VERB	COMPLEMENT
variable	CHARACTER	ACTION	———

But when you step back from the details of subjects, agents, passives, nominalizations, topic, and stress and *listen* to your prose, you should hear something beyond clarity and coherence. You should hear your voice, because the voice that your readers hear contributes substantially to the character that they think you project. Some teachers want to make voice a moral choice between a false voice and an "authentic" one. But we all speak in many voices, no one of which is more or less authentic. When we are being authoritative and aloof, then that's the voice we choose to project because that's what we're being. When we want to be businesslike and direct, we choose that voice. Your job is to choose the voice that you want your readers to hear. That's no more false than choosing how you dress and behave. Some of us learn to make those choices naturally, without thought or instruction.

The rest of us have to work at it.

Part Three

Grace

There are two sorts of eloquence; the one indeed scarce deserves the name of it, which consists chiefly in laboured and polished periods, an over-curious and artificial arrangement of figures, tinseled over with a gaudy embellishment of words. . . . The other sort of eloquence is quite the reverse to this, and which may be said to be the true characteristic of the holy Scriptures; where the eloquence does not arise from a laboured and farfetched elocution, but from a surprising mixture of simplicity and majesty.

LAURENCE STERNE

Lesson Eight

Concision

Loquacity and lying are cousins.
GERMAN PROVERB

I write for those who judge of books, not by the quantity, but by the quality of them: who ask not how long, but how good they are? I spare both my reader's time and my own, by couching my sense in as few words as I can.
JOHN WESLEY

When a Discourse is to be bound down upon Paper, and subjected to the calm leisurely Examination of nice Judgment, everything that is needless gives Offense.
BENJAMIN FRANKLIN

If you require a practical rule of me, I will present you with this: Whenever you feel an impulse to perpetrate a piece of exceptionally fine writing, obey it—wholeheartedly—and delete it before sending your manuscript to press. Murder your darlings.
ARTHUR QUILLER-COUCH

To a Snail: If "compression is the first grace of style," you have it.
MARIANNE MOORE

CLARITY, GRACE, AND CONCISION

You are a long way toward clarity when you match CHARACTERS to your SUBJECTS and ACTIONS to your VERBS and when you structure your sentences to focus your readers' attention on the right sequence of TOPICS. But even when you do all that, your readers may still think that you are a long way from grace if you write like this:

> In my personal opinion, it is necessary for all of us not to miss the opportunity to think over in a careful manner each and every suggestion that is offered us.

This writer matched most of her AGENTS and actions with subjects and verbs, but in more words than her readers needed: Every opinion is personal, so we can cut *personal.* And since this statement is obviously opinion, *in my opinion,* as well. *It is necessary* means *must. Us* implies *all. Think over* means *consider. In a careful manner* means *carefully. Each and every* is redundant. A suggestion is by definition offered, so neither do we need *that is offered.* And since the negative *not miss* negates itself, we can change the sentence to an affirmative. What's left is a leaner, more straightforward sentence. If not obviously elegant, it has at least the quality of compression, a quality that in Marianne Moore's judgement, is style's first grace:

✓ We must consider each suggestion carefully.

To get to that sentence, I applied five principles of economy:

1. Delete words that mean little or nothing.
2. Delete words that repeat other words.
3. Delete words whose meaning your reader can infer from other words.
4. Replace a phrase with a word.
5. Change unnecessary negatives to affirmatives.

Unfortunately, these principles are easier for me to state than for you to follow, because the only way to identify and prune wordiness is to inch your way through every sentence, word by word. That's hard work. It helps a bit, though, to know generally what to look for. (Don't worry about discriminating among these categories; use them just as a way to think about concision systematically.)

1. Delete Meaningless Words

Some words are verbal tics that we use as unconsciously as we clear our throats:

kind of	actually	particular	really	certain	various
virtually	individual	basically	generally	given	practically

Productivity **actually** depends on **certain** factors that **basically** involve psychology more than any **particular** technology.

✓ Productivity depends more on psychology than on technology.

> ***Here's the point:*** Don't use words whose meaning adds nothing to the sentence.

2. Delete Doubled Words

Early in the history of English, writers began to pair a native English word with a French or Latin word, because a borrowed word sounded more learned than the native one. Among the common pairs today:

full and complete	hope and trust	any and all
true and accurate	each and every	basic and fundamental
hopes and desires	first and foremost	various and sundry

> ***Here's the point:*** When you use a familiar pair of adjectives, your readers probably need only one of them.

3. Delete What Readers Infer

This is the most common redundancy.

Redundant Modifiers

Often, the meaning of a word implies its modifier:

completely finish	**past** history	**various** different
basic fundamentals	**future** plans	**personal** beliefs
final outcome	**true** facts	**consensus** of opinion
terrible tragedy	**free** gift	**each** individual

Do not try to *anticipate* **in advance** those events that will **completely** *revolutionize* society because **past** *history* shows that it is the **eventual** *outcome* of minor events that **unexpectedly** *surprises* us more.

✓ Do not try to *anticipate revolutionary* events because *history* shows that the *outcome* of minor events *surprises* us more.

Perhaps the most common redundancy is a preposition implied by its verb:

continue **on** return **back** to penetrate **into** circle **around**

Here's the point: When a word implies its modifier, drop the modifier.

Redundant Categories

Every word implies the name of its general category, so you can usually cut the word for the category. Compare:

During that *period* of **time,** the *membrane* **area** became *pink* in **color** and *shiny* in **appearance.**

✓ During that *period,* the *membrane* became *pink and shiny.*

Sometimes, when we eliminate the category, we must change an ADJECTIVE into an ADVERB:

The holes must be aligned in an *accurate* **manner.**

✓ The holes must be aligned *accurately.*

Sometimes we must change an adjective modifying a deleted category into a NOUN:

The **educational** *process* and public **recreational** *activities* are the responsibility of the **county** *government.*

✓ *The* ***county*** is responsible for ***education*** and public ***recreation.***

Here are some general nouns (boldfaced) often used redundantly:

large in **size**	*round* in **shape**	*honest* in **character**
unusual in **nature**	of a *strange* **type**	**area** of mathematics
of a *bright* **color**	at an *early* **time**	in a *confused* **state**

> ***Here's the point:*** When a general category word is attached to a specific modifier, drop the category word.

General Implications

This kind of wordiness is a general version of the others, but it is harder to spot because it can be so diffuse:

Imagine someone trying to learn the rules for playing the game of chess.

Learning implies *trying, playing* a *game* implies *rules, chess* is a kind of *game.* More concisely,

✓ Imagine someone learning the rules of chess.

> ***Here's the point:*** When one word implies others, cut the others.

Unnecessary Explanation

In technical writing for an informed audience, writers assume their readers have a good deal of knowledge.

The basic type of verb stem results from rearrangement of the phonemic content of polysyllabic forms so that the initial CV of

> the first stem syllable is transposed with the first CV of the second stem syllable.

The writer didn't define *verb stem, phonemic content, stem syllable,* or *CV* because she assumed that anyone reading that professional journal would know. On the other hand, a student reading his first linguistics textbook would probably need a definition even of *phonetic transcription*:

> To study language scientifically, we need some kind of phonetic transcription, a system to write a language so that visual symbols consistently represent segments of speech.

> ***Here's the point:*** Don't tell your readers what you are *certain* they already know.

4. REPLACE A PHRASE WITH A WORD

This kind of redundancy is the most difficult to prune, because a writer needs a large vocabulary and the wit to use it. For example,

> As you carefully read what you have written to improve wording and catch errors of spelling, punctuation, and so on, the thing to do before anything else is to see whether you could use sequences of subjects and verbs instead of the same ideas expressed in nouns instead of verbs.

That is,

✓ As you edit, first replace nominalizations with clauses.

I compressed six phrases into six words:

carefully read what you have written	→	edit
the thing to do before anything else	→	first
see where	→	find
use X instead of Y	→	replace
sequences of subjects and verbs	→	clauses
nouns instead of verbs	→	nominalizations

I can offer no principle to help you recognize phrases that you can replace with a word, much less give you that word. I can point out only that we often can, and that we should be on the alert for opportunities to do so—which is to say, try.

Here are some common phrases you can watch for (note that some of these also let you revise a nominalization into a verb; they are indicated by italicized nominalizations and verbs):

the reason for
due to the fact that
owing to the fact that
in light of the fact that
considering the fact that
on the grounds that
this is why
} because, since, why

We must explain **the reason for** the *delay* in the meeting.

✓ We must explain **why** the meeting is *delayed*.

despite the fact that
regardless of the fact that
notwithstanding the fact that
} although, even though

Despite the fact that the data were checked, errors occurred.

✓ **Even though** the data were checked, errors occurred.

in the event that
if it should transpire/happen that
under circumstances in which
} if

In the event that the information is ready early, contact this office.

✓ **If** the information is ready early, contact this office.

on the occasion of
in a situation in which
under circumstances in which
} when

In a situation in which a class is closed, you may petition for admission.

✓ **When** a class is closed, you may petition for admission.

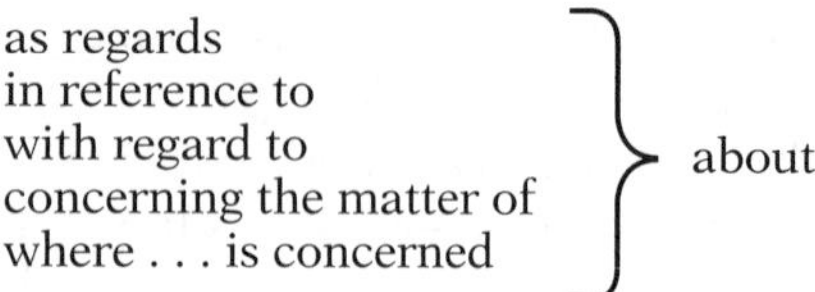
as regards
in reference to
with regard to
concerning the matter of
where . . . is concerned
} about

I should now like to say a few words **concerning the matter of** money.

✓ I should now like to say a few words **about** money.

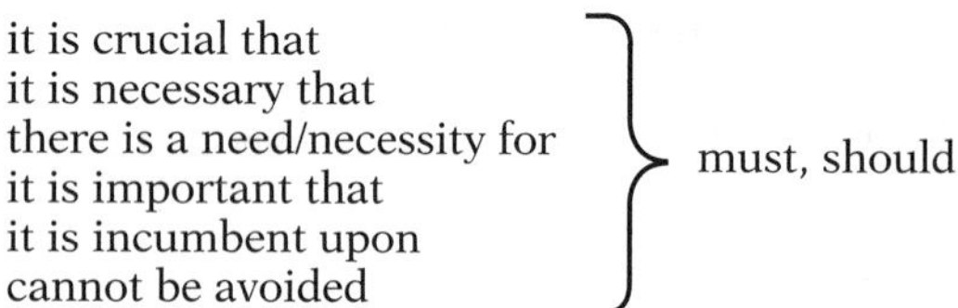
it is crucial that
it is necessary that
there is a need/necessity for
it is important that
it is incumbent upon
cannot be avoided
} must, should

There is a need for more careful *inspection* of all welds.

✓ You **must** *inspect* all welds more carefully.

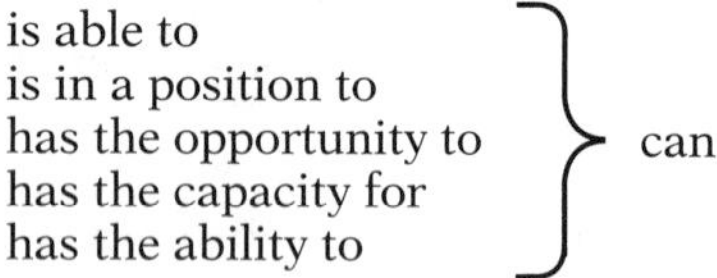
is able to
is in a position to
has the opportunity to
has the capacity for
has the ability to
} can

We are in a position to make you a firm offer.

✓ We **can** make you a firm offer.

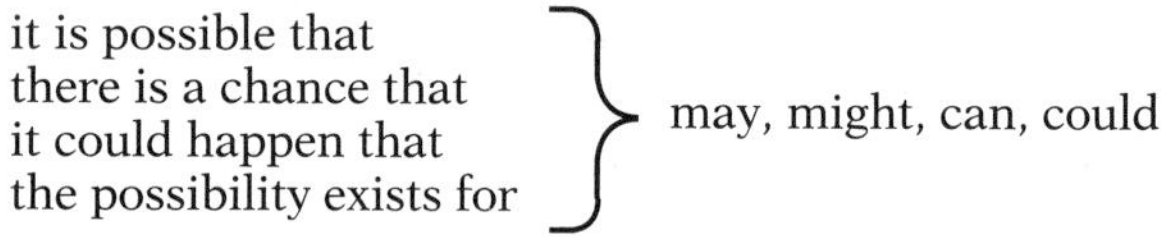
it is possible that
there is a chance that
it could happen that
the possibility exists for
} may, might, can, could

It is possible that nothing will come of these preparations.

✓ Nothing **may** come of these preparations.

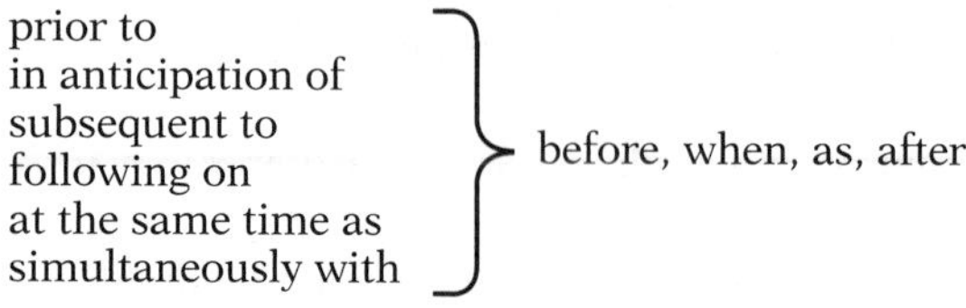
prior to
in anticipation of
subsequent to
following on
at the same time as
simultaneously with
} before, when, as, after

Prior to the *end* of the training, you should apply for your license.

✓ **Before** your training *ends,* you should apply for your license.

increase in decrease in	}	more, less/fewer, better/worse

There has been an ***increase*** in the number of university *applications.*

✓ ***More*** people are *applying* to universities.

We have noted a ***decrease*** in the number of errors.

✓ We have noted *fewer* errors.

> ***Here's the point:*** Look for the word that says the same thing as a phrase or clause.

5. *Change Negatives to Affirmatives*

When you express an idea in a negative form when a positive form would suffice, you have to use an extra word: *not different → same.* But more important, you may also force your readers to infer your meaning through a kind of algebraic computation. These two sentences mean much the same thing, but the affirmative is more direct:

Do not write in the negative.

✓ Write in the affirmative.

Do not translate a negative into an affirmative if you want to emphasize the negative. (Is that such a sentence? I could have written, *Keep a negative sentence when. . . .*) But you can rewrite most negatives, some almost formulaically:

not different	→similar	not many	→few	not remember	→forget
not notice	→overlook	not include	→omit	not consider	→ignore
not the same	→different	not often	→rarely	not have	→lack
not allow	→prevent	not admit	→deny	not accept	→reject

Some verbs, conjunctions, and propositions are implicitly negative:

> **Verbs:** *preclude, prevent, lack, fail, doubt, reject, avoid, deny, refuse, exclude, contradict, prohibit, bar*
>
> **Conjunctions:** *except, unless*
>
> **Prepositions:** *without, against, lacking, absent, but for*

As complex as simple multiple negatives can be, you will thoroughly baffle your readers if you combine them with these implicitly negative verbs, conjunctions, and prepositions. Compare these:

> **Except** when applicants have **failed to** submit applications **without** documentation, benefits will **not** be **denied.**

✓ You will receive benefits only if you submit your documents.

✓ To receive benefits, submit your documents.

And when you combine these negatives with passives and nominalizations, your readers will find such sentences almost incomprehensible:

> There should be no submission of payments without due notification of this office, unless the payment does not exceed $100.

This sentence relates two events, one a precondition for the other. First change nominalizations into verbs and PASSIVES into actives:

> Do not submit payments if you have not notified this office, unless you are paying less than $100.

Now revise the negatives into affirmatives:

✓ Submit payments to this office only if you are paying less than $100.

✓ If you submit more than $100, notify this office first.

Which do you put first—the outcome or the condition? That depends on what you think your reader has in mind. Reading these sentences, the reader would have in mind the idea of submitting payments. So begin with what your readers know and move to what they do not.

Here's the point: To be direct, choose the affirmative.

Exercise 8.1

Prune the redundancy from these sentences.

1. Critics cannot avoid employing complex and abstract technical terms if they are to successfully analyze literary texts and discuss them in a meaningful way.
2. Scientific research generally depends on fully accurate data if it is to offer theories that will allow us to advance into the future in a safe and secure way.
3. In regard to desirable employment in teaching positions, prospects for those engaged in studies at the graduate school level are at best not certain.
4. Those various agencies and offices that provide aid and assistance to those who participate in our program activities have reversed the policy that they recently announced to return to the earlier original policy.
5. In spite of the fact that the educational environment is a very significant facet to each and every one of our children in terms of his or her future development, some groups do not support reasonable and fair tax assessments that are required for providing an educational experience at a high level of quality.
6. Most likely, a majority of all patients who appear at a public medical clinical facility do not expect special medical attention or treatment, because their particular health problems and concerns are often of a minor nature and for the most part can usually be adequately treated with minimal time, effort, and attention.
7. Notwithstanding the fact that all legal restrictions on the use of firearms are the subject of heated debate and argument, it is necessary that the general public continue carrying on discussions pro and con in regard to them.

8. Under circumstances in which people with financial resources anticipate the possibility that goods and services may continue to increase in price, those individuals will ordinarily put a majority of their discretionary resources into objects of artistic value.
9. In the event that governors have the opportunity to gather and discuss matters of economic needs and issues in their respective states, it is possible that they will find a way to overcome the major problem of specifying exactly how to divide up federal resources to their different states.
10. Those engaged in the profession of teaching have for a long time had an interest in significantly improving how individuals learn and commit to memory information from written sources. The first problem in doing this is identifying common and different features among comparable passages of writing. The second addresses the complex matter of assigning some kind of value to the quality and quantity of information that a reader retains in memory after that person reads a passage.

Exercise 8.2

What single words can you find for the negative phrases in these sentences? Each was in an earlier draft of this book.

1. While the standard definition of a verb as an action word is not reliable, it is in fact not bad advice.
2. A second set of rules includes those whose observance we do not notice, and whose violation we do not notice either.
3. But we ought not accept the argument that we do not need the word *finalize,* or that it is ugly because of the *-ize.*
4. While it is not clear what counts as "too many" prepositions, it is clear that when you do not use abstract nouns, you do not need most of the prepositional phrases.
5. These choices among points of usage let those among us who wish to do so express our sense of linguistic

decorum, a decorum that many of us believe testifies to our precision. It is an impulse we ought not scorn, so long as it is not ignorant or thoughtless.

Exercise 8.3

Where appropriate, change the following negatives to affirmatives. Do any additional editing you think useful.

1. There is no possibility in regard to a reduction in the federal deficit if reductions in federal spending are not introduced.
2. Do not discontinue medication unless symptoms of dizziness and nausea alleviate for six hours.
3. No one should be prevented from participating in cost-sharing educational programs without a full hearing into the reasons for his or her not being accepted.
4. No agreement exists on the question of an open or closed universe, a dispute about which no resolution is likely as long as a computation of the total mass of the universe has still to be done.
5. So long as taxpayers do not engage in widespread refusal to pay taxes, the government will have no difficulty in paying its debts.
6. No alternative exists in this country to the eventual development of tar sand, oil shale, and coal as sources of fuel, if we wish to stop being energy dependent on imported oil.
7. Not until a resolution between Catholics and Protestants in regard to the authority of papal supremacy is reached will there be a start to a reconciliation between these two Christian religions.
8. Except when such expenses do not exceed $250, the Insured may not refuse to provide the Insurer with all relevant receipts, checks, or other evidence of costs, when requested.
9. It seems to me that in looking at the nature of advertising, it is not illogical to start out with a statement that

defines the term. This will establish a common point of reference so that we will not be subjective in our approach to a subject matter that is often the topic of emotional discussion. There is, however, no single definition or agreement for the word *advertising,* making the chances for possible objectivity not likely.

10. Regardless of the fact that we cannot not know with any degree of certainty whether or not there are life forms in the universe other than our own, evidence of a statistical nature makes it highly unlikely that life does not exist somewhere among the large number of planetary systems scattered throughout the universe as we know it.

A PARTICULAR KIND OF REDUNDANCY: METADISCOURSE

In Lesson Four, I described METADISCOURSE as the language we use to refer to elements in a rhetorical situation:

- The writer's intention: *to sum up, candidly, I believe, therefore, however*
- The reader's desired response: *note that, consider now, as you see*
- The structure of our text: *first, second, finally*

We need metadiscourse in almost everything we write. But some writers use so much that it buries their ideas:

> The last point I would like to make is that in regard to men-women relationships, it is important to keep in mind that the greatest changes have occurred in the way they now work with one another.

Only a few words in that sentence address men-women relationships:

> men-women relationships . . . greatest changes . . . the way they work with one another.

The rest is metadiscourse:

> The last point I would like to make is that in regard to . . . it is important to keep in mind that . . . .

If we prune the metadiscourse, we tighten the sentence:

> The greatest changes in men-women relationships have occurred in the way that they work with one another.

Once we see what the sentence says, we can make it yet more direct:

✓ Men and women have changed their relationships most in the way they work with one another.

Some teachers and editors relentlessly urge writers to cut all metadiscourse, but we cannot rely on simplistic advice about how much metadiscourse to use, because some successful writers use a lot; others, equally successful, little. You have to read with an eye to how it is used in your field by writers who you think are clear and concise, and do likewise.

There are, however, some types that are often ripe for pruning.

Metadiscourse that Attributes Your Writing to a Source

Some writers announce that something has been anonymously *observed* to exist, is *found* to exist, is *seen, noticed, noted,* etc.:

> High divorce rates **have been observed** to occur in areas that **have been determined** to have low population density.

✓ High divorce rates **occur** in areas with low population density.

> ***Here's the point:*** Unless you have reason to cite who specifically observed or determined that something exists, cut such phrases. Just say what is.

Metadiscourse that Announces Your Topic

These phrases tell your reader what you intend to write about:

> **This section introduces** another problem, that of noise pollution. **The first thing to say** about it is that noise pollution exists not only. . . .

Your reader can catch your topic more concisely without the metadiscourse:

✓ Another problem is noise pollution. First, it exists not only. . . .

Look closely at any sentence opening with a metadiscourse subject and verb that merely announce a topic:

In this essay, I will discuss Robert Frost's bird imagery.

I usually write that kind of sentence when I have little idea where I am going, saying in effect, "I have this topic to write about and I hope that eventually I will think of something to say about it." On the other hand, when that kind of sentence appears in a journal article, as it often does, it expresses not a hope, but a promise.

Here's the point: When you find that kind of sentence in your own prose, try rewriting it into a claim that needs no introduction. Then determine whether what's left in fact says anything significant.

In this essay, I will discuss Robert Frost's bird imagery.

✓ Robert Frost used bird imagery.

That says little.

Unfortunately, when you do this you may find that you have little to say, always a distressing moment, but less so than hearing someone else say it. When you see a sentence that banal, you know you have to think harder.

Metadiscourse that Highlights

There is one device of metadiscourse that serves to highlight phrases. Contrast that sentence with

One metadiscourse device serves to highlight phrases.

When you begin a sentence with *there is/are/was/were,* you throw weight on the words that follow. Some teachers disparage this construction, but like the passive, it has its uses. One is to stress a new idea that the next few sentences will elaborate (as in this paragraph). When you find that you have used this construction for any other purpose, try revising.

Two other constructions call similar attention to a word or phrase, usually mentioned at least once before:

> **In regard to** *a vigorous style,* the most important feature is a short, concrete subject followed by a forceful verb.
>
> **So far as** *China's industrial development* **is concerned,** it will take decades to equal that of Japan.

We use phrases and clauses such as *in regard to, where X is concerned, in the matter of, as for, as to, speaking of* to announce that we are moving to a new idea already mentioned. In any other context, however, try to maneuver that new idea into the body of the sentence with a short subject followed by a forceful verb:

✓ The most important feature of **a vigorous style** is a short, concrete subject followed by a forceful verb.

✓ **China's industrial development** will take decades to equal Japan's.

Hedging and Intensifying

Each profession has its own idiom of caution and confidence. How successfully you tread the rhetorical line between timidity and arrogance depends a good deal on how you manage phrases like *a good deal,* a phrase that a few words ago allowed me to pull back from what I would have felt was too dogmatic:

> How successfully you tread the rhetorical line between timidity and arrogance depends on how you manage phrases like *a good deal.*

But this would have been too timid:

> How successfully you tread the rhetorical line between timidity and arrogance **often seems** to depend **at least to some degree** on how you manage **certain** phrases like *a good deal.*

Between hedging and intensifying, we have to find the middle way.

Hedges Some readers think that hedging is mealymouthed. And it is true that some writers qualify so often that their hedges seem like verbal tics:

> There **seems** to be **some** evidence that **may suggest** that **certain** differences between Japanese and Western rhetoric **could** derive from historical influences traceable to Japan's long cultural isolation and Europe's equally long intercultural interactions.

That claim sounds so uncertain, that readers might wonder whether it is worth making at all. On the other hand, only a fool or someone with massive historical evidence would venture an assertion as flatly true as this:

> This evidence **proves** that Japanese and Western rhetorics differ because of Japan's long cultural isolation and Europe's equally long intercultural interactions.

In thoughtful academic writing, we more often state claims closer to this (and look closely at that clause for my own hedging):

✓ This evidence **suggests** that **aspects** of Japanese and Western rhetoric differ because of Japan's long cultural isolation and Europe's equally long intercultural interactions.

This next paragraph introduced the article announcing the most significant breakthrough in the history of genetics, the discovery of the double helix of DNA. If anyone was entitled to be assertive, it was Crick and Watson. But they chose to be diffident (hedges are boldfaced):

✓ We **wish to suggest a** [note: not ***the***] structure for the salt of deoxyribose nucleic acid (D.N.A.). . . . A structure for nucleic acid has already been proposed by Pauling and Corey. . . . **In our opinion,** this structure is unsatisfactory for two reasons: (1) **We believe** that the material which gives the X-ray diagrams is the salt, not the free acid. . . . (2) **Some** of the van der Waals distances **appear** to be too small.

—J. D. Watson and F. H. C. Crick, "Molecular Structure of Nucleic Acids"

Without the hedges, the claim is more aggressive. I boldface the stronger words:

> We **announce** here **the** structure for the salt of deoxyribose nucleic acid (D.N.A.). . . . A structure for nucleic acid has already been proposed by Pauling and Corey. . . . Their structure is unsatisfactory for two reasons: (1) The material which gives their X-ray

diagrams is the salt, not the free acid. . . . (2) Their van der Waals distances **are** too small.

We need hedges to sound modest notes of civil diffidence. They say to readers, "I stand behind my claims, but I understand that they can be only tentative, and even if I am sure of them, I don't want to seem arrogant." And we hope our readers will think "Here's someone who is thoughtful." Some common hedges:

Adverbials: *usually, often, sometimes, almost, virtually, possibly, perhaps, apparently, in some ways, to a certain extent, somewhat, in some/certain respects*

Adjectivals: *most, many, some, a certain number of*

Verbs: *may, might, can, could, seem, appear, suggest, indicate*

The verbs *suggest* and *indicate* are particularly useful in making a claim about which you are less than 100 percent certain, but confident enough to propose:

✓ The evidence **indicates** that some of these questions remain unresolved

✓ These data **suggest** that further studies are necessary.

Intensifiers Confident writers use intensifiers less often than hedges because they do not want to sound smug. When readers feel that intensifiers are being overused, they may feel that the writer is in fact rather unpleasant:

For a century now, liberals have argued against **any** censorship of art, and **all** courts have found their arguments so persuasive that **not a** person **any longer** remembers how they were countered. As a result, today, censorship is **unquestionably** a thing of the past.

Inexperienced writers often think that this kind of aggressive argument is the most effective. In fact, a more moderately stated claim is likely to be more thoughtfully received:

✓ For **about** a century now, **many** liberals have argued against censorship of art, and **most** courts have found their arguments persuasive **enough** that **few people may** remember **exactly** how they were countered. As a result, today, censorship is **virtually** a thing of the past.

Some will claim that a passage hedged that much verges on the weak-kneed. Perhaps. But it does not come at the reader like a bulldozer. It leaves room for the reader to question, think, and imagine a reasoned and equally moderate response. In fact, in some academic areas, there is a rule of thumb that if some one opens a sentence with *It is clear. . . .* or *It is obvious. . . .*, that person is about to claim something that is at least questionable. A few common intensifiers:

> **Adverbs:** *very, pretty, quite, rather, clearly, obviously, undoubtedly, certainly, of course, indeed, inevitably, invariably, always, literally*
>
> **Adjectives:** *key, central, crucial, basic, fundamental, major, principal, essential*
>
> **Verbs:** *show, prove, establish, as you/we/everyone knows/can see, it is clear/obvious that*

And of course, the most common intensifier is probably the absence of any hedge. The first sentence below has no intensifiers where the ______'s appear, but neither does it have any hedges there, and so it seems like a very strong claim:

> ______ Americans believe that the federal government is ______ intrusive and ______ authoritarian.
>
> **Many** Americans believe that the federal government is **often** intrusive and **increasingly** authoritarian.

> ***Here's the point:*** There is no simple way to determine how much to hedge or emphasize: Look at how others in your field write and do likewise.

Exercise 8.4

Here are sentences that announce a topic rather than state a thesis. Delete the metadiscourse and rewrite what remains into a full statement. Then decide whether the full statement seems to make an interesting and contestable claim. For example:

> In this study, I examine the history of Congressional legislation regarding the protection of children in the workplace.

First, delete the metadiscourse:

> . . . the history of Congressional legislation regarding the protection of children in the workplace.

Then rewrite what is left into a full sentence:

✓ Congress has legislated the protection of children in the workplace.

That appears to be a banal claim.

1. This essay will survey recent research in schemata theory as applied to the pedagogy of mathematical problem solving.
2. I will analyze Frost's use of imagery of seasons in his longer poems published at the end of his career.
3. The methodological differences between English and American histories of the War of 1812 that resulted in radically differing interpretations of the cause of the conflict are the topic of this study.
4. This study will discuss the traditional but self-contradictory values that once showed us how to be good mothers and wives.
5. We will consider scientific thinking and its historical roots in connection with the influence of Egypt on Greek thought.
6. In this study, I analyze the mistaken assumption underlying Freud's interpretation of dreams.
7. This chapter discusses needle sharing among drug users.
8. The relationship between birth order and academic success will be explored.
9. I intend to address the problem of the reasons for the failure and success of trade embargoes in this century.

Exercise 8.5

In these, edit for both unnecessary metadiscourse and redundancy.

1. On the other hand, however, we can perhaps point out that there may always be TV programming to appeal to our most prurient and, therefore, lowest interests.
2. In this particular section, I intend to discuss my position about the possible need to dispense with the standard approach to plea bargaining. I believe this for two reasons. The first reason that it is necessary to overhaul plea bargaining is that there is the possibility that it lets hardened criminals not receive their just punishment. The second reason is the following: Plea bargaining seems to encourage a growing lack of respect for the judicial system.

3. Turning now to the next question, there is in regard to the subject of wilderness area preservation activities one basic principle when attempting to formulate a way of approaching decisions about unspoiled areas that should be set aside as not open to development for commercial exploitation.
4. It is my belief that in regard at least to terrestrial-type snakes, an assumption can be made that there are probably none in unmapped areas of the world surpassing the size of those we have knowledge of.
5. Depending on the particular position that one takes on this question, the educational system has taken on a degree of importance that may be equal to or perhaps even exceed the family as a major source of transmission of social values.
6. I think that in regard to the current interest in life stages, most investigators in the area take the position that midlife is the most critical period or stage in a person's development from a mental health point of view; that is to say, at that point in our development, we are in a position to know whether or not we are going to be on the winning side of the game of life or on the losing side.

Exercise 8.6

Find a passage that seems moderate in tone. Then revise it twice, adding hedges to one, emphatics to the other. Then exchange your revisions with someone else who has done the same thing to see if you can revise that other person's work back to the original.

Productive Redundancy

Learning by Writing

Some teachers and editors look upon redundancy as an unqualified bane. But in our development as competent writers, some redundancy is important, probably even inevitable. We signal membership in a community by what we say and how we say it.

But a surer sign is in what we know to leave unsaid as our community's common knowledge. When we are still outsiders to a community, though, we don't know what not to say.

Here, for example, is the introduction to a paper written by someone who had just graduated from a good college, where he had been correctly judged to be a competent writer (I checked) but who was writing his first paper in a new community of discourse, his law school:

> It is my opinion that the ruling of the lower court concerning the case of *Haslem* v. *Lockwood* should be upheld, thereby denying the appeal of the plaintiff. The main point supporting my point of view on this case concerns the tenet of our court system which holds that in order to win his case, the plaintiff must prove that he was somehow wronged by the defendant. The burden of proof rests on the plaintiff. He must show enough evidence to convince the court that he is in the right.

To this person's legal writing teacher, everything after the first sentence was a tissue of self-evident truisms: Obviously if a court upholds a ruling, it denies the appeal; obviously a plaintiff can win only if he proves a defendant has wronged him; obviously a plaintiff has the burden of proof; obviously a plaintiff has to provide evidence. But at this point in his career, this writer was an outsider who had yet to assimilate that common knowledge, and so he could not resist stating it.

The large-scale version of this problem is the complaint that a paper seems to be all "summary" with no "analysis." Perhaps a writer who only summarizes does indeed confuse the two or cannot analyze at all. But as we learn a new subject, we all belabor the obvious. In fact, when we write out material that we are trying to learn, we master it just so that later we can leave it unsaid. It may be that before some of us—probably most of us—can analyze anything new and complex, we have to make it our own by articulating it in writing. And that often sounds like summary.

Here's the point: The difference between experienced and inexperienced writers is that the experienced writer knows that summarizing is a good idea and does it deliberately, but also knows when to discard it from the final draft. The inexperienced writer has to learn to use summary not as an end in itself, but in the service of analysis and argument.

Autobiographical Metadiscourse

Just as "belaboring the obvious" may signal a writer getting started in a field, so may some metadiscourse. When we are comfortable thinking through familiar problems, we can suppress the narrative of that mental process. But when we are inexperienced in a subject, we often feel compelled to give a running commentary about what we did or are doing:

> **I was concerned with** the structural integrity of the supports, so **I proceeded** to test the weight that the beams would carry. **I have concluded** after numerous tests that the beams can carry the prescribed weight, but no more. **I think that it is important** that we notify every section using the storage facility of this finding.

If we eliminate the narrative devices and focus attention only on what the reader needs to know, we make the passage more pointed:

✓ Every section using the storage facility must be notified not to exceed the prescribed kilogram-per-square-meter floor weight. Although tests have established the structural integrity of the beams, they are strong enough to carry only the prescribed weights.

Look again at that paper by the first-year law student. Not only did he "belabor the obvious," he made the machinery of his thinking too visible. I boldface metadiscourse and italicize the self-evident:

> **It is my opinion that** the ruling of the lower court concerning *the case* of Haslem V. Lockwood should be upheld, *thereby denying the appeal of the plaintiff.* **The main point supporting my point of view on this case concerns** *the tenet of our court system which holds that in order to win his case, the plaintiff must prove that he was somehow wronged by the defendant. The burden of proof rests on the plaintiff. He must show enough evidence to convince the court that he is in the right.*

When we delete autobiographical narrative and commonplaces that knowledgeable readers assume, we are left with something leaner:

✓ *Haslem* should be affirmed because plaintiff failed to meet his burden of proof.

It is easy to judge writing like the original as "wordy," or "empty," but we should hesitate before we assume that certain writers lack some innate ability or intelligence. They may, but they may also be at that stage in their learning where they cannot yet resist expressing the obvious or delete the story of their thinking.

Having emphasized concision so relentlessly as the first grace of style, here at the end of this lesson I should qualify what I have urged: Readers don't like graceless redundancy, but a style so concise, so tight, so compact that it has no soft edges at all can seem gracelessly brusque. I can't tell you when that happens. That's why you must pay such close attention to what your readers think, because your readers know something that you don't: They know how it feels to be your reader.

Exercise 8.7

Pick a respectable journal in your field and in its lead article, pick out every word and phrase that either hedges or emphasizes its claims. Examine it for metadiscourse. Then compare it with a recent piece of your own writing.

Summing Up

Concision alone does not guarantee grace, but it clears away the deadwood so that you can at least see your ideas clearly. If less is more, then prune these:

1. Redundant pairs

   If and when we can define our final **aims and goals, each and every** member of our group will be **ready and willing** to offer **aid and assistance.**

   ✓ *If* we define our *goals, every* member will be *ready* to *help.*

2. Redundant modifiers

   In the business **world of today, official** governmental red tape is **seriously** destroying initiative among **individual** businesses.

   ✓ Government red tape is destroying business initiative.

3. Redundant categories

   In the area of education, tight financial **conditions** are forcing school boards to cut nonessentials.

   ✓ Tight finances are forcing school boards to cut nonessentials.

4. Meaningless modifiers

   Most students **generally** find **some kind of** summer work.

   ✓ Most students find summer work.

5. Obvious implications

    Energy **used to power our industries and homes** will **in years to come** cost more **money.**

    ✓ Energy will eventually cost more.

6. Excessive detail

    A microwave oven **that you might buy in any department store** uses less energy **that is so expensive than** a conventional oven **that uses gas or electricity.**

    ✓ Microwave ovens use less energy than conventional ones.

7. A phrase for a word

    [A sail-powered craft] [that has turned on its side or completely over] must [remain buoyant enough so that it will bear the weight of] [those individuals who were aboard].

    ✓ A capsized sailboat must support its passengers.

8. Excessive metadiscourse

    It is almost certainly the case that totalitarian systems cannot allow a society to have **what we would define as** stable social relationships.

    ✓ Totalitarianism cannot allow stable social relationships.

9. Indirect negatives

    There is **no reason not to believe** that engineering malfunctions in nuclear energy systems **cannot** be anticipated.

    ✓ Malfunctions in nuclear energy systems will surprise us.

10. Hedges and emphatics

It is hard to make reliable generalizations on this matter because it depends on a good ear.

Lesson Nine

Shape

Everything should be made as simple as possible, but not simpler.
ALBERT EINSTEIN

The structure of every sentence is a lesson in logic.
JOHN STUART MILL

Sentences in their variety run from simplicity to complexity, a progression not necessarily reflected in length: a long sentence may be extremely simple in construction—indeed must be simple if it is to convey its sense easily.
SIR HERBERT READ

A long complicated sentence should force itself upon you, make you know yourself knowing it.
GERTRUDE STEIN

You never know what is enough until you know what is more than enough.
WILLIAM BLAKE

CLARITY IN COMPLEXITY

A clear and concise sentence is a singular achievement, a whole passage of them even more so. But if all your sentences were so concise that they never exceeded 20 words, you'd be like a pianist who could play only a few notes at a time: You might be able to pick out a jingle or two, but not much more. Like musical themes, some ideas are so complex that we need more than a few words to express them. A competent writer must therefore know both how to write clear short sentences, and how to combine those short sentences into one that is longer and more complex, but just as concise and just as easy to understand. And it's when sentences grow longer that we must address those matters of rhythm and movement that give a sentence a sense of grace.

Consider (1a):

1a. An understanding of the conditions that have resulted in conflicts in Southern Europe today means we must consider a variety of social, economic, and cultural factors rooted in 1000 years of European history rather than just a single force such as ethnicity or religion.

Those ideas may need all those 44 words, but surely not in a sentence so ungainly. We might try a series of shorter sentences:

1b. We wish to understand the conditions that have resulted in conflicts in Southern Europe today. To do so, we must not consider just a single force such as ethnicity or religion. We must consider a variety of social, economic, and cultural factors. These factors are rooted in 1000 years of European history.

But if (1a) is shapeless, (1b) fragments a complex concept into a string of unconnected, simplistic to the point of simpleminded assertions. Ideally, we should be able to combine those short sentences into something not just complex and clear, but *well formed,* something closer to this:

✓ 1c. To understand the conditions that have created ethnic conflicts in Southern Europe today, we must consider not just a single force such as ethnicity or religion, but a variety of social, economic, and cultural factors that are rooted in 1000 years of European history.

Sentence (1c) has exactly the same number of words as (1a), but unlike (1a) it does not sprawl; it has a shape, and shape is an indispensable quality of grace. So it is not merely the number of words that makes a sentence seem ungainly, but the lack of internal architecture. That architecture is the object of this lesson.

DIAGNOSING SPRAWL AND REVISING IT

It's easy to recognize sprawl in the writing of others—in the middle of a sentence you lose track of its idea or feel it will never end. But few of us get lost in our own sentences, so we need a way to diagnose them to compensate for our too good understanding of them. One way to do that is to put a slash mark after every PUNCTUATED SENTENCE./ Then pick out sentences longer than three typed lines and read them aloud, pausing where it feels natural to do so./ If the process of reading one of your own long sentences gives you the feeling that you are about to run out of breath before you come to a place where you can pause in order to integrate all of the parts of the sentence to get a sense of how its whole fits together to communicate a single conceptual structure, you have identified a sentence that your readers are likely to wish that you had revised. Like that one.

Sometimes, you can revise such a sentence merely by eliminating redundancy and NOMINALIZATIONS:

> If you feel you are running out of breath before you can pause to integrate its parts, you have identified a sentence that your readers are likely to wish you had revised.

If your sentence still feels too long (I don't think that one does), you can always divide it:

> As you read a long sentence, you may feel you are running out of breath before you can pause to integrate its <u>parts. If so</u>, you have identified one that your readers are likely to wish you had revised.

But sometimes you have to integrate more ideas than that into a single complex structure. For that structure to be both complex and clear, it should have four characteristics (in addition to all the others discussed in earlier lessons):

1. It gets the reader to the VERB in the MAIN CLAUSE quickly.
2. After that verb, it avoids a string of three or more consecutive SUBORDINATE CLAUSES or PHRASES of the same kind, unless those clauses and phrases are structured as described in (3) and (4) below.
3. It COORDINATES phrases and clauses after the SUBJECT.
4. It adds subordinate phrases by means of three modifying constructions that we call RESUMPTIVE, SUMMATIVE, and FREE.

1. Getting the Reader to Verbs Quickly

In every sentence, we listen in our minds' ear for a kind of grammatical "click" that signals when we connect one important part to another. That occurs in two places:

- The first connection is that point where introductory phrases and clauses end and the subject of the main clause begins.
- The more important connection is the link between that subject and its verb.

When your readers complete those two connections quickly and surely, they are less likely to think that your sentences sprawl.

- *Managing introductory phrases and clauses:* The best way to help your reader through introductory phrases and clauses is to keep them short. If you can't shorten them, try breaking them out into their own sentences:

> **Although Dr. Jones may have served as a medical consultant for ABCO, Inc., to help it develop medical policies in regard to coverage of employees engaged in high risk activities,** she may not be compelled to testify in trials involving malpractice if she was paid only as a consultant and not as a full-time company employee.

> ✓ Dr. Jones served as a medical consultant to help the company develop medical policies in regard to coverage of employees engaged in high risk activities. But she may not be compelled to testify in trials involving. . . .

Here's the point: Your readers want to get to the subject of the main clause quickly; help them do that by keeping your introductory phrases and clauses short, by breaking them out into their own sentences, or by moving them to the ends of their sentences (review pp. 107–10, 114–16).

- *Managing long subjects:* Readers also object to long subjects because they keep readers from completing the most important grammatical connection in a clause quickly, the connection between subject and verb.

  When a subject is long because it consists of nominalizations, you can revise them as suggested in Lessons Three and Four, but sometimes objects grow long from relative clauses. When that happens, you can break the relative clause out into either a subordinate or independent clause (see also p. 246):

> **A musical group specializing in early music that insists on using either instruments that are actually old or instruments that have been created according to historical standards**$_{\text{subject}}$ produces a sound markedly different from that of groups playing early music on modern instruments.

✓ [*When* **a musical group specializing in early music insists on using either instruments that are actually old or instruments that have been created according to historical standards**],$_{\text{subordinate clause}}$ they produce a sound that is markedly different from that of groups playing early music on modern instruments.

✓ [Some musical groups specializing in early music insist on using either instruments that are actually old or instruments that have been created according to historical standards.]$_{\text{independent clause}}$ [The sound they produce is markedly different from that of groups playing early music on modern instruments.]

Here's the point: Your readers want to get to a verb, any verb, quickly. So help them do that by keeping your subjects relatively short. You are likely to do that if you follow the old-new principles we discussed in Lesson Five. The more general point is that readers want to get through *everything* before the verb quickly. Shorten those parts of your clauses, and you can extend what follows the verb almost indefinitely, if you follow the next two principles.

2. Reducing Strings of Subordinate Clauses

Once your readers are past the subject and verb, especially in the MAIN CLAUSE, your next task is to get them to the end of the sentence without making them feel that you are just tacking one clause on to the next. Don't do this:

> [The problem of liberal education]$_{\text{subject}}$ [is]$_{\text{verb}}$ to institutionalize those intellectual circumstances [under which it is maximally probable] [that the reflective moment of intellectual activity will serve the purpose of permanently transforming the relationship] [that an individual has to the intellectual world] [so that persons may become freely functioning participants in intellectual activity], in order that [they may become autonomous members of the intellectual community].

A rule of thumb: Avoid stringing together three or more consecutive subordinate clauses or phrases of the same kind, especially relative clauses:

> Of the areas of science **that** *are* important not just to the future of knowledge but to life on this planet, few are more promising than genetic engineering, **which** *is* a new way of manipulating the elemental structures and units of life itself, **which** *are* the genes and chromosomes **that** direct our cells how to reproduce and become the parts **that** constitute our bodies.

The default solution is to break such a sentence into smaller ones, but there are other solutions. One is to reduce some of the relative clauses to phrases by deleting *who/that + is/was,* etc.:

> ✓ Of all the areas of science [. . .] important not just to the future of knowledge but to life on this planet, few are more promising than genetic engineering, [. . .] a new way of manipulating the elemental structures and units of life itself, [. . .] the genes and chromosomes. . . .

Occasionally, you have to rewrite the remaining verb into an *-ing* form:

> One day, we will all have numbers **that will identify** our financial transactions so that the IRS can monitor activities **that involve** economic exchange.

✓ The day is coming when we will all have numbers [. . .] **identifying** our financial transactions so that the IRS can monitor activities [. . .] **involving** economic exchange.

> ***Here's the point:*** Avoid three consecutive clauses or phrases of the same kind. Even two can be a mistake.

Exercise 9.1

Revise the sentence above about liberal education. Then find some long sentences in your textbooks and revise them.

3. Coordination

Of all the solutions to the problem of sprawl, coordination is the most demanding on the writer, but when done well, most pleasing to the reader. Coordination is in fact the architectural foundation of a well-shaped sentence. Compare these. My version is first; the original is second:

The aspiring artist may find [that even a minor, unfinished work which was botched] may be an instructive model for [how things should be done], [while for the amateur spectator, such works are the daily fare] [which may provide good, honest nourishment,] [which can lead to an appreciation of deeper pleasures] [that are also more refined].

✓ For the aspiring artist, the minor, the unfinished, or even the botched work, may be an instructive model for how things should—and should not—be done. For the amateur spectator, such works are the daily fare which provide good, honest nourishment—and which can lead to appreciation of more refined, or deeper pleasures.

—Eva Hoffman, "Minor Art Offers Special Pleasures"

My revision sprawls through a string of tacked-on clauses, mostly relative:

The aspiring artist may find that even a minor, unfinished work
which was botched may be an instructive model for
how things should be done,
while for the amateur spectator, such works are the daily fare
which may provide good, honest nourishment,
which can lead to an appreciation of deeper pleasures
that may also be more refined.

Hoffman's original gets a shape from its multiple coordinations.

✔For the aspiring artist, { the minor, / the unfinished, / or / even the botched } work,

may be an instructive model for how things { should— / and / should not— } be done.

For the amateur spectator, such works are

the daily fare { which provide { good, / honest } nourishment— / and / which can lead to appreciation of { more refined, / or / deeper } pleasures. }

Here's the point: When you have a choice between stringing clauses one after another or coordinating them, coordinate. Coordination creates balance, and balance is an important source of shape.

You enhance coordination when you observe a few simple principles.

1. *Avoid coordinations inside the subject phrase:* A subject with elaborate coordination will be long, and a long subject delays readers from getting to the verb. Compare these:

   An academic culture that **[encourages research into arcane and abstract topics] but [feels no responsibility for explaining to the public why such projects are valuable to society]**$_{\text{subject}}$ risks alienating its ultimate source of support.

   ✓ **When an academic culture encourages** research into arcane and abstract topics but feels no responsibility for explaining to the public why such projects are valuable to society, **it risks alienating** its ultimate source of support.

   (Now the problem is that long introductory clause. We can move it to the end or break it out into its own sentence.)

2. *Coordinate grammatically parallel elements:* Coordinate elements only of the same grammatical structure: clause and clause, PREDICATE and predicate, PREPOSITIONAL PHRASE and prepositional phrase, etc.

   When you coordinate parts with different grammatical structures, readers are likely to feel that you have created an offensive lack of PARALLELISM. Most careful writers would avoid this:

   The committee recommends { **revising the curriculum** to recognize trends in local employment / and / **that the division be reorganized** to reflect the new curriculum. }

   Corrected:

   ✓. . . recommends { **that the curriculum be revised** to recognize . . . / and / **that the division be reorganized** to reflect. . . . }

But some nonparallel coordinations often occur in well-written prose. Many competent writers often coordinate a noun phrase with a *how*-clause, and readers do not blink:

✔ We will attempt to delineate { **the problems** of education among developing nations and **how coordinated efforts can address** them in economical ways. }

Or an ADJECTIVE or ADVERB with a prepositional phrase:

✔ The proposal appears to have been written { **quickly,** **carefully,** and **with the help** of many.

Readers respond to coordination best when the coordinate elements balance not only grammar but thought. This seems "off":

> Many voters [believe that elected officials are abusing their privileges], [are calling for term limits], **and** [in that way get rid of them].

While those three elements may be coordinate grammatically, they aren't in thought. They are instead a sequence of cause-effect/cause-effect:

> ✓ Many voters believe **so** strongly that elected officials are abusing their privileges **that** they are calling for term limits **in order to** get rid of them.

Unfortunately, I cannot tell you how to decide when elements coordinate in grammar are not coordinate in thought. You have to be thoughtful; that's little help.

3. *Keep connections clear:* What bothers readers more than faulty parallelism is a coordination so long that they lose track of its internal connections:

> Teachers should remember that students are vulnerable, insecure, and uncertain about those everyday, ego-bruising moments that adults ignore, and that they do not understand that one day they will become as confident and as secure as the adults that bruise them.

Just enough to interrupt the flow of the sentence is that flicker of hesitation about where to connect:

> . . . and that they do not understand that one day they. . . .

To revise a sentence like this, shorten the first half of the coordination so that the second half begins closer to the point where the coordination began:

✓ Teachers should remember that students are vulnerable to ego-bruising moments that adults ignore and that they do not understand that one day. . . .

If you can't do that, repeat a word that reminds the reader where the second half of the coordination began:

✓ Teachers should try **to remember** that students are vulnerable to ego-bruising moments that adults ignore, **to remember** that they do not understand that. . . .

Of course, you can always begin a new sentence:

✓ . . . adults ignore. Every teacher should also remember that students. . . .

Readers can also see the elements of the coordination more clearly when you use CORRELATIVE CONJUNCTIONS such as *both X and Y, not only X but also Y, neither X nor Y.* Compare:

✓ Teachers should remember **not only** that students are vulnerable, insecure, and uncertain about those everyday, ego-bruising moments that adults ignore, **but also** that they do not understand. . . .

Use these sparingly though, because they imply a dramatic emphasis that not every coordination deserves.

Exercise 9.2

The best way to learn how to manage coordination is by imitating it. Try imitating any of the passages laid out above. For example:

For the amateur spectator,
such works are the daily fare

which provide { good, honest } nourishment—
and
which can lead to an appreciation of { more refined, or deeper } pleasures.

You might write,

> For the serious student, the library sometimes provides a chance to be alone and to think through problems that may be too complex or too painful to think about in a noisy and crowded dormitory.

---

4. Resumptive, Summative, and Free Modifiers

Those three terms are probably unfamiliar. But since mature writers often use those patterns to extend a sentence, we need a word to name what they do and I am about to do in the sentence that you are now reading, a sentence that I could have ended seven words ago, but that I extended to show you how resumptive modifiers work.

- *Resumptive modifiers:* A resumptive modifier lets you extend the length of a sentence but avoids a sprawling series of relative clauses. Read these aloud:

  ✓ These three terms are probably unfamiliar. But since mature writers often use those patterns to extend a sentence, we need a word to name what they do and I am about to do in the sentence that you are now reading, a sentence that I could have ended seven words ago, but that I extended to show you how resumptive modifiers work.

  These three terms are probably unfamiliar. But since mature writers often use those patterns to extend a sentence, we need a word to name what they do but I am not going to do in the sentence that you are now reading that I could have ended seven words ago but that I extended to show you how a sentence sprawls without them.

  The first sentence lets the reader take a breath after *now reading,* repeats the phrase *a sentence,* and continues for another 19 words. That second sentence seems to run on until we run out of breath.

To create the resumptive modifier, I did this:

1. When I felt I had gone on long enough, I paused with a comma:

> Since mature writers often use those patterns to extend a sentence, we need a word to name what they do and I am about to do in the sentence that you are now reading. . . .

2. Then I found an important word close to the end of that clause, *sentence,* and repeated it:

> Since mature writers often use those patterns to extend a sentence, we need a word to name what they do and I am about to do in the **sentence** that you are now reading,
> **a sentence**. . . .

3. Then to that repeated word, *sentence,* I added a relative clause:

> Since mature writers often use those patterns to extend a sentence, we need a word to name what they do and I am about to do in the *sentence* that you are now reading,
> *a sentence* **that I could have ended seven words ago, but extended to show you how resumptive modifiers work.**

You can pause and resume with adjectives as well:

> It was American writers who found a voice that was both **true** and **lyrical,**
> **true** to the rhythms of the working man's speech and **lyrical** in its celebration of his labor.

And with verbs:

> All who value independence should **resist** the trivialization of government regulation,
> **resist** the bureaucrats' obsession with administrative tidiness and their compulsion to arrange things not for our convenience but for theirs.

The pause and repeated word makes it seem almost as if you are starting the sentence over.

- *Summative modifiers:* This modifier lets you avoid the sprawl that sometimes occurs when you tack on a *which*-clause referring to everything that preceded, as in this slightly awkward sentence:

  > Economic changes have reduced Russian population growth to almost zero,
  > **which in years to come will have serious social implications.**

  A summative modifier doesn't repeat a word; instead, it requires you to find a word that sums up what has gone before:

  > ✓ Economic changes have reduced Russian population growth almost to zero,
  > **a demographic event** that will have serious social implications.

  To create a summative modifier, do this:

  1. End a segment of a sentence with a comma:

     > Economic changes have reduced Russian population growth to almost zero,

  2. Find a noun that sums up the substance of the preceding:

     > Economic changes have reduced Russian population growth to almost zero,
     > **a demographic event**. . . .

  3. Continue with a relative clause:

     > Economic changes have reduced Russian population growth to almost zero,
     > a demographic event **that will have serious social implications.**

- *Free modifiers:* Like the other two kinds of modifiers, a free modifier can also appear at the end of a clause, but instead of repeating a key word or summing up what went before, it specifically modifies the subject of the closest verb:

✓ Free modifiers resemble resumptive and summative modifiers, **letting** [i.e., the *free modifier* lets] you extend the line of a sentence while avoiding a train of ungainly phrases and clauses.

Compare these two:

Socrates, who questioned the foundations of political behavior, forced Athenians to examine the duty they owed their state and encouraged youth to question the authority of their elders while he maintained that he wanted only to puzzle out the truth.

✓ Socrates questioned the foundations of political behavior,
forcing Athenians to examine the duty they owed their state,
encouraging youth to question the authority of their elders,
claiming all the while that he wanted only to puzzle out the truth.

Free modifiers most often begin with an *-ing* PRESENT PARTICIPLE, as these did, but they can also begin with a PAST PARTICIPLE form of the verb:

✓ Leonardo da Vinci was a man of powerful intellect,
driven by an insatiable curiosity and
haunted by a vision of artistic perfection.

A free modifier can also begin with an adjective:

✓ In 1939, we began to assist the British against Germany,
aware that we faced another world war.

We call these modifiers *free* because they can both end and begin a sentence:

✓ Driven by an insatiable curiosity, Leonardo da Vinci was. . . .

✓ Aware that we faced another world war, in 1939 we began. . . .

Exercise 9.3

In these sentences, create resumptive, summative, and free modifiers. In the first five, start a resumptive modifier with the word in italics. Then use the word in brackets to create another sentence with a summative modifier. For example:

> Within ten years, we could meet our *energy needs* with solar power. [a possibility]
>
> *Resumptive:*
>
> ✓ Within ten years, we could meet our *energy needs* with solar power, ***needs* that will soar as our population grows.**
>
> *Summative:*
>
> ✓ Within ten years, we could meet our energy needs with solar power, ***a possibility* that few anticipated ten years ago.**
>
> *Free:*
>
> ✓ Within ten years, we could meet our energy needs with solar power, **freeing ourselves of dependence on foreign oil.**

But before you begin adding resumptive and summative modifiers, edit these sentences for redundancy, wordiness, nominalizations, and other problems.

1. Many different school systems are making a return back to traditional *education* in the basics. [a change]
2. Within the period of the last few years or so, automobile manufacturers have been trying to meet new and more stringent-type quality control *requirements.* [a challenge]
3. The reasons for the cause of aging are a *puzzle* that has perplexed humanity for millennia. [a mystery]
4. The majority of young people in the world of today cannot even begin to have an understanding of the *insecurity* that a large number of older people had experienced during the period of the Great Depression. [a failure]
5. The successful accomplishment of test-tube fertilization of embryos has raised many *issues* of an ethical nature that continue to trouble both scientists and laypeople. [an event]

In these next sentences, prune the redundancy and the abstraction and then create coordinate modifiers of your own. For example, here is a coordinate resumptive modifier built into (5) above:

✓ . . . ethical *issues* that trouble both scientists and laypeople, *issues* that yield easily to neither religious principles nor legal theory.

6. Many who lived during the period of the Victorian era were appalled when Darwin put forth the suggestion that their ancestry might have included creatures such as apes.
7. The concept of systematic skepticism is in effect a kind of denial that there can ever be any kind of certain knowledge of reality so long as it goes on being screened and influenced by human perception.
8. The point when scientific inquiry began to develop is to be found in the individual observations of primitive peoples about the natural things that seemed to occur in a regular way.
9. In the period known to scholars and historians as the Renaissance, increases in affluence and stability in the area of political affairs had the consequence of allowing streams of thought of different kinds to merge and flow together.

Exercise 9.4

Find sentences in a paper that you have already written and out of them create several resumptive, summative, and free modifiers.

Movement and Momentum

If your readers are to feel that your long sentences are as clear as a series of short ones, you have to give them a chance to take a breath, but you do not want to slow their movement through a sentence by repeated interruptions.

Maintaining the Largest Grammatical Connections

To help your readers move through a clause easily, you must maintain its two most important internal grammatical links: subject >< verb and verb >< OBJECT. When readers cannot complete those links quickly and surely, they will feel your sentences hesitate.

1a. A semantic theory, if it is to represent in real-time processing terms on-line cognitive behavior, must propose more neurally plausible psychological processes than those described here.

✓ 1b. If a semantic theory is to represent on-line cognitive behavior in real-time terms, it must propose psychological processes that are more neurally plausible than those described here.

Both sentences make a reader pause, but in (1a) that long *if*-clause after the subject, *semantic theory,* forces the reader to hold her mental breath until she reaches the verb, *must propose.* And even as she reads that interrupting *if*-clause, she had to suspend the sense after its verb, *represent,* because another interruption, *in real-time processing terms,* kept her from getting to its object, *on-line cognitive behavior.* The interruptions look like this:

A semantic theory > < must propose

if it is to represent > <on-line cognitive behavior

in real-time terms

And then the *more* at the end is split off from its *than:*

more > <than those described

neurally plausible psychological processes

On the other hand, the revised sentence (1b) lets the reader move uninterrupted from element to element:

✓ If a semantic theory >< is to represent >< on-line cognitive behavior >< in real time terms, it >< must propose psychological processes more neurally plausible >< than those suggested here.

Readers do not hesitate when you interrupt those links with short modifiers:

✓ Scientists > **deliberately** < write in a style that is impersonal and objective.

But longer phrases and clauses always disrupt "flow":

> Scientists > , **because they write in a style that is impersonal and objective,** < do not easily communicate with lay people.

Move the phrase or clause to the beginning or end of its sentence, depending on what comes next.

Readers will have different expectations after reading these next two sentences. The first suggests that the following sentences will address difficulties in communication; the second that the following sentences will address scientific style:

✓ **Because they write in a style that is impersonal and objective,** scientists do not easily communicate with lay people. They fail. . . .

✓ Scientists do not easily communicate with lay people **because they write in a style that is impersonal and objective.** That impersonality. . . .

Maintaining the Smallest Grammatical Connections

This is a fine point: To avoid even the smallest hitch in the rhythm of a sentence, look for adjective phrases that you have split from the nouns they modify. The boldfaced words and phrases belong together.

> We have **as accurate** > a projection < **as any available.**
>
> A **similar** > theory < **to the one proposed** by Chang is based on **different** > principles < **from ours.**
>
> We must create a **bolder** > plan < **than this one** to find **sufficient** > capital < **to complete such** > projects < **as those you describe.**

In each case, we split an adjective from its modifying phrase by putting the adjective before a noun and the phrase after:

as accurate >	a projection	< **as any available**
similar >	theory	< **to the one proposed**
different >	basis	< **from ours**
bolder >	plan	< **than this one**
sufficient >	capital	< **to complete**
such >	projects	< **as those you**

The reader feels a smoother rhythm if we move the adjective *after* the noun, directly connecting the adjective to the phrase that modifies it:

> We have a projection **as accurate** >< **as any available.**
>
> A theory **similar** >< **to the one proposed** by Chang is based on principles **different** >< **from ours.**
>
> We must create a plan **bolder** >< **than this one** to find capital **sufficient** >< **to complete** projects **such** >< **as those you describe.**

Some words that we frequently split off from their phrasal modifiers:

more than	less than	other than	as . . . as
equal to	similar to	different from	such as

Exercise 9.5

These sentences are unfortunately interrupted. First, eliminate wordiness and correct the interruption. Then devise summative, resumptive, and free modifiers. Finally, create a coordinate member to balance the modifier you've added. See how long a sentence you can write before it collapses.

1. The construction of the Interstate Highway System, owing to the fact that Congress, on the occasion when it originally voted funds for it, did not anticipate the rising cost of inflation, ran into serious financial problems.
2. Such prejudicial conduct or behavior, regardless of the reasons offered to justify it, is rarely not at least to some degree prejudicial to good order and discipline.
3. TV talk shows, because they have an appeal to our fascination with real life conflict because of our voyeuristic

impulses, are about the most popular shows that are regularly scheduled to appear on TV.

4. The merit selection of those who are judges, given the low quality and character of elected officials, is an idea whose time came long ago.
5. The field of physics, using devices that can actually accelerate particles to a speed almost as fast as the speed of light, is exploring the ultimate nature and makeup of matter.
6. The continued and unabated emission of carbon dioxide gas into the atmosphere, unless there is a marked reduction prior to the end of the century, will eventually result in serious changes in the climate of the world as we know it today.
7. Insistence that there is no proof by scientific means of a causal link between tobacco consumption and various disease entities such as cardiac heart diseases and malignant growth, despite the fact that there is a strong statistical correlation between smoking behavior and such diseases, continues to be the officially stated position of cigarette companies.

Exercise 9.6

These sentences have awkwardly split adjective phrases. Reunite the phrases and revise for directness. The separated phrases in (1) and (2) are boldfaced.

1. An **identical** ecological impact statement **to that submitted the previous year** indicates that it will again contain **difficult** data **to evaluate.**
2. Under the circumstances in which **similar** EKG readings are obtained **to those obtained earlier, other** conditions **than cardiac disease** must come under suspicion. To determine those conditions, the diagnostician must follow the **same** procedures **as those outlined above** and must be closely adhered to on the expectation that **as effective** results **as those outlined there** can be achieved in such cases.
3. As a result of the reorganization of the marketing research division, more rapid information processing

than that which has been possible in the past should allow more reliable identification of different market segments from those that have been traditionally aimed at. This will be relatively easy information to process as a result of the fact that there has already been accumulated such demographic data as the average financial income, expenditure patterns, etc., for many different markets. As a result of all this, greater efficiency than that which we achieved in our earlier operation may be a reasonable expectation.

Some Other Problems with Long Sentences

In long sentences, even writers can lose track of the grammatical connections between the modifier and the modified.

Dangling Modifiers

Modifiers can dangle anywhere in a sentence, but they dangle most often at its beginning or end. Again, a modifier "dangles" when its implied subject differs from the explicit subject of the clause it attaches to. Free modifiers in particular are subject to dangling, so be sure that their implied subjects are identical to the explicit subjects:

> The results of the tests underwent extensive reviews, **hoping to find some cause of the flaw.**

The modifier, *hoping to find,* dangles because its implicit subject (whoever hopes) differs from the explicit subject of the clause it attaches to (*the results of the tests*). To revise, make the implied and explicit subjects identical:

✓ **We** reviewed the results of the tests extensively, **hoping** to find. . . .

The most common dangling modifier begins as if the writer intended to write a direct sentence:

✓ Realizing the need for more time, **the agency** delayed its decision.

But before reaching the subject of the main clause, the writer makes the verb passive or nominalizes it, thereby changing the explicit subject so that it is no longer the same as the implicit subject of the introductory phrase:

Realizing the need for time, **the decision** was delayed.

Realizing the need for time, there was **a delay** in the agency's decision.

There are some dangling modifiers that readers generally ignore. Few notice, much less care, when the implied subject of the modifier is different from the explicit subject of the main clause when either is METADISCOURSE:

✓ [For someone] *to start the motor,* **it** is essential to engage the switch.

Misplaced or "Squinting" Modifiers

A second problem with modifiers is that sometimes readers can't see which of two things they modify. An ambiguous modifier can look forward or back:

Overtaxing oneself in physical activity **too frequently** results in injury.

We make the modifier unambiguous by moving it:

✓ Overtaxing oneself **too frequently** in physical activity results in injury.

✓ Overtaxing oneself in physical activity results **too frequently** in injury.

An ambiguous modifier at the end of a clause can modify either a neighboring or a more distant phrase:

Scientists have learned that their observations are as subjective as those in any other field **in recent years.**

We can move the modifier to a less ambiguous position:

✓ **In recent years,** scientists have learned that. . . .

✓ Scientists have learned that **in recent years** their. . . .

Exercise 9.7

These sentences suffer from a variety of problems. Revise as you see fit.

1. Having no previous familiarity with it, the metal detection device did not function as expected.
2. With every expectation of success, new efforts to resolve the differences that have resulted in interference with communication are necessary.

3. Realizing that the undergraduate curriculum must be completely reevaluated in the next few weeks, proposals have suddenly appeared on the agenda that had received earlier attention but were rejected.
4. After making an audit of all internal operations in the summer of 1996, a second audit examined the record of foreign affiliates that had not been previously audited by their local headquarters.

These devices can help you shape a long yet graceful sentence, but not even the best syntax can salvage it if its content is incoherent. This next sentence appeared one Sunday in The *New York Times* travel section. The sentence before had introduced the professional women of Amsterdam's red-light district:

> They are so unself-conscious about their profession that by day they can be seen standing naked in doorways, chatting with their neighbors in the shadow of the Oudekerstoren Church, which offers Saturday carillon concerts at 4 P.M. and a panoramic view of the city from its tower in summer.

This syntactically well-formed sentence opens with a coherent clause:

> They are so unself-conscious about their profession that by day they can be seen standing naked in doorways. . . .

It continues with a free modifier:

> . . . chatting with their neighbors in the shadow of the Oudekerstoren Church. . . .

then concludes with a relative clause containing a balanced pair of direct objects:

> . . . which offers {
> Saturday carillon concerts at 4 P.M.
> and
> a panoramic view of the city from its tower in the summer.

But the movement of ideas is goofy (or evidence of a sly sense of humor).

Here's the point: With no controlling idea, coherent syntax provides only meaningless decoration. A graceful sentence merges substantive thought with coherent structure.

Summing Up

1. Revise sentences consisting of a series of similar dependent clauses.

   a. Trim relative clauses:

   Work **that is** not done on time must be submitted on a date **which will be** set by those **who are** responsible for scheduling.

   ✓ Work [ ] not done on time must be submitted on a date [ ] set by those [ ] responsible for scheduling.

   b. Coordinate rhetorically parallel elements:

   Besides the fact that no civilization has experienced such rapid alterations in the conditions of daily life, the life of the mind has changed greatly too.

   ✓ No civilization has experienced such rapid alterations **in the conditions of daily life** *or* **in the life of the mind.**

   c. Use resumptive, summative, and free modifiers:

   ✓ When we discovered that the earth was not the center of the universe, it reshaped **our understanding** of who we are, **an understanding** that was changed again by Darwin, again by Freud, and again by Einstein.

   ✓ After a period of uncertainty, American productivity has risen to new heights, **an achievement** that only a decade ago was considered an impossible dream.

   ✓ Global warming has become a central political issue of the twentieth century, **raising questions whose answers will affect the standard of living in every Western nation.**

2. To maintain the momentum in a long sentence, don't break links between subject and verb or verb and object.

   The Protagoras, *despite its questionable logic and superficial philosophical content,* **remains** one of Plato's most appealing dialogues.

   ✓ *Despite its questionable logic and superficial philosophical content,* **the Protagoras remains** one of Plato's most appealing dialogues.

3. Watch for modifiers that may seem to modify something other than what you intended:

   Reexamining the issues that had been earlier discussed, a new perspective on them arose among the committee.

   ✓ Reexamining the issues that had been earlier discussed, the committee took a new perspective on them.

Lesson Ten

Elegance

In literature the ambition of the novice is to acquire the literary language; the struggle of the adept is to get rid of it.
George Bernard Shaw

Anything is better than not to write clearly. There is nothing to be said against lucidity, and against simplicity only the possibility of dryness. This is a risk well worth taking when you reflect how much better it is to be bald than to wear a curly wig.
Somerset Maugham

But clarity and brevity, though a good beginning, are only a beginning. By themselves, they may remain bare and bleak. When Calvin Coolidge, asked by his wife what the preacher had preached on, replied "Sin," and, asked what the preacher had said, replied "He was against it," he was brief enough. But one hardly envies Mrs. Coolidge.
Frank L. Lucas

Read over your compositions, and wherever you meet with a passage which you think is particularly fine, strike it out.
Samuel Johnson

Teaching What Cannot Be Taught

Anyone able to express complex ideas clearly should rejoice to have achieved so much. But while most readers prefer bald clarity to the density of institutional prose, they sometimes feel that the relentless simplicity of the plain style can eventually become dry, even arid. Plainness has the spartan virtue of unsalted meat and potatoes, but such fare is rarely memorable. A touch of class, a flash of elegance can mark the difference between bland clarity and a thought so elegantly shaped that it not only fixes itself in the minds of your readers, but gives them a flicker of pleasure every time they recall it.

I wish I could tell you how to write such sentences, but I can't. In fact, I am inclined to agree with the quotations from the previous page—the best eloquence is disarming simplicity—and when you think you have written something quite fine, strike it out. And yet there are a few specific devices used by writers thought to be graceful, devices that combine the virtues of making thoughts both clear and elegant.

But I also know that listing those devices is about as useful as telling you the ingredients in the bouillabaisse of a great cook and then expecting you to make it. Knowing the names of the ingredients and knowing how to mix them is the difference between reading cookbooks and Cooking. It's a matter of practice and taste, and maybe it's a gift.

This lesson is for those who are concerned with more than spartan plainness, who enjoy prose not as a transparent medium but as an aesthetic experience, who take a special pleasure when they read a well-turned sentence, especially when it is one of their own.

Balance and Symmetry

The most common kind of balance and symmetry depends on coordination, but a flexible stylist can balance almost any kind of construction.

Coordination

One mark of a style that readers judge to be particularly elegant is coordinated balance and antithesis. I've described how to extend the line of a sentence with COORDINATION (pp. 191–95), a device that alone can grace a sentence with rhythm. Here is a passage by Walter Lippmann and my revision. Even a tin ear can identify which is which:

✓ The national unity of a free people depends upon a sufficiently even balance of political power to make it impracticable for the administration to be arbitrary and for the opposition to be revolutionary and irreconcilable. Where that balance no longer exists, democracy perishes. For unless all the citizens of a state are forced by circumstances to compromise, unless they feel that they can affect policy but that no one can wholly dominate it, unless by habit and necessity they have to give and take, freedom cannot be maintained.

The national unity of a free people depends upon a sufficiently even balance of political power to make it impracticable for an administration to be arbitrary against a revolutionary opposition that is irreconcilably opposed to it. Where that balance no longer exists, democracy perishes, because unless all the citizens of a state are habitually forced by necessary circumstances to compromise in a way that lets them affect policy with no one dominating it, freedom cannot be maintained.

In Lippmann's original, when we hear his CLAUSES echo one another, we see more clearly the architecture of his thought. In my version, the sentences limp from one uncoordinated PHRASE and clause to the next.

But Lippmann shapes his prose with more than simple coordination. Like other especially elegant writers, he *balances* parts of phrases against other phrases, parts of clauses against other clauses, giving the whole passage an intricate architecture of balanced and symmetrical members whose parts echo one another.

If we extend the concepts of TOPIC and STRESS from a whole sentence to its internal phrases and clauses, we can see how this kind of architectural elegance depends on creating balanced topics and stresses even in relatively short segments. I have boldfaced what we could take as topics of phrases and italicized stresses. Note that each is a significant word that balances another significant word in its corresponding coordinate phrase.

The national unity of a free people depends upon a sufficiently even balance of political power to make it impracticable

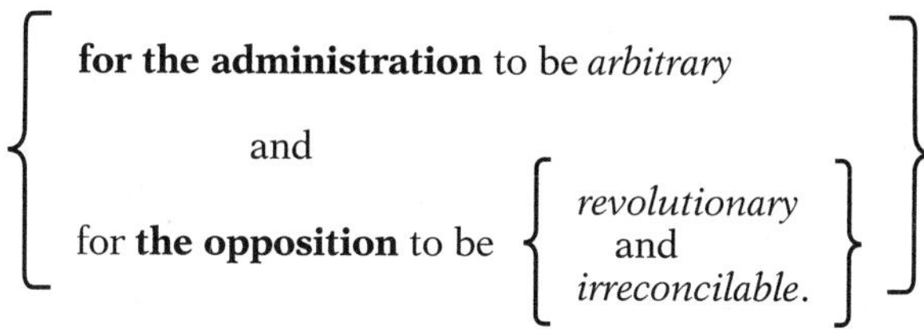

Lippmann first balances the opposing topics of *administration* and *opposition,* and closes by balancing the stressed meanings and sounds of *arbitrary, revolutionary,* and *irreconcilable.* He follows this with a short concluding sentence whose stressed words are not coordinated, but nevertheless balance each other (to indicate noncoordinated balance, I use square brackets):

Where [that balance *no longer exists,*
democracy *perishes.*]

Then in an especially intricate design, he creates a complex balance of many sounds and meanings out of internal topics and stress:

For {
unless all the **citizens** of a state are forced . . . to *compromise,*

unless **they** feel { that **they** can *affect policy* but that **no one** can *wholly dominate it* }

unless by { *habit* and *necessity* } **they** have to { *give* and *take,* }

freedom cannot be *maintained.*
}

Here is what Lippmann did:

- He repeats references to *citizens* as the SUBJECT/topic of each clause (note that he had to use a passive in the first one: *citizens are forced*).

- He balances the sound and sense of *forces* against *feel,* and the meaning of *affect policy* against the meaning of *dominate it.*
- In the last *unless*-clause, he balances *habit* against *necessity,* and the stressed *give* against *take.*
- Then in order to parallel the clauses of that short preceding sentence, *balance no longer exists* = *democracy perishes,* he concludes this long sentence with an equally short clause whose meaning and structure of topic and stress parallel that pair in the preceding sentence:

balance	*no longer exists*
democracy	*perishes*
freedom	*cannot be maintained.*

To the reader who can hear this design, it is an impressive achievement.

Uncoordinated Balance

Readers can hear the same balanced effect in grammatical structures that are not coordinate. In the first example below, the whole subject balances an object, and in the second, the PREDICATE of a RELATIVE CLAUSE in a subject balances the predicate of the whole sentence:

Scientists whose research	*creates revolutionary views of the universe*
	invariably upset
those of us who	*construct our vision of reality out of our common sense experience of it.*

A government	unwilling to *listen* to the *moderate* hopes of its *citizenry*
	must eventually *answer* to the *harsh* justice of its *revolutionaries.*

Here a direct object parallels the object of a PREPOSITION:

Those of us concerned with our school systems
will not sacrifice

[the *intellectual growth* of our *innocent children*
to
the *social engineering* of *incompetent bureaucrats.*]

Here is a more complicated example:

(1a) Were I trading [(2a) scholarly principles
for
(2b) financial profit,]

(1b) I would not be writing [(3a) short books on
(3b) minor subjects for
(3c) small audiences.]

This sentence balances

- A SUBORDINATE CLAUSE (la), *Were I trading,* against the MAIN CLAUSE (1b), *I would not be writing,*
- The object of that subordinate clause (2a) *scholarly principles,* against the object in the prepositional phrase (2b) *financial profit,*
- The object in the main clause (3a) *short books,* against the objects of prepositions in two following prepositional phrases, (3b) *minor subjects* and (3c) *small audiences.*

None of these is coordinated, but each is balanced. Used to excess, these patterns can seem merely clever, but used prudently, they can emphasize an important point or conclude the line of an argument with a flourish that readers will notice.

But if these patterns impress a reader, they can help a writer even more: The sheer act of trying to write a sentence like this forces you to think of things you would not have thought of otherwise. When you begin a sentence with

> In his earliest years, Picasso was not only a master draftsman of the traditional human form, but a. . . .

you force yourself to wonder, what else might he have been. Or not have been.

CLIMACTIC EMPHASIS

Light and Heavy Words

Readers want to hear in a sentence appropriate emphasis when they come to its stressed position (pp. 146–47), so they may feel a sentence is anticlimactic if it ends on words that carry slight grammatical weight. Prepositions feel light—a reason why we sometimes avoid leaving one at the end of a sentence. Sentences should carry readers forward toward strength. Compare:

> Studies into intellectual differences among races is a project that only the most politically naive psychologist **is willing to give support to.**

✓ Studies into intellectual differences among races is a project that only the most politically naive scientist **is willing to support.**

ADJECTIVES and ADVERBS are heavier than prepositions, but lighter than NOUNS. The heaviest words are NOMINALIZATIONS. Readers can have a problem with them when they begin a sentence, but at the end, nominalizations provide a kind of satisfyingly climactic thump, particularly when they are paired. Compare these two versions of a sentence from Winston Churchill's "Finest Hour" speech. Always elegant and emphatic, Churchill ended his sentence with a parallelism climaxed by a balanced pair of heavy nominalizations:

✔ . . . until in God's good time, the New World,
with all its power and might, steps forth to
{ the **rescue** / and / the **liberation** } of the old.

He could have written more simply, and more banally:

> . . . until in God's good time, the New World rescues us.

Elegant Stress: Four Devices

Occasionally, you may want to end your sentences in a way that is self-consciously dramatic. Here are four ways to do so.

1. of + Nominalization This one may seem odd, but it's true: Writers looking for a grand effect combine coordinations and nominalizations at the end of a sentence with prepositional phrases beginning with *of*. That pattern appears at the end of the Churchill quotation. The lightly stressed *of* (and an equally light *a* or *the*) quickens the rhythm just before it is brought down hard by the weight of the last word: *the rescue and the liberation* ***of*** *the old.* You can hear this pattern clearly in the first few sentences of William Gibbon's *Decline and Fall of the Roman Empire:*

> ✓ In the second century of the Christian era, the Empire of Rome comprehended the fairest **part of the earth,** and the most civilized **portion of mankind.** The frontiers of that extensive monarchy were guarded by ancient renown and disciplined valour. The gentle but powerful influence of laws and manners had gradually cemented the **union of the provinces.** Their peaceful inhabitants enjoyed and abused the **advantages of wealth and luxury.** The image of a free constitution was preserved with decent reverence: the Roman senate appeared to possess the sovereign authority, and devolved on the emperors all the **executive powers of government.**

In comparison, this is flat:

> In the second century of the Christian era, the Roman Empire comprehended the **earth's fairest, most civilized part.** Ancient renown and disciplined valour guarded **its extensive frontiers.** The gentle but powerful influence of laws and manners had gradually **cemented and unified the provinces.** Their peaceful inhabitants enjoyed and abused luxurious wealth while decently preserving what seemed **to be a free constitution.** Appearing to possess the sovereign authority, the Roman senate devolved on the emperors all executive **governmental powers.**

2. Echoing Salience When readers end a sentence on a word or phrase that semantically echoes or contrasts with an earlier word or phrase, they will hear special emphasis on that second word or phrase. (These examples are all from Peter Gay's *Style in History.*)

> ✓ I have written these essays to anatomize this familiar yet really strange being, **style the centaur;** the book may be read as an extended critical commentary on Buffon's famous saying that the **style is the man.**

When these stressed words also alliterate, they elevate the contrast and the emphasis.

✓ Apart from a few mechanical tricks of rhetoric, **manner** is indissolubly linked to **matter; style** shapes, and in turn is shaped by, **substance.**

✓ It seems frivolous, almost inappropriate, to be **stylish** about **style.**

Gay echoes *manner* in *matter* and *style* in *substance,* enhancing the emphasis on both *matter* and *substance* (which also echo one another in meaning).

3. ***Elaborated Coordinations*** Especially elegant coordinations generally move a reader from shorter segments to longer and more complex ones, especially when the last member of a coordinate pair or triplet branches into yet another coordination, in the way a tree branch branches and then branches again.

This passage has a problem:

> It is appropriate that we devote a few final words to a matter that reaches beyond the techniques of research, to the intimate and inescapable connections between **those values that we reflect in our deepest ethical choices** and **objective research.**

That sentence seems to end abruptly; this next revision moves from shorter to longer by reordering the elements and adding a parallelism to the second one:

✓ It is appropriate to devote a few final words to a matter that reaches beyond the techniques of research, to the intimate and inescapable connections between **objective research** and **those values that we reflect in our deepest ethical choices** and **our most profound intellectual commitments.**

The difference between a flat rhythm and one that builds to a climax depends partly on the reader moving not from long to short, but from short to long. Compare:

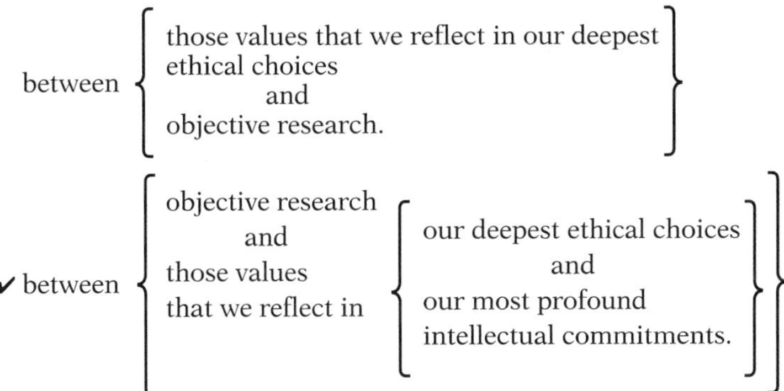

4. *Chiasmus* A different—and admittedly rather rarefied—kind of balanced repetition is *chiasmus,* from the Greek word for "crossing." It contrasts with parallelism because the second half of the construction *reverses* the order of elements in the first half (the elements may or may not be coordinate). For example, this would be coordinate and parallel because the balanced parts are in the same order (AB : AB):

✔ A concise style can improve both { our own[A] thinking[B] and our readers'[A] understanding.[B] }

But some writers looking for a special effect like to reverse the order of elements in the second part so that they mirror those in the first half, thereby throwing a kind of surprising emphasis on the last element in the pattern. This next would be a chiasmus because the pattern is not AB : AB, but AB : BA:

✔ A concise style can improve both { our own[A] thinking[B] and the understanding[B] of our readers.[A] }

This next example is more complex. It is parallel because the balanced elements in each part appear in the same order: ABCDE: ABCDE

> You[A] reveal[B] your own[C] rhetorical[D] skill[E]
> by the way
> you[A] respect[B] your opponent's[C] most deeply held[D] beliefs.[E]

In this next version, however, only the first two elements are parallel. The last three now mirror one another: AB CDE : AB EDC

> You[A] reveal[B] your own[C] highest rhetorical[D] skill[E]
> by the way
> you[A] respect[B] the beliefs[E] most deeply held[D] by your opponent.[C]

Admittedly, appreciating this pattern takes some practice; successfully creating it takes a lot more.

Extravagant Elegance

When writers combine nominalizations with balanced and parallel constructions, when they draw on resumptive and summative modifiers to extend the line of a sentence, we know they are aiming at something special, as in this next passage by Joyce Carol Oates:

> Far from being locked inside our own skins, inside the "dungeons" of ourselves, we are now able to recognize that our minds belong, quite naturally, to a collective "mind," a mind in which we share everything that is mental, most obviously language itself, and that the old boundary of the skin is not boundary at all but a membrane connecting the inner and outer experience of existence. Our intelligence, our wit, our cleverness, our unique personalities—all are simultaneously "our own" possessions and the world's.
>
> —Joyce Carol Oates, "New Heaven and New Earth"

Note the two resumptive modifiers: *inside the dungeons of ourselves* and *a mind in which we share.* Note too the doubled nominalization at the end of the first long sentence, *experience of existence* and the coordinate nominalizations at the end of the second: *our own possessions and the world's.*

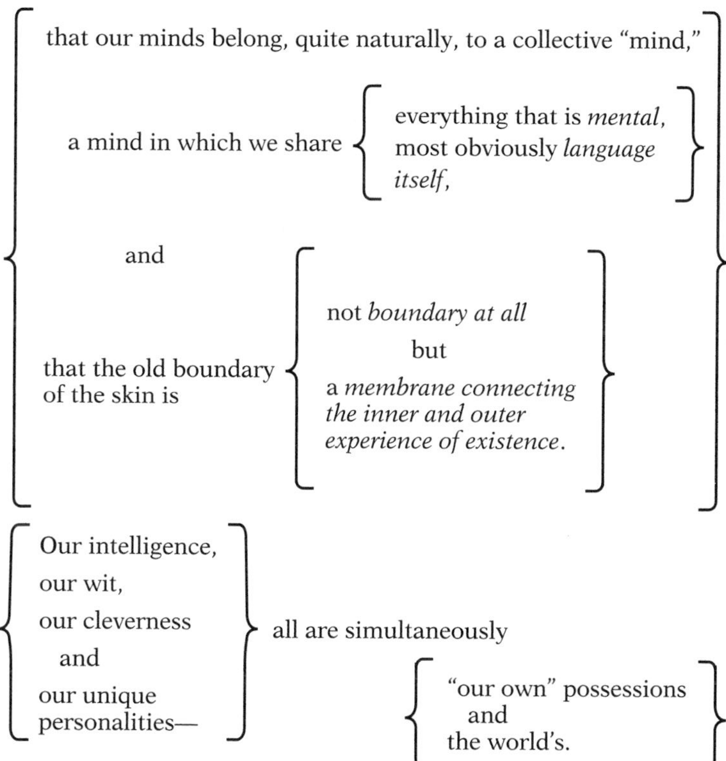

In the second sentence, note also the SUMMATIVE subject, *all* (see p. 246).

In the most elaborate prose, the parallelisms and balances, the free and resumptive modifiers seem to go on forever but they don't exhaust our attention. This is the last sentence from Frederick Jackson Turner's *The Frontier in American History:*

> This then is the heritage of the pioneer experience—a passionate belief that a democracy was possible which should leave the individual a part to play in free society and not make him a cog in a machine operated from above; which trusted in the common man, in his tolerance, his ability to adjust differences with good humor, and to work out an American type from the contributions of all nations—a type for which he would fight against those who challenged it in arms, and for which in time of war he would make sacrifices, even the temporary sacrifice of individual freedom and his life, lest that freedom be lost forever.

Here is the structure of that passage:

This then is the heritage of the pioneer experience—
[a free modifier] a passionate belief that a democracy was possible

which should
- leave the individual a part to play in free society
- and
- not make him a cog in a machine operated from above;

which trusted
- in the common man,
- in his tolerance,
- his ability
  - to adjust differences with good humor,
  - and
  - to work out an American **type** from the contributions of all nations—

[this is a kind of resumptive modifier, restating "tolerance"]

[resumptive modifier #1] → a **type**
- for which he would fight against those who challenged it in arms,
- and
- for which in time of war he would make **sacrifices**,

[resumptive modifier #2] → even the temporary **sacrifice** of
- his individual freedom
- and
- his life,

lest that freedom be lost forever.

Note the chiasmus in the last few words:

> temporary$_1$ sacrifice$_2$ freedom$_3$ life$_4$ freedom$_3$ lost$_2$ forever$_1$

Exercise 10.1

You can develop a knack for this kind of elegance in two ways: Practice writing balanced sentences from scratch or imitate balanced and parallel sentences that you read. Try imitating a few of these examples, not word for word, just the general pattern:

> Survival in the wilderness requires the energy and wit to overcome the brute facts of an uncooperative Nature but rewards the person who acquires that power with the satisfaction of having done it once and with the confidence of being able to do it again.

First, think of a subject close enough to this one to make your imitation easy—the academic life:

> Life as a college student offers four years of intellectual excitement but imposes a sense of anxiety on that person who looks ahead and knows that its end is in sight.

Exercise 10.2

Here are the first halves of some sentences. Finish them with balancing last halves. For example, given this:

> Those who keep silent over the loss of small freedoms. . . .

finish with something like this:

> . . . . will be silenced when they protest the loss of large ones.

1. Those who keep silent over the loss of small freedoms. . . .
2. While the strong are often afraid to admit weakness, the weak. . . .
3. We should pay more attention to those politicians who tell us how to make what we have better than to those. . . .

4. When parents raise children who do not value the importance of hard work, the adults those children become will. . . .
5. Some teachers mistake neat papers that rehash old ideas for. . . .

You can find other models in dictionaries of quotations.

Exercise 10.3

These sentences end on weak adjectives and adverbs or clumsy possessives. Edit them for clarity and concision, then revise them so that they end on more heavily stressed words, particularly with prepositional phrases beginning with *of.* For example:

> Our interest in paranormal phenomena testifies to the fact that we have empty spirits and shallow minds.

> ✓ Our interest in paranormal phenomena testifies to the **emptiness** *of* our spirits and the **shallowness** *of* our minds.

In the first three, I have boldfaced words you might nominalize.

1. If we invest our sweat in these projects, we must avoid appearing to be working only because we are **interested** in ourselves.
2. The blueprint for the political campaign plan was concocted by those who were least **sensitive** to what we **needed** most critically.
3. Throughout history, science has made progress because dedicated scientists have gotten around a **hostile** public that is uninformed.
4. Not one tendency in our governmental system has brought about more changes in American daily life than federal governmental agencies that are very powerful.
5. In the year 1923 several representatives from the side of the victorious Allied nations went to Versailles with the intention of seeking to dismember Germany's economic potential and to destroy her armaments industry.
6. The day is gone when school systems' boards of education have the expectation that local taxpayers will automatically go along with whatever extravagant things that incompetent bureaucrats decide to do.

7. Irreplaceable works of native art are progressing into slow deterioration in many of our most prestigious museums for the reason that their curators have no recognition of how extremely fragile even recent artifacts can be.

NUANCES OF LENGTH AND RHYTHM

Ordinarily, the length of sentences is an issue only when they are all 10 or 15 words long, or much longer. While one 20-word sentence after another is no ideal, they will seem cumulatively less monotonous than sentences regularly longer or shorter. But in artful prose, length is controlled and varied. Some stylists write short sentences to strike a note of urgency:

> Toward noon Petrograd again became the field of military action; rifles and machine guns rang out everywhere. It was not easy to tell who was shooting or where. One thing was clear; the past and the future were exchanging shots. There was much casual firing; young boys were shooting off revolvers unexpectedly acquired. The arsenal was wrecked. . . . Shots rang out on both sides. But the board fence stood in the way, dividing the soldiers from the revolution. The attackers decided to break down the fence. They broke down part of it and set fire to the rest. About twenty barracks came into view. The bicyclists were concentrated in two or three of them. The empty barracks were set fire to at once.
>
> —Leon Trotsky, *The Russian Revolution,* trans. Max Eastman

Or terse certainty:

> The teacher or lecturer is a danger. He very seldom recognizes his nature or his position. The lecturer is a man who must talk for an hour. France may possibly have acquired the intellectual leadership of Europe when their academic period was cut down to 40 minutes. I also have lectured. The lecturer's first problem is to have enough words to fill 40 or 60 minutes. The professor is paid for his time, his results are almost impossible to estimate. . . . No teacher has ever failed from ignorance. That is empiric professional knowledge. Teachers fail because they cannot "handle the class." Real education must ultimately be limited to men who INSIST on knowing, the rest is mere sheep-herding.
>
> —Ezra Pound, *ABC of Reading*

Or fire:

> Let us look at this American artist first. How did he ever get to America, to start with? Why isn't he a European still, like his father before him?
>
> Now listen to me, don't listen to him. He'll tell you the lie you expect. Which is partly your fault for expecting it.
>
> He didn't come in search of freedom of worship. England had more freedom of worship in the year 1700 than America had. Won by Englishmen who wanted freedom and so stopped at home and fought for it. And got it. Freedom of worship? Read the history of New England during the first century of its existence.
>
> Freedom anyhow? The land of the free! This the land of the free! Why, if I say anything that displeases them, the free mob will lynch me, and that's my freedom. Free? Why I have never been in any country where the individual has such an abject fear of his fellow countrymen. Because, as I say, they are free to lynch him the moment he shows he is not one of them. . . .
>
> All right then, what did they come for? For lots of reasons. Perhaps least of all in search of freedom of any sort: positive freedom, that is.
>
> —D. H. Lawrence, *Studies in Classic American Literature*

In this last example, Lawrence invests his prose with even more urgency by breaking sentences into FRAGMENTS and what could have been longer paragraphs into quick, breathless utterances.

Self-conscious stylists can also write one long sentence after another. Here is just part of a sentence describing a protest march:

> In any event, up at the front of this March, in the first line, back of that hollow square of monitors, Mailer and Lowell walked in this barrage of cameras, helicopters, TV cars, monitors, loudspeakers, and wavering buckling twisting line of notables, arms linked (line twisting so much that at times the movement was in file, one arm locked ahead, one behind, then the line would undulate about and the other arm would be ahead) speeding up a few steps, slowing down while a great happiness came back into the day as if finally one stood under some mythical arch in the great vault of history, helicopters buzzing about, chop-chop, and the sense of America divided on this day now liberated some undiscovered patriotism in Mailer so that he felt a sharp searing love for his country in this moment and on this day, crossing some divide in his own mind

wider than the Potomac, a love so lacerated he felt as if a marriage were being torn and children lost—never does one love so much as then, obviously, then—and an odor of wood smoke, from where you knew not, was also in the air, a smoke of dignity and some calm heroism, not unlike the sense of freedom which also comes when a marriage is burst—Mailer knew for the first time why men in the front line of battle are almost always ready to die; there is a promise of some swift transit. . . .

—Norman Mailer, *Armies of the Night*

This single PUNCTUATED SENTENCE consists of several GRAMMATICAL SENTENCES. But it does not sprawl.

Mailer opens with staccato phrases to suggest the confusion of the scene, but he controls those phrases by coordinating them.

- He continues the sentence by coordinating free modifiers: *arms linked (line twisting,. . .) speeding up. . . .*
- After serveral more free modifiers, he continues with a resumptive modifier: *a love so lacerated. . . .*
- After another grammatical sentence, he adds another resumptive modifier: *a smoke of dignity and some calm heroism. . . .*

A sentence like this makes us feel we are overhearing someone thinking aloud, letting the shape of his sentence lead him from one discovery to the next.

Exercise 10.4

Combine some of Lawrence and Pound's short sentences into longer sentences like Mailer's. How do they sound? Break up Mailer's long sentence into shorter ones in the style of Lawrence and Pound. How do they differ? Imitate the style of Lawrence, Pound, and Mailer. Then transform your Lawrence imitation into a Mailer imitation, and your Mailer imitation into a Lawrence imitation.

It is only by seeing how you can express the same content in different styles that you can see how different styles can seem to change content (a self-conscious chiasmus there).

METAPHOR

Clarity, vigor, symmetry, rhythm—prose so graced is a great achievement. And yet, while those virtues might excite admiration for our craft, they do not reveal the reach of our imagination. This next passage displays all these stylistic devices and graces, but it goes beyond craft. It reveals a truth about pleasure through a figure of speech embedded in a comparison that is itself metaphorical:

> The secret of the enjoyment of pleasure is to know when to stop. . . . We do this every time we listen to music. We do not seize hold of a particular chord or phrase and shout at the orchestra to go on playing it for the rest of the evening; on the contrary, however much we may like that particular moment of music, we know that its perpetuation would interrupt and kill the movement of the melody. We understand that the beauty of a symphony is less in these musical moments than in the whole movement from beginning to end. If the symphony tries to go on too long, if at a certain point the composer exhausts his creative ability and tries to carry on just for the sake of filling in the required space of time, then we begin to fidget in our chairs, feeling that he has denied the natural rhythm, has broken the smooth curve from birth to death, and that though a pretense of life is being made, it is in fact a living death.
>
> —Alan W. Watts, *The Meaning of Happiness*

Watts could have written this:

> . . . however much we like that moment, we know that its perpetuation would interrupt and spoil the movement of the melody. We begin to fidget in our chairs, feeling that he has denied the natural rhythm, has interrupted the regular movement from beginning to end, and that though a pretense of wholeness is being made, it is in fact a repeated end.

The two passages are equally clear and graceful. But the first illuminates music—and pleasure—in a way that the second cannot. That metaphor of birth and of the smooth curve of life into death startles us with a flash of unexpected truth. The figure invites us to look at both things—death and music—in a new way.

Similes do the same, but less intensely, their *like* or *as* moderating the force of the comparison. Compare these:

> The schoolmaster is the person who takes the children off the parents' hands for a consideration. That is to say, he establishes a child prison, engages a number of employee schoolmasters as turnkeys, and covers up the essential cruelty and unnaturalness of the situation by torturing the children if they do not learn, and calling this process, which is within the capacity of any fool or blackguard, by the sacred name of Teaching.
>
> —George Bernard Shaw, *Sham Education*

> The schoolmaster establishes something like a child prison, engages a number of schoolmasters to act like turnkeys, covers up the essential cruelty and unnaturalness of the situation by doing things to children that are like torture if they do not learn, calling this process, which is within the capacity of any fool or blackguard, by the sacred name of Teaching.

That second passage says about the same thing, but less intensely.

Metaphor can vivify all kinds of prose. Historians rely on it:

> This is what may be called the common-sense view of history. History consists of a corpus of ascertained facts. The facts are available to the historian in documents, inscriptions, and so on, like fish on the fishmonger's slab. The historian collects them, takes them home, and cooks and serves them in whatever style appeals to him. Acton, whose culinary tastes were austere, wanted them served plain. . . . Sir George Clark, critical as he was of Acton's attitude, himself contrasts the "hard core of facts" in history with the "surrounding pulp of disputable interpretation"—forgetting perhaps that the pulpy part of the fruit is more rewarding than the hard core.
>
> —E. H. Carr, *What Is History?*

So do biologists:

> Some of you may have been thinking that, instead of delivering a scientific address, I have been indulging in a flight of fancy. It is a flight, but not of mere fancy, nor is it just an individual indulgence. It is my small personal attempt to share in the flight of the mind into new realms of our cosmic environment. We have evolved wings for such flights, in shape of the disciplined scientific imagination. Support for those wings is provided by the atmosphere of knowledge created by human science and learning: so far as this supporting atmosphere extends, so far can our wings take us in our exploration.
>
> —Julian Huxley, "New Bottles for Old Wine,"
> *Journal of the Royal Anthropological Institute*

And philosophers:

> Quine has long professed his skepticism about the possibility of making any sense of the refractory idioms of intentionality, so he needs opacity only to provide a quarantine barrier protecting the healthy, extensional part of a sentence from the infected part.
>
> —Daniel C. Dennett, "Beyond Belief"

And physicists, when they write about ideas for which they have no standard language:

> Whereas the lepton pair has a positive rest mass when it is regarded as a single particle moving with a velocity equal to the vector sum of the motions of its two components, a photon always has zero rest mass. This difference can be glossed over, however, by treating the lepton pair as the offspring of the decay of a short-lived photonlike parent called a virtual photon.
>
> —Leon M. Lederman, "The Upsilon Particle," *Scientific American*

These metaphors serve different ends. Shaw used the prison metaphor of turnkeys and torture to invest his argument with an emotional intensity that literal language could not capture. Carr used fish and fruit both to emphasize and to illuminate. He could have expressed his ideas more prosaically, but the literal statement would have been longer and weaker. Dennett and Lederman required no heightened emphasis; they used their comparisons to explain.

But if a striking metaphor evidences imagination, it can betray those of us whose imagination falls short of its demands. Of metaphor, Aristotle wrote,

> By far the greatest thing is to be a master of metaphor. It is the one thing that cannot be learned from others. It is a sign of genius, for a good metaphor implies an intuitive perception of similarity among dissimilars.

Those of us short on genius can still use metaphor, but we have to be careful that the metaphor does not distort the idea that we want to express:

> Societies give birth to new values through the osmotic flow of daily social interaction. Conflicts evolve when old values collide with new, a process that frequently spawns yet a new set of values that synthesize the conflict into a reconciliation of opposites.

We get the picture, but darkly. The birth metaphor suggests a traumatic event, but the values, it is claimed, result from osmotic flow, a process of invisibly small events. Conflicts do not "evolve"; they more often occur in an instant, as suggested by the metaphor of collision. The spawning image picks up the metaphor of birth again, but by this point the image is collectively ludicrous.

Had the writer thought more carefully, he might have expressed himself more exactly in literal language:

> As we interact in small ways, we gradually synthesize new social values. When one person behaves according to an old value and another according to a new, the values may conflict, creating a third value that reconciles the other two.

More embarrassing are those passages that confuse elegance with excess—Huxley's passage comes close when he writes about wings of inquiry flapping in an atmosphere of knowledge. Metaphors also invite trouble if you aren't sensitive to the way their literal meanings can unexpectedly revive, as in this student example:

> The classic blitzkrieg relies on a tank-heavy offensive force, supported by ground-support aircraft, to destroy the defender's ability to fight by running amuck [*sic*] in his undefended rear, after penetrating his forward defenses.

The problem with trying to be elegant is that our failures can be so spectacular. And when we fail spectacularly, we are reluctant to try again. I can only encourage you to accept with good humor those first awkward attempts and failures that we have all experienced.

A Last Word

The satisfactions of style include the pleasure we take in the compliments of our readers. But I also know that for many writers the pleasure of crafting a good paragraph, even a single sentence, is often in the sheer achievement of it. What it finally comes down to, I think, is the responsibility we feel for our language and the satisfaction we take in meeting it. It is a satisfaction expressed well, I think, by the philosopher Alfred

North Whitehead, from his book, *The Aims of Education and Other Essays.*

> Finally, there should grow the most austere of all mental qualities; I mean the sense for style. It is an aesthetic sense, based on admiration for the direct attainment of a foreseen end, simply and without waste. Style in art, style in literature, style in science, style in logic, style in practical execution have fundamentally the same aesthetic qualities, namely, attainment and restraint. The love of a subject in itself and for itself, where it is not the sleepy pleasure of pacing a mental quarter-deck, is the love of style as manifested in that study. Here we are brought back to the position from which we started, the utility of education. Style, in its finest sense, is the last acquirement of the educated mind; it is also the most useful. It pervades the whole being. The administrator with a sense for style hates waste; the engineer with a sense for style economizes his material; the artisan with a sense for style prefers good work. Style is the ultimate morality of mind.

A Summary of Summaries

1. Make your style direct by putting characters in your subjects, then join them immediately to verbs naming significant actions.
2. Make your style emphatic by ending your sentences on your most rhetorically salient words.
3. Make your sentences flow by maintaining the crucial connections between major grammatical elements.
4. Make your prose cohesive and coherent by helping your readers see the connection in the string of topics through a series of sentences.
5. Make your sentences concise by reducing redundancy to a minimum.
6. Give your sentences shape by keeping introductory clauses and phrases relatively short, creating coordinate structures after the subject, and extending the line of a sentence with resumptive, summative, and free modifiers.

Appendix

Punctuating for Clarity and Grace

I know there are some Persons who affect to despise it, and treat this whole Subject with the utmost Contempt, as a Trifle far below their Notice, and a Formality unworthy of their Regard: They do not hold it difficult, but despicable; and neglect it, as being above it. Yet many learned Men have been highly sensible to its Use; and some ingenious and elegant Writers have condescended to point their Works with Care; and very eminent Scholars have not disdained to teach the Method of doing it with Propriety.

JAMES BURROW

In music, the punctuation is absolutely strict; the bars and rests are absolutely defined. But our prose cannot be quite strict, because we have to relate it to the audience. In other words we are continually changing the score.

SIR RALPH RICHARDSON

One who uses many periods is a philosopher; many interrogations, a student; many exclamations, a fanatic.

J. L. BASFORD

There are some punctuations that are interesting and there are some that are not.

GERTRUDE STEIN

Most of us view commas and semicolons about as aesthetically interesting as sorting socks. In fact, many think good punctuation is simply a matter of following rules. It is not, of course. Chosen and deployed thoughtfully, your punctuation can help your readers not only see the structure of your longer and more complex sentences but respond to their intended nuances, even note modest moments of elegance. It takes more than a few commas to turn a monotone into the Hallelujah Chorus, but a little care can produce gratifying results.

Some Basic Concepts

I begin with the least you have to know about punctuation, then explore its finer points. I'll address the matter not by describing how to use periods, commas, and so on, but as a functional problem: How do you punctuate the end of a sentence, its beginning, and its middle? I address them in that order because how you end a sentence determines how most readers judge your basic literacy.

Punctuated and Grammatical Sentences

I'll call anything that begins with a capital letter and ends with a period or question/exclamation mark a "punctuated sentence." But we have to distinguish two kinds of punctuated sentences because our readers do; the one you are reading, for example, is one long punctuated sentence, but it does not feel as long as another long sentence you will read in a moment; I have simply chosen to punctuate as a single sentence what I might have chosen to punctuate as a series of shorter ones; all those semicolons and the comma before *but* could have been periods, for example—and that dash could have been a period as well.

I can write a different kind of punctuated sentence, a sentence that I could not break into shorter sentences merely by replacing commas and semicolons with periods, because it is a sentence consisting of several SUBORDINATE CLAUSES, all of them depending on one MAIN or INDEPENDENT CLAUSE—a sentence like this one that you have almost finished but that probably feels longer than that sentence in the previous paragraph, even though it is much shorter.

We have to distinguish those two kinds of punctuated sentences, because readers read them in different ways: They may complain about the length of both, but they read a long sentence comprising a series of short independent clauses more easily than they read a long sentence comprising a series of subordinate clauses. The reason has to do with how we process the grammar of independent and subordinate clauses: At those points where a period *could* occur, we know that we can stop processing the grammar of that segment and start anew on the next, as if there actually were a period there (I rewrite a bit to make sense; underlines indicate where I changed the punctuation):

> We have to distinguish two kinds of punctuated sentences because readers do. The one you are reading, for example, is a single short punctuated sentence. It does not feel as long as another long sentence you will read in a moment. I have simply chosen to punctuate as separate sentences what I earlier punctuated as one long one. That period and the two before it, for example, could have been semicolons. And that period could have been a dash.

On the other hand, even though that second long sentence lets you pause about as often as the first, it forces you to keep sorting out long stretches of its grammar, right to the end. Just as that first sentence does, it starts with an independent clause:

> I can write a different kind of punctuated sentence. . . .

But instead of continuing with a series of independent grammatical sentences, it continues with a series of subordinate clauses:

> . . . a sentence [that I could not break into shorter punctuated sentences merely by replacing a comma and semicolons with periods]$_{1}$, [because it is a sentence consisting of several subordinate clauses, all of them depending on one main or independent clause]$_{2}$—a sentence like this one [that you have almost finished]$_{3}$ but [that probably feels longer than that sentence in the previous paragraph]$_{4}$ [even though it is shorter]$_{5}$.

In the first sentence consisting of short independent units, you can stop sorting out the grammar at the end of each of those units and start over. But in the second, you have to keep figuring out to the end how all the subordinate parts fit together, and that requires a lot more mental work.

Exercise A.1

What is the difference in style between a long punctuated sentence that uses commas, semicolons, and colons to separate grammatical sentences and a passage comprising the same grammatical sentences separated by periods? Revise that second long sentence beginning with "I can write a different kind of punctuated sentence" on p. 234 so at least some of the subordinate clauses are independent clauses. Then set those independent clauses off first with commas, semicolons, and colons. Finally punctuate that revised sentence a second time with periods. How have you changed the style of the sentence? Which revision changes the style more radically: periods, or commas and semicolons?

Simple, Compound, and Complex Sentences

At this point, you may be thinking about that schoolbook definition of "simple," "compound," and "complex": If a sentence consists of a single independent clause, it is *simple.*

> SIMPLE: English dictionaries date back almost 400 years.

If it consists of two or more independent clauses, it is *compound:*

> COMPOUND: [English dictionaries date back almost 400 years]$_1$,[but the greatest of them all is the *Oxford English Dictionary*]$_2$.

If it has an independent clause and at least one subordinate clause, it is *complex.*

> COMPLEX: [While there are many good dictionaries],$_{\text{subordinate}}$ [the greatest of them all is the *Oxford English Dictionary*].$_{\text{independent}}$

The trouble with that schoolbook terminology is that it can mislead us, because we often think that a grammatically simple sentence *feels* more stylistically complex than one that is grammatically complex:

> GRAMMATICALLY SIMPLE: Our review of the test resulted in a decision as to its suspension as a result of complaints from teachers.
>
> GRAMMATICALLY COMPLEX: When we reviewed the test, we decided to suspend it because teachers complained about it.

In what follows, I have to use terms a bit different from these schoolhouse terms.

- The term *grammatical sentence* will refer to a single independent clause plus all of its attached subordinate clauses, if any. The term therefore covers both simple and complex sentences.
- What schoolteachers call a *compound* sentence comprises at least two grammatical sentences.
- A *punctuated* sentence may therefore consist of a single grammatical sentence or of several.

Those are the basics; now we can discuss how to apply them.

Punctuating Ends of Grammatical Sentences

Beyond all other considerations, readers have to know where one grammatical sentence stops and another begins:

> In 1957 and again in 1960, Congress passed civil rights laws that remedied problems of registration and voting this had significant political consequences throughout the South.

We have nine ways to fix that sentence.

Three Common Forms of End Punctuation

1. Period (or Question/Exclamation Mark) Alone The simplest way to signal the end of a grammatical sentence is, of course, with a period:

> ✓ In 1957 and 1960, Congress passed laws that remedied problems of registration and voting. This had significant political consequences throughout the South.

But if you end up with too many short punctuated sentences, readers may feel your prose is choppy. Some writers change short grammatical sentences into subordinate clauses or phrases:

✓ **When Congress passed laws in 1957 and 1960 to remedy problems of registration and voting,** those laws had significant political consequences throughout the South.

✓ The laws **that Congress passed in 1957 and 1960 remedying problems of registration and voting** had significant political consequences throughout the South.

But be cautious: Overdo it and you create the kind of long sentence that seems never to end. To avoid that kind of complexity, you can bring grammatical sentences together in other ways, without seeming choppy.

2. Semicolon Alone A semicolon is like a permeable period; when readers see a semicolon end a grammatical sentence, they assume that they should understand the next sentence to be closely linked to the one they just finished:

✓ In 1957 and again in 1960, Congress passed laws that remedied problems of registration and voting; those laws had significant political consequences throughout the South.

If readers can't see any clear link between the two grammatical sentences, they will experience a small twinge of confusion as they try to figure it out:

> In 1957 and again in 1960, Congress passed laws in order to remedy problems of registration and voting; by 1995 Southern states had thousands of sheriffs, mayors, and other officials from their African-American communities.

A few shared concepts would make the connections clearer:

✓ In 1957 and again in 1960, Congress passed civil rights laws in order to remedy racial problems of registration and voting, particularly in the South; by 1995 Southern states had elected thousands of sheriffs, mayors, and other officials from their African-American communities.

A SPECIAL PROBLEM WITH *HOWEVER:* There is a common occasion on which even well-educated writers confuse readers by using a comma where they need a semicolon or period: when they end one grammatical sentence and begin another with *however*. This is wrong:

> [Taxpayers have supported public education through taxes], **however,** [they are beginning to resist because taxes have been rising so steeply].

That first grammatical sentence must end with a period or a semicolon to signal readers that a second one follows:

✓ [Taxpayers have supported public education through taxes]$_1$; [**however,** they are beginning to resist because taxes have been rising so steeply]$_2$.

Writers probably use a comma there because they often see *however* inside a grammatical sentence, where it should be set off by commas:

✓ [Taxpayers have been willing to support public education through taxes]. [They are beginning to resist, **however,** because taxes have been rising so steeply].

A fairly reliable rule: If you have more than ten or so words before a *however* and as many after, you probably need to change a comma before the *however* to a semicolon or period, because you are likely to have grammatical sentences on both sides of *however.* But double-check to be sure.

3. Comma + COORDINATING CONJUNCTION Readers recognize the end a grammatical sentence when they see a comma, and

- a grammatical sentence follows;
- that sentence begins with a coordinating conjunction: *and, but, yet, for, so, or, nor.*

✓ In the 1950s religion came to be viewed as a bulwark against communism, **so** it was not long after that that atheism was felt to threaten national security.

✓ American intellectuals have often followed Europeans, **but** our culture has proven inhospitable to their brand of socialism.

Again, prefer a period if the two grammatical sentences are long and have their own internal punctuation.

When readers begin a coordinated series of three or more grammatical sentences, they will accept just a comma between the first two, but only if they are short and have no internal punctuation:

✓ Baseball satisfies our love of leisurely skill, basketball speaks to our admiration for speed and grace, and football appeals to our lust for violence.

If either of the first two clauses has internal punctuation, separate them with semicolons:

✓ Baseball, the oldest indigenous American sport and essentially a rural one, satisfies our admiration for precise skill; basketball, our newest sport and now more urban than rural, speaks to our love of speed and grace; and football, a sport both rural and urban, appeals to our lust for violence.

AN EXCEPTION: When you introduce a coordinated pair of short grammatical sentences with a modifier that applies to both of them, omit the comma between them:

✓ By 1995, the economies of the Soviet Union's former satellites had begun to rebound but Russia's had yet to hit bottom.

Four Less Common Forms of End Punctuation

1. Period + Coordinating Conjunction Some readers think it an error to begin a punctuated sentence with a coordinating conjunction. But they are wrong; this is entirely correct:

✓ Education can not guarantee a democracy. But without it, democracy cannot survive.

A *however* there would be too heavy. Like any rhetorical device, of course, this way of linking sentences can become pointless when used to excess. No more than once every page or so is about right, especially for *and*. *And* implies the last in a series or a quick afterthought, an effect that a reader eventually tires of.

2. Semicolon + Coordinating Conjunction Writers rarely end one grammatical sentence with a semicolon and begin the next with a COORDINATING CONJUNCTION, so generally avoid this:

✓ In the 1950s religion came to be viewed as a bulwark against communism; so it was not long after that atheism was felt to threaten national security.

More commonly, they use a comma there. Of course, readers will be grateful for a semicolon if the two grammatical sentences are long with their own internal commas:

✓ Problem solving, one of the most active areas of cognitive psychology, has made great strides in the last decade, particularly in regard to understanding the problem-solving strategies of experts; so it is no surprise that educators have followed that research with interest.

But they would probably appreciate a period even more.

3. Comma Alone Though readers ordinarily do not expect to see just a comma separate two grammatical sentences, they will not be confused if the two are short, balanced in length, and closely linked in meaning—cause-effect, first-second, if-then, this-but-not-that, etc.. Be sure, though, that neither has internal commas. This would be confusing:

> Women, who have always been underpaid, no longer accept that discriminatory treatment, they are now doing something about it.

This is clearer:

✓ Women have always been underpaid, they are now doing something about it.

But a warning: Though writers of the best prose do this, many teachers consider it an error, so be sure of your readers before you experiment.

4. Conjunction Alone Nor is it uncommon to signal the close linkage of two short grammatical sentences with a coordinating conjunction alone, omitting the comma:

✓ Oscar Wilde brazenly violated one of the fundamental laws of British society **and** we all know what happened to him.

Two Special Cases: Colon and Dash

1. Colon Careful readers will think you are a more than common writer if you end a sentence with an appropriate colon:

They take it as shorthand for *to illustrate, for example, that is, let me expand on what I just said, therefore:*

✓ Only one question remains: What if we lose money?

✓ Dance is not widely supported: No company operates at a profit, and there are few outside major cities.

A colon also lets you signal more obviously than with a comma that you are self-consciously balancing the structure, sound, and meaning of one clause against that of another:

✓ Civil disobedience is the public conscience of a democracy: mass enthusiasm is the public consensus of a tyranny.

Avoid inserting a colon where it breaks up the structure of a clause:

> Genetic counseling requires: a thorough knowledge of statistical genetics, an awareness of choices open to parents, and the psychological competence to deal with emotional trauma.

Put the colon after a whole subject-verb-object structure:

✓ Genetic counseling requires the following: a thorough knowledge of statistical genetics, an awareness of choices open to parents, and the psychological competence to deal with emotional trauma.

If what follows the colon is a grammatical sentence, capitalize the first word or not, depending on how much you want to emphasize what follows.

2. Dash You can signal the same balance more informally with a dash—it suggests the casual immediacy of an afterthought:

✓ Stonehenge is a wonder—only a genius could have conceived it.

Try that with a colon: it makes a difference.

Summary: Nine Ways to End a Grammatical Sentence

1. Comma alone	I win, you lose.
2. Conjunction alone	I win **and** you lose.

3. Dash	I win—you lose.
4. Comma + coordinating conjunction	I win**, and** you lose.
5. Semicolon	I win**;** you lose.
6. Colon	I win**:** you lose.
7. Semicolon + coordinating conjunction	I win**; and** you lose.
8. Period + coordination conjunction	I win**. And** you lose.
9. Period	I win**.** You lose.

Readers take these ways of ending grammatical sentences as increasingly emphatic (personal taste varies). If you choose punctuation that separates grammatical sentences only slightly—just a comma or conjunction—be certain your readers can recognize that they are closely linked, because they will look for that linkage.

Punctuating Beginnings

Punctuation at the beginning of a sentence is not an issue when the sentence begins directly with its SUBJECT, as this one does. However, as with this one, when it forces a reader to plow through several introductory modifying phrases and clauses, especially when they have their own internal punctuation, and those readers might be confused by it all (as you probably are right now), forget trying to punctuate it right: Rewrite:

> If you open a sentence with complicated phrases and clauses, you are likely to confuse your readers, so rewrite it.

There are a few other rules that your readers will expect you always to follow, but more often you have to rely on your judgment to decide how best to help them.

Five Reliable Rules

1. Always punctuate if a reader might misunderstand the structure of the sentence. Do **not** do this:

   > When a lawyer concludes her argument has to be easily remembered by a jury.

2. Never put a semicolon at the end of an introductory element, no matter how long and complicated. Readers ordi-

narily take semicolons to mean they have come to the end of a grammatical sentence (but see p. 252). Do **not** do this:

> Although the Administration knew that Iraq's invasion of Kuwait threatened American interests in Saudi Arabia; it did not immediately order military.

Always use a comma there.

3. Do not put a comma after a SUBORDINATING CONJUNCTION. Do **not** do this:

> Although, the practice of punctuation is not complicated, it is rarely mastered.

4. Do not put a comma after coordinating conjunctions (*and, but, yet, for, so, or, nor*) if the next element is the subject. Do **not** do this:

> But, we cannot know whether life on other planets realizes that we're here and simply prefers to ignore us.

Some writers who punctuate heavily put a comma after *and, but, yet, for, so, or, nor* if an introductory word or phrase follows:

✓ Yet, during this period, prices continued to rise.

Such heavy punctuation retards a reader just a bit, but that is your choice. These are also correct and for the reader, perhaps a bit swifter:

✓ Yet during this period, prices continued to rise.

✓ Yet during this period prices continued to rise.

5. Put a comma after an introductory word or phrase that comments on the whole of the following sentence or that connects one sentence to another.

These include elements like *fortunately, possibly, perhaps,* etc. and *however, nevertheless, regardless, instead,* etc. Since readers hear sentences in their minds' ear, they expect a pause after such words.

✓ Fortunately, we found that these groups are as healthy as others.

If, however, you find yourself starting sentence after sentence with a word or two and a comma, consider revising.

That kind of opening retards a reader just when she should be picking up speed. A series of such sentences makes a whole passage feel hesitant.

Three common exceptions: We typically omit a comma after *now, thus,* and *hence:*

✓ Now it is clear that many will not support this position.

✓ Thus the only alternative is to choose some other action.

Three Reliable Principles

1. Readers need no punctuation after a short introductory phrase directly before a subject:

   ✓ Once again we find similar responses to such stimuli.

   ✓ In 1945 few realized how the war had transformed us.

   It is not wrong to put a comma there, but again, it slows a reader just when you may want him to be picking up speed.

2. Readers often need a comma after a *long* introductory phrase or clause:

   ✓ When a lawyer begins her opening statement with a dry recital of the law and how it must be applied to the case before the court, the jury is likely to nod off.

   But there are other considerations: How long will a reader feel is too long, and how closely do you want your reader to connect the meanings of the two clauses? Readers don't need a comma when the clause is shorter than, say, ten or so words, its subject is the same as the subject of the main clause, and its meaning closely depends on the meaning of the main clause:

   ✓ When Hitler realized that he had lost the war he ordered his army to raze every city through which it retreated.

   But if the subjects of the clauses differ and the ideas contrast, a comma helps the reader sense the opposition. Compare:

✓ Since we accepted the IRS data we dropped further appeals.

✓ Although the IRS overruled us, we will still follow our original procedures.

3. Readers do not expect a comma to separate a subject from its VERB. Do not do this:

> A sentence that consists of many complex subordinate clauses and long phrases and that all precede a verb, may seem to some students to demand a comma somewhere.

As we've said before, readers generally don't like long subjects, so the best policy is to keep your subjects short, making a comma unnecessary under any circumstances. Readers need a comma between a subject and a verb only when a phrase or clause clearly *interrupts* that expected connection. (See the next section on interruptions.)

Occasionally, you cannot avoid a long subject because it consists of a list of items with internal punctuation:

> The president, the vice president, the secretaries of the departments, senators, members of the House of Representatives, and Supreme Court justices, take an oath that pledges them to uphold the Constitution.

In these circumstances, help your readers sort out the subject from the rest of the sentence by creating a *SUMMATIVE subject.*

- First, insert a colon or a dash at the end of that long subject.
- Then insert a word that summarizes the preceding list:

✓ The president, the vice president, the secretaries of the departments, senators, members of the House of Representatives, and Supreme Court justices: **all** take an oath that pledges them to uphold the Constitution.

Use a dash or a colon depending on how formal you want to seem.

PUNCTUATING MIDDLES

This is where explanations get messy, because to punctuate inside a grammatical sentence—more specifically, inside a clause—you have to consider not only grammar, but the nuances of rhythm, meaning, and emphasis that you want your readers to hear in their mind's ear.

> ***Here's the point:*** You can rely on four principles:
>
> 1. Inside the boundaries of a clause, you always use paired marks of punctuation—commas, parentheses, or dashes. Never use semicolons (but see p. 252).
> 2. Set off what prominently interrupts grammatical connections with commas, parentheses, or dashes. Never use semicolons.
> 3. Set off loose commentary with commas, parentheses, or dashes. Never use semicolons.
> 4. Use commas to separate items in a series; use semicolons to set off items in a series only when they have internal commas.

Interruptions

When you insert a long phrase or short clause between a subject and its verb or between a verb and its OBJECT, your readers have a marginally harder time making the two grammatical connections that hold those three basic elements of a sentence together. So in general, avoid interruptions (see pp. 201–04). But if for reasons of emphasis or nuance, you decide you want to interrupt those connections, you have to help your reader recognize the interruption by setting it off with *paired* commas or dashes:

> A sentence >, if it consists of many complex subordinate clauses and long phrases and that all precede a verb**,** < may seem to need a comma somewhere.

Readers need commas before and after shorter ADVERBIAL PHRASES, depending on what kind of emphasis you want them to feel. The general principle of emphasis is this: Readers feel that emphasis falls on whatever immediately follows a pause. Compare the different emphases in these:

✓ Modern poetry has in recent years become more relevant to the average reader.

✓ Modern poetry has, in recent years, become more relevant to the average reader.

✓ Modern poetry has become, in recent years, more relevant to the average reader.

✓ The antagonism between Congress and the president has created utter distrust among every group of voters.

✓ The antagonism between Congress and the president has created, among every group of voters, utter distrust.

Loose Commentary

"Loose commentary" is different from an interruption, because you can usually move what interrupts someplace else in the sentence. But loose commentary modifies what it is next to, and so it cannot be moved. So it needs to be set off with commas, parentheses, or dashes.

It is difficult to explain exactly what counts as "loose commentary" because it depends on both grammar and meaning. One familiar distinction is between RESTRICTIVE and NONRESTRICTIVE CLAUSES (see pp. 23–25) and APPOSITIVES.

We use no commas with **restrictive** modifiers because they are not loose commentary; they are necessary to understand the sentence:

✓ Tax deduction for child support belongs to the parent with whom the child resides.

But we always set off **non**restrictive modifiers with *paired* commas (unless the modifier ends the sentence), because they are loose commentary, not necessary to understand the meaning of the sentence:

✓ We had to rebuild the larynx, which is the source of speech, with cartilage from the shoulder.

You can achieve a more casual effect with a dash:

✓ We had to rebuild the larynx—which is the source of speech—with cartilage from the shoulder.

An appositive is actually just a truncated nonrestrictive clause:

✓ We had to rebuild the larynx, the source of speech, with cartilage from the shoulder.

A dash is particularly useful when the "loose commentary" itself has internal commas. Readers find this confusing:

All the nations of Eastern Europe, Poland, Hungary, Romania, Czechoslovakia, Bulgaria, and Yugoslavia, have been in the middle of an East-West tug-of-war.

They understand this kind of structure more easily if they can see that loose modifier set off with dashes or parentheses:

✓ All the nations of Eastern Europe—Poland, Hungary, Romania, Czechoslovakia, Bulgaria, and Yugoslavia—have been in the middle of an East-West tug-of-war.

Use parentheses when you want your reader to hear your comment as a *sotto voce* aside:

✓ The brain (at least that part that controls nonprimitive functions) may comprise several little brains operating simultaneously.

or as an explanatory footnote inside a sentence:

✓ Lamarck (1744–1829) was a French naturalist and pre-Darwinian evolutionist.

✓ The poetry of the *fin de siècle* (end of the century) was characterized by a world-weariness and fashionable despair.

When loose commentary closes a sentence, use a comma to separate it from the rest of the sentence; if the meaning of the modifier is crucial to the meaning of the sentence, omit the comma. Contrast these:

✓ I wandered through Europe, seeking a place where I could write undisturbed.

✓ I spent my time seeking a place where I could write undisturbed.

✓ Offices will be closed July 2–6, as announced in the daily bulletin.

✓ When closing the offices, secure all safes as prescribed in the Operating Manual.

✓ Historians have overlooked the effect of social changes, at least in this country.

✓ These records must be maintained at least until the IRS has reviewed them.

Punctuating Coordinated Elements

Punctuating Two Coordinate Elements

Generally speaking, do not insert a comma between only two coordinated elements. Compare these:

As computers have become sophisticated, and powerful they have taken over more clerical, and bookkeeping tasks.

✓ As computers have become sophisticated and powerful they have taken over more clerical and bookkeeping tasks.

Three Exceptions

1. To achieve a dramatic contrast, put a comma after even a short coordinate element if you want to emphasize a contrast between the first and second one:

   ✓ The ocean is nature's most glorious creation, and its most destructive.

   This use of a comma is especially emphatic before a *but:*

   ✓ Organ transplants are becoming more common, but not less expensive.

2. If you want your readers to feel the cumulative power of a coordinated pair (or more), drop the *and* and insert a comma. Compare these:

   ✓ Lincoln never had a formal education and never owned a large library.

✓ Lincoln never had a formal education, never owned a large library.

✓ The lesson of the pioneers was to ignore conditions that seemed difficult or even overwhelming and to get on with the business of subduing a hostile environment.

✓ The lesson of the pioneers was to ignore conditions that seemed difficult or even overwhelming, to get on with the business of subduing a hostile environment.

3. Put a comma between long coordinate pairs only if you think you have to give your readers a chance to breathe or to sort out the grammar. Compare:

   It is in the graveyard that Hamlet finally realizes that the inevitable end of life is the grave and clay and that regardless of one's station in life the end of all pretentiousness and all plotting and counter-plotting must be dust.

   A comma after *clay* signals a natural pause:

   ✓ It is in the graveyard that Hamlet finally realizes that the inevitable end of all life is the grave and clay, and that regardless of one's station in life, the end of all pretentiousness and all plotting and counter-plotting must be dust.

More importantly, the comma after *clay* sorts out the structure of a potentially confusing *grave and clay and that regardless.*

In this next sentence, because the first half of a coordination is long, a reader might have a problem connecting the second to its origin:

> Conrad's *Heart of Darkness* brilliantly dramatizes those primitive impulses that lie deep in each of us and stir only in our darkest dreams but asserts the need for the values that control those impulses.

A comma after *dreams* would clearly mark the end of one coordinate member and the beginning of the next:

✓ Conrad's *Heart of Darkness* brilliantly dramatizes those primitive impulses that lie deep in each of us and stir only in our darkest dreams, but asserts the need for the values that control those impulses.

On the other hand, if you find yourself trying to make sense out of a complicated sentence with punctuation alone, you probably need to revise the whole sentence.

Punctuating a Series of Three or More Coordinated Elements

Finally, there is the matter of punctuating a series of three or more coordinated elements. First decide whether in a series of three you are someone who as a matter of principle does or does not put a comma before the *and*. Either is acceptable. Compare these:

✓ His wit, his charm and his loyalty made him our friend.

✓ His wit, his charm, and his loyalty made him our friend.

Both are correct, but be consistent. If any of the items in the series has its own internal commas, then readers rely on semicolons to see how they should group the items:

✓ In mystery novels, the principal action ought to be economical, organic, and logical; fascinating, yet not exotic; clear, but complicated enough to hold the reader's interest.

Exercise A.2

These passages lack their original punctuation. Slash marks indicate grammatical sentences. Punctuate them three times, once using the least punctuation possible, a second time using as much varied punctuation as you can, and then a third time as you think best. You might also analyze these passages for features of elegance, especially how their sentences end. You can even improve some.

1. Scientists and philosophers of science tend to speak as if "scientific language" were intrinsically precise as if

those who use it must understand one another's meaning even if they disagree / but in fact scientific language is not as different from ordinary language as is commonly believed / it too is subject to imprecision and ambiguity and hence to imperfect understanding / moreover new theories or arguments are rarely if ever constructed by way of clear-cut steps of induction deduction and verification or falsification / neither are they defended rejected or accepted in so straightforward a manner / in practice scientists combine the rules of scientific methodology with a generous admixture of intuition aesthetics and philosophical commitment / the importance of what are sometimes called extrarational or extralogical components of thought in the *discovery* of a new principle or law is generally acknowledged/ . . . but the role of these extralogical components in persuasion and acceptance in making an argument convincing is less frequently discussed partly because they are less visible / the ways in which the credibility or effectiveness of an argument depends on the realm of common experiences on extensive practice in communicating those experiences in a common language are hard to see precisely because such commonalities are taken for granted / only when we step out of such a "consensual domain" when we can stand out on the periphery of a community with a common language do we begin to become aware of the unarticulated premises mutual understandings and assumed practices of the group even in those subjects that lend themselves most readily to quantification / discourse depends heavily on conventions and interpretation conventions that are acquired over years of practice and participation in a community.

—from Evelyn Fox Keller, *A Feeling for the Organism: The Life and Work of Barbara McClintock*

2. In fact of course the notion of universal knowledge has always been an illusion / but it is an illusion fostered by the monistic view of the world in which a few great central truths determine in all its wonderful and amazing proliferation everything else that is true / we are not to-

day tempted to search for these keys that unlock the whole of human knowledge and of man's experience / we know that we are ignorant / we are well taught it / and the more surely and deeply we know our own job the better able we are to appreciate the full measure of our pervasive ignorance / we know that these are inherent limits compounded no doubt and exaggerated by that sloth and that complacency without which we would not be men at all / but knowledge rests on knowledge / what is new is meaningful because it departs slightly from what was known before / this is a world of frontiers where even the liveliest of actors or observers will be absent most of the time from most of them / perhaps this sense was not so sharp in the village that village which we have learned a little about but probably do not understand too well the village of slow change and isolation and fixed culture which evokes our nostalgia even if not our full comprehension / perhaps in the villages men were not so lonely / perhaps they found in each other a fixed community a fixed and only slowly growing store of knowledge of a single world / even that we may doubt / for there seem to be always in the culture of such times and places vast domains of mystery if not unknowable then imperfectly known endless and open.

—J. Robert Oppenheimer, "The Sciences and Man's Community,"
from *Science and the Common Understanding*

SUMMING UP

Rather than summarize this detailed material, I offer just a few simple principles: Always signal the end of a grammatical sentence (p. 242); always observe the five reliable rules (p. 243). Beyond that, just use your good judgment: Punctuate in ways that will help your readers see those connections and separations that they have to see to make sense of your sentences. That means that you must put yourself in the place of your reader, not easy to do, but something every competent writer must learn to do. On the other hand, write a clearly structured sentence in the first place, and your punctuation will take care of itself.

Glossary

Grammar is the ground of all.
William Langland

Most of the grounds of the world's troubles are matters of grammar.
Montaigne

There is a satisfactory boniness about grammar which the flesh of sheer vocabulary requires before it can become vertebrate and walk the earth. But to study it for its own sake, without relating it to function, is utter madness.
Anthony Burgess

Thou hast most traitorously corrupted the youth of the realm in erecting a grammar school. . . . It will be proved to thy face, that thou hast men about thee that usually talk of a noun and a verb, and such abominable words as no Christian ear can endure to hear.
William Shakespeare, 2 Henry VI

What follows is no tight theory of grammar, just definitions useful for the terms in the text. Where the text discusses something at length, I refer you to those pages in the interest of saving space here.

Action: A word that includes movement, feeling, cognition, etc. Prototypically, an action is expressed by a verb: *move, hate, think, discover.* But actions also appear in NOMINALIZATIONS: *movement, hatred, thought, discovery.* Associated with actions are conditions, typically expressed by adjectives: *able, intelligent, plausible.* These may also be nominalized: *ability, intelligence, plausibility* (pp. 49–50).

Active: Distinguish between what feels active and what, by grammatical definition, is a VERB in the active voice (pp. 80–81).

> Discovery of the deficit **required** termination of the project.
>
> When the deficit **was discovered,** the project **was terminated.**

A grammatically active verb has a SUBJECT that is typically the AGENT of its action, occurs in its PAST PARTICIPLE form only after *have* and has an OBJECT after the verb: ***I have*** *brok**en** the code.*

Adjective: A word you can put *very* in front of: *very old, very interesting.* Exceptions: *major, additional, resumptive,* etc. Since this is also a test for ADVERBS, you can further identify adjectives by trying them out between *the* and a noun: *The* **occupational** *hazard, the* **major** *reason,* etc. Unfortunately, some nouns occur in the same position—*the* **chemical** *hazard.*

Adjectival Clause: A clause that modifies a noun. Also called RELATIVE CLAUSES, they usually begin with a relative pronoun: *which, that, whom, whose, who.* There are two kinds: RESTRICTIVE and NONRESTRICTIVE.

> The book **that** *I read* was good. My car, **which** *you saw,* is gone.

Adjectival Phrase: An ADJECTIVE and what attaches to it: *so* ***full*** *that it burst.*

Adverb: Adverbs modify all parts of speech except NOUNS:

Adjectives:	**extremely** large, **rather** old, **very** tired
Verbs:	**frequently** spoke, **often** slept, left **here**

Adverbs:	**very** carefully, **somewhat** often, **a bit** late
Articles:	**precisely** the man I meant, **just** the thing we need
Clause:	**Fortunately,** we were on time

Adverbial Clause: A kind of SUBORDINATE CLAUSE. It modifies a verb or adjective, indicating time, cause, condition, etc., and usually begins with subordinating conjunctions like *because, when, if, since, while, unless:*

If you leave, I will stop. **Because** he left, I did too.

Adverbial Phrase: The adverb and what attaches to it: *too **fast** to catch.*

Agent: A kind of CHARACTER. Prototypically, agents are flesh-and-blood, but for our purposes, an agent is the *seeming* source of any ACTION, the entity without which the action could not occur.

She criticized the program in this report.

Often, we can convert the means by which we do something into a seeming agent:

This report criticizes the program.

Do not confuse agents with SUBJECTS. They prototypically are subjects, but an agent can be in a grammatical OBJECT: *I underwent an interrogation by **the police*** (pp. 72–77).

Appositive: A word or phrase that modifies a noun but that is not necessary to identify it uniquely. An appositive is just a reduced NONRESTRICTIVE CLAUSE:

This report, **which is a devastating criticism of the program,** is true.

This report, **a devastating criticism of the program,** is true.

Article: Easier to list than define: *a, the, this, these, that, those.*

Character: Prototypically, a flesh-and-blood human who acts or is acted on. If the character acts, it is an AGENT; if acted on, a GOAL. We also count as characters inanimate entities if a writer repeatedly refers to them, particularly in the SUBJECT/TOPIC of several consecutive sentences. By this definition, abstract NOUNS can count as a kind of character. Thus *cognitive complexity* is a character if we repeatedly use it as the subject of VERBS (pp. 72–77).

Clause: A clause has two defining characteristics:

1. It is a sequence of at least one SUBJECT + VERB.
2. The verb agrees with the subject in number and can be made past or present.

By this definition, these next are all clauses:

She left that they leave if she left why he is leaving

These next are not, because the verbal form cannot be turned into a past tense nor does it agree in number with the putative subject:

for her to **go** her **having gone**

Complement: What ever completes a VERB:

I am **home.** You seem **tired.** She helped **me.**

Compound Noun: Spelling alone does not signal when consecutive nouns constitute a compound noun. Some are separate words: *space capsule, retirement home;* some are hyphenated: *mother-in-law, eighty-two;* some are one word: *airport, bookkeeper.* A reliable test is pronunciation: If the first word is stressed, it is a compound word: *doghouse, skyscraper, book dealer.* On the other hand, some phrases that seem to be compounds are stressed on the second word: *garden path, stone wall, father confessor* (pp. 94–95).

Conjunction: Usually defined as a word that links other words, PHRASES, or CLAUSES. (But so do VERBS and PREPOSITIONS.) They are easier to illustrate than define (the first two are also categorized as subordinating conjunctions):

ADVERBIAL conjunctions:	because, although, when, since, etc.
RELATIVE conjunction:	who, whom, whose, which, that
SENTENCE conjunction:	thus, however, therefore, nevertheless
COORDINATING conjunction:	and, but, yet, for, so, or, nor

CORRELATIVE coordinating conjunctions:	both X and Y, not only X but Y, either X or Y, neither X nor Y, X as well as Y

Coordination: The process of joining grammatically equal elements (pp. 191–195):

Same part of speech: *you* **and** *I, red* **and** *black, run* **or** *jump.*

PHRASES: *In the house* **but** *not in the basement.*

CLAUSES: *when I leave* **or** *when you arrive.*

Correlative Conjunction: Ordinarily, the second conjunction of a pair of correlative conjunctions should precede a word, PHRASE, or CLAUSE that exactly parallels the first:

Not:

He **both** *had the data* **and** *the equipment* to display it.

✓ He had **both** *the data* **and** *the equipment* to display it.

Not:

We will **either** *arrive on Monday* **or** *on Wednesday.*

✓ We will arrive **either** *on Monday* **or** *on Wednesday.*

✓ We will arrive on **either** *Monday* **or** *Wednesday.*

Dangling Modifier: A phrase whose implicit subject is different from the explicit subject of the CLAUSE that the modifier attaches to:

To understand this answer, the question has to be analyzed carefully.

The implicit subject of *to understand* is some unnamed person, but the explicit subject of the following clause is *the question.* To fix this, one or the other has to be changed (pp. 206–07):

✓ For anyone to understand this answer, the question has to be analyzed.

To understand the answer, you have to analyze the question.

Dependent Clause: Any CLAUSE that cannot be punctuated as a MAIN CLAUSE, one beginning with a capital letter and ending with a period or question mark. A dependent clause usually begins with a subordinating conjunction such as *because, if, when, which, that,* etc.:

Why he left. Because he left. Which he left.

Direct Object: The noun that follows a transitive verb and that can be made the subject of a PASSIVE verb:

I found the **money.** → **The money** was found by me.

Distinguish this from indirect objects: *I gave **my friend** the money.*

Finite Verb: A verb that can be made past or present. These are finite verbs because we can change their tense from past to present and vice versa:

She **wantS** to leave. → She **wantED** to leave.

These are not finite verbs because we cannot change them:

She wants to **leaveS.** → She wants to **leaveD.**

Fragment: A PHRASE or DEPENDENT CLAUSE that begins with a capital letter and ends with a period, question mark, or exclamation mark:

Because I left. Though I am here. What you did.

These are complete sentences:

✓ She left because I did.

✓ Though I am here, he is not.

✓ I know what you did.

Free Modifier: A modifier that may appear either after a main clause or before. It usually begins with a verb in its PRESENT or PAST PARTICIPLE form, less often with an ADJECTIVE (pp. 198–99):

The dean ended the meeting, **hoping that everyone was happy.**

Hoping that everyone was happy, the dean ended the meeting.

The dean ended the meeting, **happy that the matter was settled.**

Gerund: A NOMINALIZATION created by adding *-ing* to a VERB:

When she **solved** the problem, she helped me.

Her **solving** the problem helped me.

Goal: That toward which the ACTION of a VERB is directed. In most cases, goals are expressed as DIRECT OBJECTS.

I see **you.** I broke **the dish.** I built **a house.**

But in some cases, the literal goal can be the SUBJECT of an ACTIVE VERB:

I underwent an interrogation. **She** received a warm welcome.

Grammatical Sentence: A single independent CLAUSE plus all attached modifiers (pp. 234–36).

Hedge: A word that softens the certainty of a claim: *possibly, probably, may, indicate, suggest, appear, seem.* The opposite of an INTENSIFIER (pp. 175–77).

Independent Clause: A CLAUSE that does not modify any other element in a sentence.

Infinitive: A VERB that cannot be made past or present. It is often but not always preceded by the word *to:*

He decided to **stay.** I watched him **leave.**

Intensifier: A word that heightens truth or certainty: ***very*** *old,* ***certainly*** *true,* ***completely*** *useless.* The opposite of a HEDGE (pp. 177–78).

Intransitive Verb: A verb that does not take an OBJECT and so cannot be made PASSIVE. These are not transitive verbs:

He **exists.** They **left** town. She **became** a doctor.

Linking Verb: A VERB with a COMPLEMENT that modifies its SUBJECT.

He **is** my brother. They **became** teachers. She **seems** reliable.

Main Clause: There are two kinds of clauses: *main* (or *independent*) and *subordinate* (or *dependent*). A main or independent clause can be punctuated as an independent sentence:

I left. Why did you leave? We are leaving.

A subordinate or dependent clause cannot be punctuated as an independent sentence. It must be attached to a main or independent clause. These would be incorrectly punctuated:

Because she left. That they left. Whom you spoke to.

Metadiscourse: Writing about the writer writing and the reader reading. This includes connecting devices such as *therefore, however, for example,* and expressions of the author's attitude and intention: *I believe, in my opinion;* comment about what the writer is about to assert: *most people believe, it is widely assumed, allegedly;* remarks addressed directly to the reader: *as you can see, consider now the problem of* (pp. 89–91, 172–178).

Nominalization: A noun derived from an adjective or verb (pp. 49–50):

decide → **decision,** depart → **departure,** happy→ **happiness**

Nominalize: To turn an adjective or verb into a noun (pp. 49–50):

decide → decision, depart→ departure, happy→ happiness

Nonrestrictive Clause: A clause that does not uniquely identify the noun phrase it modifies:

My birthday, ***which I keep a secret,*** *was last month.*

Since we have only one birthday, any clause I attach to that word must be nonrestrictive because the word is already uniquely identified. Since it is nonrestrictive, it must begin with *which* (not *that*) and be set off with commas (pp. 23–25).

Noun: A word that fits the frame: *The [____] is good* or *[____] is good.* Some are concrete: *dog, rock, car;* others abstract: *ambition, space, speed.* The nouns that most concern us are NOMINALIZATIONS, nouns derived from VERBS or ADJECTIVES: *act → action, wide → width.*

Object: There are three kinds:

1. Direct object: the NOUN following a TRANSITIVE VERB:

I *read* **the book.** We *followed* **the car.**

2. PREPOSITIONAL object: the noun following a preposition:

in **the house,** *by* **the walk,** *across* **the street,** *with* **fervor**

3. Indirect object: the noun between a verb and its direct object: *I gave* ***him*** *a tip.*

Parallelism: PHRASES or CLAUSES are parallel when they have similar grammatical elements, similar sound patterns, and/or similar or deliberately contrasting semantic elements (pp. 191–94, 211–20):

I have neither { the time to explore these questions / nor / the temper to examine their implications. }

Passive: A passive verb has three and sometimes four characteristics: (1) the SUBJECT is the GOAL of the ACTION of the VERB; (2) the main verb appears after a form of *be;* (3) the verb is in its PAST PARTICIPLE form; (4) the AGENT of the action may be in a PREPOSITIONAL PHRASE after the verb (pp. 80–86):

> The cryptologists broke the code.
>
> → The code^{1} **was**^{2} brok**en**^{3} [by **cryptologists**^{4}].

Past Participle: Usually the same form as the past tense *-ed: jumped, worked, investigated.* Irregular verbs have irregular forms: *seen, broken, swum, stolen,* etc. Past participle forms of TRANSITIVE VERBS also function as modifiers:

> a **broken** arm, a **twisted** leg, a **scratched** face

Phrase: A group of words constituting a unit but not including a SUBJECT and a FINITE VERB.

Possessive: *my, your, his, her, its, their* or a noun ending with *-'s* or *-s': the* ***dog's*** *tail.*

Predicate: Whatever follows the whole SUBJECT, beginning with the VERB PHRASE, including the COMPLEMENT and whatever attaches to it.

> He [**went downtown yesterday to buy a hat**]. $_{\text{predicate}}$

Preposition: Easier to list than define: *in, on, up, over, of, at, by,* etc.

Prepositional Phrase: The preposition plus its OBJECT: *in the house, by the door.*

Present Participle: The *-ing* form of a VERB. It has three functions:

1. The PROGRESSIVE form of a verb following a form of *be:* He *was* **running.**
2. A modifier: ***Running*** streams are beautiful.
3. A GERUND: ***Running*** can kill you. (though the participle *-ing* and the gerund *-ing* descend into Modern English from different ancestors.)

Progressive: The PRESENT PARTICIPLE form of the verb:

> *Running* streams are beautiful.

Punctuated Sentence: Whatever begins with a capital letter and ends with a period, question mark, or exclamation point (pp. 234–36).

Relative Clause: A CLAUSE that modifies a noun:

> I read the book **that you reviewed.**

Relative Pronoun: *who, which, whose, that.*

Restrictive Clause: A restrictive clause is also called a "defining" clause. A restrictive clause uniquely identifies a thing. Most of us own more than one book, so when I refer to a book that I had not yet mentioned, I'd have to "restrict" my reference to a particular book: *Let me tell you about a book* ***that I just bought.*** In this case, we introduce the clause with *that* or *which* (but check p. 25 for this debatable question), and we do not set it off with commas (pp. 23–25).

Resumptive Modifier: A modifier that repeats a word toward the end of a CLAUSE and continue with a RELATIVE CLAUSE (pp. 196–97):

> We need to create new opportunities,
> **opportunities that will be open to everyone.**

Run-on Sentence: A PUNCTUATED SENTENCE consisting of two or more GRAMMATICAL SENTENCES not separated by either a coordinating conjunction or any mark of punctuation this entry illustrates a run-on sentence.

Simple Subject: The simple subject is the smallest unit inside the WHOLE SUBJECT that determines whether a verb will be singular or plural:

The **books** that each person must read are listed.

Stress: The last part of a CLAUSE that receives the strongest emphasis (pp. 146–51):

The program succeeded not because of luck but because of **hárd wórk.**

Subject: The subject is what the VERB agrees with in number:

Two men *are* at the door. **One man** *is* at the door.

We can see in these sentences that *there* is the subject of neither verb.

There *was a* man at the door. **There** *were two men* at the door.

Distinguish the WHOLE SUBJECT from its SIMPLE SUBJECT.

Subjunctive: A form of the VERB that we use when we talk about events that are contrary to fact: *If he* ***were*** *President. . . .*

Subordinate Clause: Subordinate clauses usually begin with a SUBORDINATING CONJUNCTION such as *if, when, unless,* or *which, that, who:*

There are three kinds of subordinate clauses: nominal (NOUN), ADVERBIAL, and ADJECTIVAL.

I know **that I left.** I left **because** he did. I am the man **who left.**

Subordinating Conjunction: *Because, if, when, since, unless, which, although, who, that, whose,* etc.

Summative Modifier: A modifier that modifies a whole clause. It begins with a word that sums up what has gone before and continues with a relative clause (pp. 198–99):

Japan is downsizing its industrial base,
a process that will affect world trade.

Summative Subject: A SUBJECT that sums up in a single word a series of preceding words (p. 248):

Poland, Hungary, Bulgaria, Romania—**they all** know the meaning of government oppression.

Theme: The key concepts that run through a series of sentences (pp. 116–18, 143–44).

Topic: The unit of information that the rest of the sentence comments on. It is the psychological SUBJECT of a sentence. The topic of a sentence is usually also its grammatical subject:

China will eventually become a major industrial nation.

We cannot define topic any more exactly because it may be in an introductory PREPOSITIONAL PHRASE.

In regard to **China,** it will eventually become. . . .

Topics can appear in other constructions, especially after METADISCOURSE.

I believe that **China** will eventually become. . . .

There is general agreement as to **China's** eventually becoming a major industrial nation.

(pp. 107–111)

Topic String: The sequence of TOPICS through a single passage (pp. 107–11).

Transitive Verb: A VERB with a DIRECT OBJECT. The direct object prototypically "receives" an ACTION. The prototypical direct object can be made the SUBJECT of a PASSIVE verb:

We **read** the book. → The book **was read** by us.

By this definition, *resemble, become, stand* (as in *He stands six feet tall*) are not transitive.

Verb: The word that must agree with the SUBJECT in number and that can be inflected for past or present:

The book **is** ready. The books **were** returned.

A verb can also appear in its infinitive form: *I want to **leave**. I saw him **leave**.*

Whole Subject: You can identify a whole subject once you have identified the VERB: Put a *who* or a *what* in front of the verb and turn the sentence into a question. The fullest answer to the question is the whole subject:

> The ability of the city to manage education is an accepted fact.
>
> Question: **What** is an accepted fact?
>
> Answer (and whole subject): The ability of the city to manage education.

This doesn't work with sentences beginning with *there.*

Possible Answers to Exercises

There is no perfect revision to any of these exercises, so do not feel that your revision has to match my suggested one word-for-word. I have no doubt that many of you will come up with revisions better than these.

3.8

When you nominalize many verbs, you frustrate your readers—they expect that characters will appear as subjects and their crucial actions as verbs. But when you drop characters out of sentences altogether, you frustrate them even more. You no doubt felt that when you read this version of Red Riding Hood. . . . I was able to drop Little Red Riding Hood and the Wolf from the story when I nominalized the verb *walk* into. . . .

3.9

Nominalizations are italicized; verbs and adjectives boldfaced.

2a. *Smoking, pregnancy,* **may lead,** *injury;* 2b. **write, understand**
4a. *Complaints, apathy,* **provide,** *suggestions, dispelling;* 4b. **have claimed, watch, tend, become, able, has demonstrated, be.**
6a. **need, know, are being logged, can save;** 6b. **is,** *need, analysis, intensity, use,* **provide,** *projection.*
8a. **examine, influence,** *advertising, advertising,* **respond,** *influences,* **create, appeals;** 8b. **is,** *review, responses, judgments, well-formedness, knowledge, reading.*

3.10

Don't worry if your revisions are slightly different from these.

1. There have been arguments by some as to the elevation of global temperatures as a result of carbon dioxide in the atmosphere.
3. Attempts by AIDS researchers at identifying the HIV virus have resulted in the failure of the development of a vaccine that will result in the immunization of those at risk.
5. A discovery by educators of uses of computer-assisted instruction could result in the teaching of subjects of greater complexity and faster learning by students.
7. Many professional athletes have arrived at the discovery that they lack a preparation for life after stardom because of their protection by their teams from problems that the rest of us make adjustment to every day.

3.11

2. When pregnant women smoke, they may injure their fetus.
4. Although editorial writers complain that voters are apathetic, they have not suggested how to dispel that apathy.
6. We must analyze how intensively students are using our libraries so that we can reliably project what new resources we need.
8. In this study, we review how readers respond to rhetorical patterns and judge texts to be well-formed when they know the subject matter of the text before they read.

3.12

2. President Nixon's aides asserted that he was immune from. . . .
4. When the author analyzed our data, he did not cite sources that would support his criticism of our argument.
6. The Pope appealed to the industrialized nations of the world to assist the starving in Somalia.
8. When the participants agreed on the program, they assumed that the federal government had promised funds.
10. The two sides agreed that they needed to revise the treaty.
12. The laboratory personnel must thoroughly prepare the specimen sections.
14. Though we were disappointed when the board rejected our proposal, we were not surprised because we expected that it had decided to delay new initiatives.

3.13

2. When you precisely plot the location of the fragments of the vase, you will reconstruct it more accurately.
4. When a student is not socialized into a field, she may have writing problems because she does not know enough about how professionals in the field construct arguments.
6. When we evaluated the outcomes of the programs, we emphasized objective measures, even though we knew that the raters often disagreed with one another.

4.1

2. We will never solve the problem of UFOs until we understand better whether extraterrestrial life is possible.
4. In an emergency room, a doctor has to decide on the scene whether to force medication on an irrational patient who is unable to provide legal consent.
6. As we view network television less and cable and rental cassettes more, networks increasingly recognize that our tastes and viewing habits have changed and that they must program accordingly.
8. Recent critics have accurately described how the press has failed to report on the Middle East fairly. When we compare how journalists from different countries cover the same event, we see how inaccurately the news is reported by politically biased newspapers. When they omit facts and slant stories, journalists reveal that they have failed to carry out their mission objectively. As a result, because the public does not know the truth, it bases its opinion more on emotion than on reason.

4.2

2. OK.
4. OK.
6. Before Ann Richards was elected governor of Texas, her Republican opponent attacked her as a liberal Democrat who once used drugs, but in her campaign, she also used negative advertising.
8. Schools will improve science education sufficiently to provide American industry with skilled workers and researchers only when taxpayers / state governments / the federal government [take your pick] provide more money.

4.4

2. The model has been statistically analyzed.
4. We are considering whether we should create a database, but we have not yet evaluated how useful it would be.

6. We intend this book to help readers understand not only how the grammars of Arabic and English differ, but also how Arabic vocabulary reflects a different worldview.
8. Tissue rejection was studied by methods developed when it was discovered that dermal sloughing increases when cells regenerate.

4.5

2. We now make almost all home mortgage loans for 30 years. With inflated prices of housing, you cannot repay a loan more quickly.
4. Many Victorian scientists and theologians argued against Darwinian evolution because it contradicted what they assumed about their place in the world. It defined humans not as divinely privileged but as a product of nature.
6. We can most clearly explicate why smoking is socially significant if we analyze how adolescents interact. In particular, we should study how their social class determines how they relate.
8. We have undervalued how the brain solves problems because we have not studied it in scientifically reliable ways.

4.6

As you probably have heard, over the last several weeks, some of our students have been racially and sexually harassing other students. Even though on other campuses some students also harass other students, we are just as offended when some of our students harass others here. In most of the 10 to 12 incidents here, students have written graffiti or verbally insulted someone. In only two cases did one of our students physically contact another, and in neither case did that student injure the other one. A commitment exists to providing an environment where life, work and study can take place without fear of racial, sexual, religious or ethnic taunting or harassment. It has been made clear that bigotry and intolerance will not be permitted and that a commitment to diversity is unequivocal. Steps are being taken to improve security in campus housing. There is pride here in a tradition of diversity. . . .

4.7

2. The blood pressure of diabetic patients may be reduced if renal depressors are applied.
4. On the basis of these principles, we can formulate rules that allow readers to extract information from narratives.
6. The Federal Trade Commission should enforce guidelines for the durability of tires on new automobiles.

8. When we visited offices and reviewed assessments of what the agency needed for training, we identified issues that we can use to create an initial questionnaire for the staff.

5.1

One of the best skis for beginning and intermediate skiers is the Hart Queen. Its inner core consists of a thin layer of tempered ash from the hardwood forests of Kentucky. Built into its outer construction are two innovations for strength and flexibility. For increased strength, the layer of ash is reinforced with two sheets of ten-gauge steel. For increased flexibility, the two sheets are wrapped with fiberglass. The Queen can be used with most conventional bindings, but the best binding is the Salomon Double. The foot and ankle are firmly cradled in a cushion of foam and insulation that still permits freedom of movement.

5.2

2. In their natural states, most animals lack the power to create and communicate a new message to fit a new experience. Their genetic code enables them to communicate only a limited number and kind of messages. Bees, for example, can communicate information only about distance, direction, source, and richness of pollen in flowers. In all significant respects, animals of the same species are able to communicate a limited repertoire of messages delivered in the same way, for generation after generation.

5.5

1. Though modern mass communication offers many advantages, it also poses many threats. If it should be controlled by a powerful minority, it could manipulate public opinion through biased reporting. And while it provides us with a knowledge of public affairs through its national coverage, it may accentuate divisiveness and factionalism by connecting otherwise isolated, local conflicts into a single larger conflict when it shows us conflicts about the same issues occurring in different places. It will always be true that human nature produces differences of opinion, but the media may reinforce the threat of faction and division when they publish uninformed opinion in national coverage. According to some, media can suppress faction through education when they communicate the true nature of conflicts, but history has shown that the media give as much coverage to people who encourage conflict as to people who try to remove it.

3. When Truman considered the Oppenheimer committee's recommendation to stop the hydrogen bomb project, he had to consider many

issues. Russia and China had just proclaimed a Sino-Soviet bloc, so one issue he had to face was the Cold War. He was also losing support for his foreign policy among Republican leaders in Congress, and when the Russians tested their first atom bomb, the public demanded that he respond strongly. It was inevitable that Truman would conclude he could not let the public think he had allowed Russia to be first in developing the most powerful weapon yet. In retrospect, according to some historians, Truman should have risked taking the Oppenheimer recommendation, but he had to face political issues that were too powerful to ignore.

5.6

This is only one of many possible versions. Yours could be quite different.

We create a "moral climate" when we accept an objectivized moral standard for approving of people if they conform and shunning them if they don't, thereby discouraging nonconformity.

6.1

As the Illinois Commerce Commission has authorized, we are charging you. . . . **We** have not raised rates . . . but **we** are restructuring the rates now . . . so that **we** can charge you for what **we** pay to provide you with service. **We** are charging you a sum that **we** have prorated over the period during which **we** changed our rates. When **we** prorate, **we** base part of the bill on former Service Charges, which **we** identify on your bill as . . . Service Charges, which **we** identify as "New Rate."

As the Illinois Commerce Commission has authorized, **you** will have to pay. . . . **You** have not had to pay. . . , but **you** will now pay rates that have been restructured consistent with the policy of the Public Utilities Act that lets us base what **you** pay on what it costs to provide you with service. **You** will pay a sum that is prorated over the period during which the rates changed. When **you** pay prorated rates, **you** pay part of the bill based on former Service Charges, which **you** can identify on your bill as "Old Rate," and part of the bill that **you** can identify as "New Rate."

6.2

Your car may have a defective part that connects the suspension to the frame. If you brake hard and the plate fails, you won't be able to steer.

We may also have to adjust the secondary latch on your hood because we may have misaligned it. If you don't latch the primary latch, the secondary latch might not hold the hood down. If the hood flies up while you are driving, you won't be able to see. If either of these things occurs, you could crash.

6.3

The introduction to this paper does not. . . . The beginning of the body does not hint how the first paragraph relates to. . . . It does not mention. . . . Finally, this paper is not organized because it just presents one point. . . . It never explains why the points appear in the order they do or how paragraphs are connected.

When I read the introduction, I could not see the problem or question that I saw later. When I started the body of the paper, I couldn't see how I should connect the first paragraph to the introduction. I didn't see any concepts from the introduction in that first paragraph of the body. Finally, I could not follow this paper because I felt I was just going through one point after another. I never understood why I was reading the points in the order I was or how I should connect each paragraph to the next one.

6.4

Men are less interested than women in talking in class. . . . They also feel more at ease with teachers who. . . . Men are seemingly less concerned than women. . . . They also ignore the openness and supportiveness of the instructor. . . . and give less importance than women do to the teacher's attempts. . . .

6.5

The people of this village, I have said, hear something from the cathedral at Chartres that I cannot, but it is important to understand that I hear something that they cannot. Perhaps it is the power of the spires, the glory of the windows that strike them; but God has made Himself known longer to them, after all, than to me, and in a different way; the slippery bottomless well to be found in the crypt, down which heretics were hurled to death, terrifies me, along with the obscene, inescapable gargoyles jutting out of the stone and seeming to say that the devil and God can never be divorced. I doubt that the devil enters the villagers minds when they look at the cathedral because the devil has never been identified with them. But the status which myth imposes on me in the West must be accepted before I can hope to change it.

6.6

Fourscore and seven years ago, **this continent** witnessed the birth of a new nation. . . . Now **a great civil war** engages us. . . . **That war** has given us this great battlefield for a meeting place. **A portion of that field** is ready to receive its dedication. . . . **This** is an altogether fitting. . . . But in a larger sense, **this ground** will not let us dedicate. . . . **It** has already received that consecration. . . . **The words we say here**. . . . [You finish the rest.]

7.1

Sets of words that provide conceptual connective tissue are highlighted.

2. The next century the situation changed, because after Peter the Great seven out of eight reigns of the Romanov line were plagued by **turmoil** over **disputed** *succession* to the THRONE.

   The **problems** began in 1722, when Peter the Great passed a law of *succession* that terminated the principle of heredity and required the SOVEREIGN to appoint a *successor.* But because many TSARS, including Peter, died before they named *successors,* those who aspired to RULE had no authority by appointment, and so their *succession* was often **disputed** by the boyars, lower level aristocrats. There was **turmoil** even when *successors* were appointed. In 1740, Ivan VI was adopted by Czarina Anna Ivanovna and named as her *successor* at age two months, but his *succession* was **challenged** by Elizabeth, daughter of Peter the Great. In 1741, she **defeated** Anna and *ascended* to the THRONE herself. In 1797 Paul tried to eliminate these **disputes** by codifying a new law: *primogeniture in the male line.* But **turmoil** continued. Paul was **strangled** by conspirators, one of whom was probably his son, Alexander I.

7.2

Your revisions may well differ from these, depending on what you think is most important in each sentence.

2. These studies may produce a new judicial philosophy that could affect our society well into the twenty-first century.
4. According to everyone in the industry, "turnkey" means responsibility not only for the manufacture and installation of a new piece of equipment, but for its satisfactory performance, as well.
6. Clearly, those who have overbuilt suburban housing developments in floodplains have in recent years caused widespread flooding and economic disaster.
8. Economically speaking, however, it is feasible to rent rather than buy textbooks for basic courses that do not change from year to year such as mathematics, foreign languages, and English.

10. Speakers should adhere to the guidelines set forth in the MLA style sheet and the NCTE guidelines for nonsexist language to the best of their ability.

7.3

2. The apparent issue here is whether during contract bargaining, management has the duty to disclose the date it intends to close down its operation. The rationale for management's duty to bargain in good faith is to minimize conflict. Though the case law on this matter is scanty, companies are obligated during bargaining to disclose major changes in an operation in order to allow the union to put forth proposals on behalf of its members.
4. One current hypothesis to explain this kind of severe condition is that a toxin elaborated by the vibrio increases mucosal and vascular permeability. In favor of this hypothesis are changes in small capillaries located near the basal surface of the epithelial cells and the appearance of numerous microvesicles in the cytoplasm of the mucosal cells. It is believed that when capillaries become more permeable, fluid is hydrodynamically transported into the interstitial tissue and then through the mucosa into the lumen of the gut.

8.1

2. Science needs accurate data if its theories are to advance the world safely.
4. Agencies that assist our participants have replaced their recently announced policy with their original one.
6. Most patients in a public clinic do not expect special attention because their problems usually seem minor and can be treated with minimal understanding and attention.
8. When investors think that prices will rise, they usually put most of their discretionary resources into art objects.
10. Educators have long wanted to help readers remember information better, but they have not been able to identify the features that make passages differ in difficulty. The first problem is to identify common and different features among comparable passages. The second is that they have not been able to evaluate the quality and quantity of information that a reader remembers.

8.2

2. A second set of rules includes those whose observance we ignore, and whose violation we ignore, as well.

4. While it is unclear what counts as "too many" prepositions, it is clear that when you avoid abstract nouns, you need fewer of them.

8.3

2. Stop taking the medicine only if you are not dizzy and nauseous for six hours.
4. Cosmologists disagree on an open or closed universe, a dispute that will likely continue until they compute its mass.
6. If we wish to be independent of imported oil, we must develop oil shale and coal as sources of fuel.
8. The Insured must provide the Insurer with all relevant receipts, checks, or other evidence of costs that exceed $100.
10. Though we are not certain whether life exists elsewhere in the universe, statistical evidence makes it likely that somewhere among its immense number of planetary systems, it does.

8.4

2. At the end of his career, Frost used imagery of seasons in his longer poems.
4. The traditional values that once showed us how to be good mothers and wives were self-contradictory.
6. When Freud interpreted dreams, he was mistaken in his assumptions.
8. Order of birth may or may not relate to academic success.

8.5

2. In this section, I argue that we must dispense with plea bargaining because it lets hardened criminals avoid punishment and encourages contempt for the judicial system.
4. We cannot assume that ground snakes in unmapped areas are larger than those in mapped areas.
6. Most investigators of life stages think that midlife is most critical for our mental health because most of us decide then whether we are winning or losing the game of life.

9.1

A liberal education should institutionalize those circumstances under which a student is most likely to use a reflective moment to transform her relationship to the intellectual world. In that way, she freely participates in intellectual activity and thereby becomes an autonomous member of her intellectual community.

9.3

Again, your revisions will be completely different from these.

2. For the last few years, automobile manufacturers have been trying to meet more stringent mileage requirements, **a challenge** that has tested American ingenuity/**requirements** that Detroit has strenuously tried to change/hoping that new technologies will provide them with a breakthrough in engine design.
4. Most young people cannot grasp the insecurity that many people felt during the Great Depression, **a failure** that makes it impossible for them to share their grandparents' experiences/**an insecurity** that shaped them for the rest of their lives/believing that the stories they hear from their grandparents are exaggerations.
6. Many Victorians were appalled when Darwin suggested that their ancestors might have included creatures such as apes, **a concept** that offended not only their personal self-respect, but their fundamental religious beliefs, as well/**creatures** that they had seen as utterly different from themselves/choosing to believe instead that they were created by God 6000 years before.
8. Scientific inquiry began when primitive people began to think about the regularities of nature, regularities that were invisible to most such people because they were so familiar, but to a few others seemed worth considering.

9.5

2. For whatever reason, such conduct is prejudicial to good discipline.
4. Given the low quality of elected officials, the merit selection of judges is an idea whose time came long ago.
6. Unless we reduce the emission of carbon dioxide by the end of the century, we will change the climate of the world.

9.6

1. An ecological impact statement identical to that submitted the previous year indicates that it will again contain data difficult to evaluate.
3. Because we have reorganized the marketing research division, we can process information more quickly and thereby identify more reliably market segments different from those that we have traditionally aimed at. We will be able to process this information relatively easily because for many markets, we have already accumulated data such as income, spending, etc. We may therefore expect to operate more efficiently than last year.

9.7

2. Though we expect to succeed, we will need to resolve immediately the differences that have interfered with communication.
4. After we audited internal operations in the summer of 1996, we audited foreign affiliates that had not been audited by their local headquarters.

10.2

2. While the strong are often afraid to admit weakness, the weak often fail to assert the strength they possess.
4. When parents raise children who do not value the importance of hard work, the adults those children become will not know how to work hard for what they claim to value.

10.3

2. The political campaign plan was concocted by those with the least sensitivity to our most critical needs.
4. Nothing has changed America more than the power of federal government.
6. Boards of education can no longer expect that taxpayers will support the extravagancies of incompetent bureaucrats.

A.2

1. Scientists and philosophers of science tend to speak as if "scientific language" were intrinsically precise, as if those who use it must understand one another's meaning, even if they disagree. But, in fact, scientific language is not as different from ordinary language as is commonly believed; it, too, is subject to imprecision and ambiguity and hence to imperfect understanding. Moreover, new theories (or arguments) are rarely, if ever, constructed by way of clear-cut steps of induction, deduction, and verification (or falsification). Neither are they defended, rejected, or accepted in so straightforward a manner. In practice, scientists combine the rules of scientific methodology with a generous admixture of intuition, aesthetics, and philosophical commitment. The importance of what are sometimes called extrarational or extralogical components of thought in the *discovery* of a new principle or law is generally acknowledged. . . . But the role of these extralogical components in persuasion and acceptance (in making an argument convincing) is less frequently discussed, partly because they are less visible. The ways in which the credibility on effectiveness of an argument depends on the realm of

common experiences, on extensive practice in communicating those experiences in a common language, are hard to see precisely because such commonalities are taken for granted. Only when we step out of such a "consensual domain"—when we can stand out on the periphery of a community with a common language—do we begin to become aware of the unarticulated premises, mutual understandings, and assumed practices of the group. Even in those subjects that lend themselves most readily to quantification, discourse depends heavily on conventions and interpretation—conventions that are acquired over years of practice and participation in a community.

2. In fact, of course, the notion of universal knowledge has always been an illusion; but it is an illusion fostered by the monistic view of the world in which a few great central truths determine in all its wonderful and amazing proliferation everything else that is true. We are not today tempted to search for these keys that unlock the whole of human knowledge and of man's experience. We know that we are ignorant; we are well taught it, and the more surely and deeply we know our own job the better able we are to appreciate the full measure of our pervasive ignorance. We know that these are inherent limits, compounded, no doubt, and exaggerated by that sloth and that complacency without which we would not be men at all.

   But knowledge rests on knowledge; what is new is meaningful because it departs slightly from what was known before; this is a world of frontiers, where even the liveliest of actors or observers will be absent most of the time from most of them. Perhaps this sense was not so sharp in the village—that village which we have learned a little about but probably do not understand too well—the village of slow change and isolation and fixed culture which evokes our nostalgia even if not our full comprehension. Perhaps in the villages men were not so lonely; perhaps they found in each other a fixed community, a fixed and only slowly growing store of knowledge—a single world. Even that we may doubt, for there seem to be always in the culture of such times and places vast domains of mystery, if not unknowable, then imperfectly known, endless and open.

Acknowledgments

D. H. Lawrence, *Studies in Classic American Literature.* New York: The Viking Press, 1961.

Norman Mailer, *Armies of the Night.* New York: The New American Library, Inc., 1971.

From *Science and the Common Understanding* by J. Robert Oppenheimer. Copyright © 1954 by J. Robert Oppenheimer, renewed © 1981 by Robert B. Meyner. Reprinted by permission.

Excerpt from Foreword, *Webster's New World Dictionary,* Second College Edition, 1974, p. viii. Copyright © 1974 by William Collins and World Publishing Company. Reprinted by permission of Simon & Schuster, Inc.

From "The Aims of Education" in *The Aims of Education and Other Essays* by Alfred North Whitehead. Copyright © 1929 by Macmillan Publishing Co., Inc., renewed 1957 by Evelyn Whitehead. Reprinted by permission.

Index